CARAVAN SITES AND MOBILE HOME PARKS: THE LEGAL FRAMEWORK

Second edition

- by -

Andrew Barsby
Barrister
(non-practising)

A. W. & C. BARSBY
LEGAL RESEARCH AND PUBLISHING
2001

A. W. & C. BARSBY
LEGAL RESEARCH AND PUBLISHING

2 Lynwood Avenue, Epsom, Surrey, KT17 4LQ
Tel: +44 (0)1372 742372
Fax: +44 (0)1372 721900

http://www.barsby.com

ISBN 0 9521625 7 1

Printed and published in England by A. W. & C. Barsby

Publishers' Preface

"Publishing....but better"

Perhaps the best way to describe what we do is "publishing...but better":

- It is *direct*: we build close links with the people and organisations who use our books. This gives us vital feedback about whether our books succeed in explaining the law clearly and helpfully, and it gives users a service tailored to their needs.

- It is *interactive*: if our books don't provide the help which readers are looking for, we can respond with clarification and more information about the law. Our Internet site—*www.barsby.com*—with its "Notes and Queries" pages linked to the printed text, enables us to do this. It also allows us to update the text when there are changes in the law, and to provide links to other sites where information about the law can be found.

- It is *efficient*: we write and publish—in print and on the Internet—as part of a continuous, seamless operation. The result is not just books but a unique legal information resource which is easily accessible, practical and helpful.

Caravan Sites and Mobile Home Parks

Since the first edition of this book was published, in 1996, there have been no major changes to the legislation dealing specifically with caravan sites. But in many small ways the law has moved on, and a new edition is by now well overdue.

We have not sought to change the essential balance of the book. This sets out to provide a practical guide to the law relating to caravan sites and mobile home parks. The book takes a neutral point of view. It is written mainly for non-lawyers—site owners, those living in caravans, and professionals in local government and elsewhere—who want to understand the subject in some detail. The book will also be of use to lawyers, however, since it summarises the law and contains references to the legislation, cases and other materials.

A chapter has been added to deal specifically with gipsies, and we have set out in an Appendix the legislation, and some of the guidance, published by the Department of the Environment, Transport and the Regions on planning law, which affects caravan sites and mobile home parks.

The book has a new graphic design, based on the design developed for our book on land law generally, *Protecting Your Property*[1]. This is explained in chapter 1—see paragraph 1-62. Additional material will be found on our Internet site—see 1-64 on how to use the site. Comments and queries are always welcome, since these enable us to add to and clarify the text in response to users' needs. We are particularly anxious to hear of County Court decisions in cases concerning caravans and mobile homes, since these may otherwise not be reported. In this connection we should like to thank particularly Helen Clarke, barrister, for kindly providing notes of the cases of *Charlton v Howard* and *Oaktree Parks Ltd v Hughes*.

We are most grateful for the help we have received, from individuals and organisations, including those within the industry, during the preparation of the text. Any mistakes remain our responsibility.

The book should not be regarded as a substitute for legal advice, where that is appropriate. The law described is that of England and Wales (though see paragraph 1-56 for the legal position in Wales). Scotland has its own legal system; though Part I of the Caravan Sites and Control of Development Act 1960 applies to Scotland[2].

A. W. & C. Barsby
Epsom
September 2001

Postscript Despite the changes made to government departments as a result of the General Election of June 2001, we have retained references to the "Department of the Environment, Transport and the Regions", or the "DETR" for short, since this name will continue to appear in much of the written material for some time to come.

---

1. ISBN 0 9521625 6 3 (2000).
2. By s. 32, which sets out how the Act is modified in its application to Scotland.

Stationing a caravan on land

The legislation on caravan sites refers to "stationing" a caravan on land, which means simply positioning or putting it on land. The word is significant because it does not include attaching a caravan permanently to the land and thus making it, for legal purposes, part of the land. 1-8

The law assumes that things attached to the land are part of it. This is true particularly of buildings, but is also true of other things attached to the land, including trees. So where the law is concerned with what is happening on land, whether it is a question of deciding who has rights over the land, or who is responsible for it, there is generally no need for the law to refer specifically to buildings or other things which are part of the land: it is enough to refer to the land itself. Often the law refers to "premises", meaning a specific piece of land[1]. A caravan site can be "premises", as can a pitch; but a caravan stationed on a pitch would not generally be regarded as part of the premises[2]. 1-9

There is usually no difficulty in deciding whether a structure is attached to and forms part of the land: most buildings are designed and constructed with just that intention. But sometimes the position is less clear-cut. In the case of *Elitestone Ltd v Morris*[3] the courts had to consider the case of a wooden bungalow which was resting on, but not attached to, concrete pillars. The House of Lords decided that whether a structure is part of the land depends in part on the extent to which it is attached to the land, and in part on the purpose of attaching it to the land. Here the bungalow could only have been moved by destroying it, and the House of Lords considered that the purpose in constructing it must have been that it should become part of the land. 1-10

Caravans *can* be permanently attached to the land, so that they are, so far as the law is concerned, buildings, and this sometimes happens. The consequence is that the caravan is outside the scope of the legislation on caravans and is treated by the law like any other building. This will be relevant, for example, to: 1-11

See particularly 7-41.

- Planning law.

See 3-48.

---

1. A deed is required to transfer land, and the part of a deed describing the land being transferred is known as the "premises" The word has come to mean land in the ownership of a particular person, and the law is often concerned with land in this sense. Less frequently, the law is concerned with land according to its physical characteristics, for example woodland or a street, regardless of who owns the land.
2. For an exception to this rule see *Norton v Knowles* [1967] 3 All ER 1061, explained at 7-51.
3. [1997] 1 WLR 647.

◆ Landlord and tenant law.

See 7-38.

1-12 But the usual intention is that caravans should not become part of the land. Although they may be in the same position for long periods, and may be connected to mains services, the intention is generally that they should still be moveable, so that they can be transferred to another pitch on the same site, or to another site altogether. The courts recognize that this is the case, and generally do not regard a caravan as part of the land unless they have been unequivocally fixed in position.

See also 2-19 on twin-unit caravans.

1-13 Generally, then, caravans are stationed on land, but not attached so far as the law is concerned; and as a result the legislation on caravan sites applies.

Legal arrangements for stationing a caravan

1-14 A person in search of land on which to put a caravan has, legally speaking, several alternatives. She can buy or lease some land herself, or she can obtain permission from the owner of land to put her caravan on the land. On organised caravan sites it is the latter sort of arrangement which is the usual one, the agreement which gives the necessary permission being generally known as a "pitch agreement". Such agreements are often subject to standard conditions.

See further chapter 7 on general questions concerning leases and licences.

See 1-36 for standard conditions issued by industry bodies.

1-15 Legally, there is a difference between ownership of land or a tenancy on the one hand, and permission on the other. A person who owns or leases land is regarded as having an interest in the land itself. Permission to use land—known legally as a "licence" —is not regarded by the law as being an interest in land, but rather as a right against the person who gave the permission. The three Acts mentioned above generally make no distinction between licences and tenancies in relation to land on which a caravan is stationed: they apply equally to both sorts of arrangement. (If the legislation applied to one sort of arrangement but not the other, this would provide a way of avoiding the law.)

This is not to be confused with a site licence, which is a different sort of permission: see the *Glossary* at the end of this chapter.

But see 5-9 on the scope of the Mobile Homes Act 1983.

1-16 A licence to use land can be granted by means of a contract. A pitch agreement is a contract, under which the occupier of the caravan has a number of obligations, including the payment of the pitch fee, and in return is given permission to place his caravan on the site. However, the owner of land can also give permission on its own, without entering into a contract, and a licence of this sort is sometimes known legally as a "bare" licence. This might be the case in an informal arrangement by which a landowner let a friend or relative station a caravan on land.

Caravans and caravan sites: terminology

Legislation on caravan sites, and on planning, generally uses the terms "caravan", and "caravan site". The Mobile Homes Act 1983 uses "mobile home", which it defines to mean the same thing as "caravan". This terminology presents difficulties, since the use of language has changed over the years. "Caravan" is still used for holiday caravans which are towed from place to place. But "residential park home" is now the accepted term for a caravan on a mobile home site acting as a permanent home for the residents; and "caravan holiday home" for a static caravan on a holiday site serving the same purpose as a holiday cottage. Since this book is about the law, the language used follows the legislation, rather than the current usage. "Caravan" and "caravan site" are thus used as general terms, "mobile home" and "mobile home park" in dealing with the Mobile Homes Act 1983. "Resident" is generally used for a person living in a caravan, but "occupier" is used when this fits in with the language of the legislation being explained. 1-17

The legal definition of "caravan" includes what would be called caravans and mobile homes in the everyday sense of those words, and also some things which would not generally be thought of as caravans, such as motorhomes. 1-18

See 2-12 onwards.

By "caravan site", the legislation does not mean that there should be more than one caravan, or that the site should be run as a business. A householder wanting to put a single caravan on her land for use by members of her family will be starting a caravan site, though she may well be exempt both from the site licensing requirements and from the need for planning permission. 1-19

See 2-30 and 3-13 on exemptions.

Sites which are operated on a commercial basis can be classified as: 1-20

- Touring sites, where people touring with caravans can stay for a short period.

- Holiday sites, not open all year round, containing static caravans for holiday use.

- Residential sites, open all year round, containing static caravans for permanent residential use.

See chapter 6.

These uses may of course be mixed on a particular site. Some special rules apply to gipsy sites set up by local authorities.

Scope of caravan sites legislation

But see 6-9 onwards for gipsy sites, to which special rules apply.

1-21 Taking into account the points explained above, the scope of the 1960, 1968 and 1983 Acts can be summarised as follows:

Table 1: Caravan sites legislation

Act	Touring sites	Holiday sites	Residential sites
Caravan Sites and Control of Development Act 1960	Applies	Applies	Applies
Caravan Sites Act 1968	Does not apply	Does not apply	Applies [see 4-9]
Mobile Homes Act 1983	Does not apply	Does not apply	Applies [see 5-6]

Applying the law to caravans

1-22 Given that caravans are usually not part of the land in the same way as buildings, but may be used in the same way (in particular, they may be used as dwellings) the question arises of how the law should treat them. In some cases there are separate rules, which may be similar to the rules which apply to buildings. For example:

See 4-20 onwards for these provisions.

- The Caravan Sites Act 1968 has, in Part I, provisions which are similar to the Protection from Eviction Act 1977, and protect some residents from harassment and unlawful eviction.

See 8-3 onwards.

- The provisions on fitness for human habitation, which apply to houses, do not apply to caravans. But some of the same ground is covered by the law on statutory nuisances.

1-23 Sometimes, the general law is made to apply to caravans in the same way it would apply if the caravan were a building. So, for example:

- The Occupiers' Liability Acts make the occupier of land responsible, in certain circumstances, for accidents which happen to people coming on to land. These Acts do not just apply to land, but also to movable structures on land—which includes caravans.

See 10-10 onwards.

- Burglary, which is an offence under the Theft Act 1968 applies not just to land and buildings but to an "inhabited vehicle or vessel", whether or not the person inhabiting the vehicle or vessel is there at the time.

See 9-24 for burglary of caravans.

1-24 There is no general rule which lays down whether caravans should be treated in the same way as houses. Sometimes the picture is confused. In planning law, caravans are "dwellings", for the purposes of planning policy on housing; but they are not "dwelling houses", since in this context a house is generally taken to mean a building. But in other areas of the law, a caravan may occasionally be treated as a "dwelling-house", depending on the context[1].

Things which are not caravans

1-25 Several sorts of structure which may be used for human habitation and are movable (so not buildings), are outside the definition of "caravan".

1-26 *Moveable dwellings* As mentioned above, the use of land as a caravan site was originally regulated by the Public Health Act 1936, s. 269. This no longer applies to caravans, because things which are caravans are now excluded from the definition of "moveable dwelling" by s. 30 of the Caravan Sites and Control of Development Act 1960. But s. 269 still applies to tents[2], vans, sheds and other structures used for human habitation which are not within the definition of "caravan" (s. 269(8)). The latter includes structures which are outside the definition of "caravan", because, for example, they

See 1-3.

1. See, for example, in relation to capital gains tax, *Makins v Elsom* [1977] 1 WLR 21, where a caravan was regarded as a "dwelling house".
2. The Department of the Environment (as it was then called) published a consultation paper in 1987 entitled "Proposed Legislation Unifying Tent and Caravan Site Licensing in England and Wales". However this proposal has not yet been put into effect.

consist of more than two sections; or because, although they can be moved, they cannot be moved lawfully on a public road.

See 2-12 onwards for caravans generally, and 2-19 for twin-unit caravans.

1-27 A licence is required in order to use land as a site for a moveable dwelling for more than 42 consecutive days, or for 60 days in any 12 consecutive months. For a breach of s. 269 the maximum fine is level 1, and £2 for each day the offence continues after conviction (s. 269(7)). This offence can thus be used to deal with unauthorised camping in tents.

See 1-47 for the standard scale of maximum fines.

And see 6-17 onwards for unauthorised camping and the Criminal Justice and Public Order Act 1994.

1-28 *Houseboats* Because of the wide definition of "caravan" in the legislation, a houseboat could be said to be a caravan for those purposes. But a houseboat is not "stationed" on land by being moored in a river or lake, even, it seems, if the houseboat is moored so that it rests against the bank, or if the water is tidal and the houseboat sometimes rests on the bed of the river[1]. Apart from the position of houseboats under the legislation on caravan sites, the courts have also had to consider their position under legislation on landlord and tenant[2].

Central and local government

1-29 The government department with overall responsibility for caravan sites is the Department of the Environment, Transport and the Regions (the "DETR"), which is also responsible for the planning system. Its functions include making delegated legislation (see above), issuing guidance about planning policy, and dealing with appeals from the decisions of local authorities. The DETR publishes *Mobile Homes, A guide for residents and site owners*, which is part of the DETR's series of guides on housing.

See further chapter 3 for the DETR's functions in relation to planning.

1-30 The day-to-day responsibility for caravans and sites, and for planning law, is in the hands of local government. Decisions about the granting of site licences and planning are thus taken at local level, subject to the possibility of appeals to the courts or (in the case of planning decisions) to the DETR. In the context of both site licensing and planning the appropriate local authority is usually the District Council, but this is not an invariable rule—some functions belong to County Councils or their equivalents in towns and cities.

See 2-49 for the local authority under the 1960 Act.

1. *Roy Crimble Ltd v Edgecombe*, New Law Journal, 3 September 1981, p. 928.
2. On the question of whether a houseboat can be a "dwelling-house" for the purposes of landlord and tenant law, see *Chelsea Yacht and Boat Club Ltd v Pope*, *The Times* 7 June 2000, [2000] 1 WLR 1941.

The industry

Representative bodies include: 1-31

- The British Holiday and Home Parks Association ("BH&HPA"), whose members own sites.

- The National Caravan Council ("NCC"), which is the representative body for the caravan industry in the UK, and whose members include site owners, dealers, manufacturers and suppliers of specialist services to the industry.

- The National Park Homes Council ("NPHC"), which is a division of the NCC, and the representative body of the mobile homes industry in the UK.

- National residents' associations.

The BH&HPA and the NPHC, together with the national residents' associations, publish the *Park Homes Charter*, which describes the rights and obligations of residents and site owners o residential sites. A resident who has a complaint should take it up with the site owner, and may be able to obtain help from the national residents' associations, the local authority's trading standards department, or a Citizens' Advice Bureau or other advice centre. Failing that, a conciliation scheme is available which applies to site owners who are members of the BH&HPA or the NPHC. The BH&HPA's and NPHC's rules back up the conciliation scheme by providing for the possibility of disciplinary measures against members who do not comply. 1-32

Finally, a dispute about pitch fees may be referred to arbitration, under a scheme drawn up by the Chartered Institute of Arbitrators, the Park Home Pitch Fee Arbitration Scheme. 1-33

See 1-51 onwards for arbitration generally.

In relation to holiday sites, the BH&HPA and NCC together publish a *Code of Practice for Selling and Siting Holiday Caravans*, and a complementary Code for Letting Caravans. The Codes represent a statement of the minimum standards expected of members of the BH&HPA and NCC. They are approved by the Office of Fair Trading, ("OFT") under consumer legislation. At the time of writing, the OFT has, however, announced that at the end of 2001 approval will be withdrawn from these Codes of Practice (and other Codes, in other industries) and a higher standard will be introduced. The Codes are thus currently under review. 1-34

A caravan owner who has a complaint should first of all discuss it with the site owner. If that does not resolve the dispute, assistance can 1-35 be sought under the BH&HPA/NCC conciliation scheme. If this does not resolve the dispute, there are separate arbitration schemes, drawn up by the Chartered Institute of Arbitrators, the Holiday Caravan Pitch Fee Arbitration Scheme (for pitch fee disputes) and the Holiday Caravan Arbitration Scheme (for other sorts of dispute on holiday sites).

1-36 Standard-form licence agreements are published by the BH&HPA and NCC, for use by site owners in making agreements with residents. There are different versions for agreements subject to the Mobile Homes Act 1983 (incorporating the terms laid down by the Act) and for holiday agreements.

See 5-13 onwards for the contents of Mobile Homes Act agreements.

1-37 The standard form licence agreement under the Mobile Homes Act, known as a "written statement", includes the following provisions:

- Obligations on the resident to pay the pitch fee and outgoings on the pitch, not to use the mobile home for business purposes, to keep the mobile home tidy, not to build, to comply with site rules, not to cause a nuisance to other residents.

- Obligations on the site owner to keep the site in good condition, to give notice of proposed changes of site rules, so that residents may meet and vote on the changes, and to maintain services and facilities.

- A right for the site owner to increase the pitch fee

See 7-14 onwards for pitch fee reviews.

1-38 For holiday caravan pitches, the standard form agreement includes the following provisions:

- Obligations on the resident to pay the pitch fee, to comply with the site rules, to keep the caravan in a good state of repair and use it only as holiday accommodation, not to build, and to permit the site owner to move the caravan; also to act courteously towards other residents, to supervise children and not to create any noise or disturbance or carry on any business on the site.

- Obligations on the site owner to provide services and to supply electricity and bottled gas at prescribed rates.

- Rights for the site owner to increase the pitch fee and to move the caravan, on three months' notice if necessary to redevelop or maintain the site, the move being to an equally pleasant pitch.

◈ A right for the site owner to change the site rules by giving notice in writing.

In 1999 the NHPC persuaded the Independent Housing Ombudsman, who operates under the Housing Act 1996, to introduce membership of the Ombudsman scheme for owners of permanent residential sites. Membership is voluntary, and is open to site owners who meet certain conditions—they must have adopted the *Park Homes Charter*, and have a complaints procedure open to all residents. 1-39

Before seeking to involve the Ombudsman, a resident must go through the site owner's complaints procedure. The Ombudsman is able to deal with complaints by residents about their relationship with the site owner, including such matters as the maintenance of the site and decisions by the site owner about relocation of caravans; but he cannot act where some other way of resolving a dispute, such as legal proceedings, is in hand. The Ombudsman may be able to deal with a complaint informally, or (if both sides agree) may undertake mediation—working to help the parties reach a settlement between themselves—or arbitration. In some cases he may carry out a more formal investigation. Intervention by the Ombudsman may lead to an apology by the site owner, payment of compensation, carrying out of work by the site owner, or a change in the site owner's methods of operating the site. The scheme is free to residents, and is confidential. 1-40

Standards of construction

There is no legislation laying down technical requirements for caravans and mobile homes. But the British Standards Institute has produced a number of relevant standards: 1-41

◈ BSEN 1647 for static holiday caravans.

◈ BSEN 1645 for touring caravans

◈ BSEN 721 for covered ventilation in holiday and touring caravans.

◈ BSEN 3632 for residential mobile homes.

In addition, the NCC operates a certification scheme, independently assessing and approving caravans in the UK.● 1-42

● See also 10-30 on the Consumer Protection Act 1987.

Possessing and occupying land

1-43 The law is often concerned not with the ownership of land as such, but with a related question, namely who is in control of land (or of a building, or a caravan). Whoever is in control is often made responsible for what happens on the land, and may also be given rights by the law. In order to identify who is in control, the law speaks of a person "occupying" land, or being "in possession of it". These are slightly different legal concepts, but in practice both generally signify being in control of the land.

But see 2-6 onwards: under the 1960 Act, "occupier" has a special meaning.

1-44 The person in possession or occupation of land will often be the owner, or a person with some other interest in the land, such as a tenant. Equally, a person with a licence (that is, permission) can be in possession or occupation of land, as can a trespasser. (In the latter case, the true owner may need to go to court and obtain a possession order—sometimes known as an eviction order—to remove the trespasser and restore the owner to possession of the land.)

Civil and Criminal law

1-45 *Civil law* The civil law is concerned with providing compensation and other remedies, such as injunctions for civil wrongs. Compensation, known to lawyers as "damages", is financial. An injunction is an order from the court to do or not to do something; disobeying an injunction is a contempt of court, which the court can punish with up to two years' imprisonment. It is generally a matter for the person concerned, not local government or other officials, whether action should be taken in the civil courts in order to obtain these remedies; though public bodies may sometimes be able to take civil proceedings to enforce the law.

See for example 7-29.

1-46 *Criminal law* Criminal proceedings are designed to punish breaches of the criminal law. By contrast, they are mainly for the police and other public bodies. Private prosecutions are possible, but rare, partly because in order to succeed it is generally necessary for the allegation to be proved to a high standard—"beyond reasonable doubt".

1-47 Many of the offences mentioned in this book can be dealt with only by magistrates' courts, or "summarily". There is a standard scale for the maximum fines which can be imposed, which applies in most, though not all, cases. (The law allows these maximum levels to be updated from time to time.) More serious offences can be dealt with by the Crown Court, or "on indictment". In the Crown Court, maximum sentences are heavier, and the standard scale of fines does not apply.

For most summary offences, a table lays down the levels of maximum fines which can be imposed: 1-48

There are some exceptions: see for example 3-43 on fines for breach of planning control.

Level	Maximum fine
1	£200
2	£500
3	£1,000
4	£2,500
5	£5,000

Some offences are "either-way" offences, meaning that depending on how serious the offence is it can be dealt with either in a magistrates' court or in the Crown Court. The legislation lays down a figure known as the "statutory maximum" which applies when one of these offences is dealt with in the magistrates' court. Currently the statutory maximum is £5,000. 1-49

Law enforcement generally In one sense the civil law and criminal law are quite separate: they exist for different purposes, and have different procedures and different courts. But in practice the position is often more involved, because the criminal law is used to re-inforce civil procedures. Site licensing, for example, is essentially a civil matter, but using land as a caravan site without a licence is made a criminal offence, since this is a more effective way of ensuring that the law is obeyed. 1-50

Arbitration Dealing with civil disputes in the courts can be expensive and complicated. Arbitration offers an alternative: it means that the parties in dispute together appoint an independent person to decide who is right, working within the legal framework provided by the Arbitration Act 1996. Arbitration has for many years been used to settle large commercial disputes. Its use for smaller disputes is becoming increasingly popular, and is now officially encouraged. The Mobile Homes Act 1983 provides that disputes arising between a site owner and a resident can, if the parties agree, be settled by an arbitrator rather than the County Court. Written agreements under the Act can thus provide for arbitration in the event of a dispute; and even if they do not do so it is open to the site owner and resident to agree that a particular dispute shall be settled in this way rather than by proceedings in the County Court. 1-51

See 5-19.

The position is in effect the same for agreements relating to holiday sites. As noted above arbitration is also given a specific rôle where there is a breach of the *Park Homes Charter* or the Codes of Practice relating to holiday sites.

See 1-33 and 1-35.

Human rights

1-52 Basic human rights are set out in the European Convention on Human Rights (the "ECHR"), which became part of the law of England and Wales on 2 October 2000, as a result of the Human Rights Act 1998. The Act gives people a range of basic rights, including:

- The right to a fair trial in civil and criminal proceedings.
- The right to respect for private and family life.
- The right to freedom of expression.
- The right to peaceful enjoyment of possessions.

1-53 As its effect is considered by the courts, the Human Rights Act will have an effect on many areas of the law. The Act works by laying down that:

- It is unlawful for public authorities (which includes central and local government) to act in a way which is incompatible with the ECHR.
- Whenever possible legislation must be interpreted in a way which gives effect to the ECHR.
- The higher courts can issue a "declaration of incompatibility" if an Act appears to conflict with the ECHR (though the Act remains in force until it can be altered).
- The courts can decide that delegated legislation which conflicts with the ECHR is of no effect.

1-54 The Human Rights Act has proved to be of particular relevance to gipsies, because of their special position.

See 6-36 onwards.

Conventions used in the book

A number of conventions have been adopted in order to keep the text as short and clear as possible. First, powers given by legislation to government departments are described as though they belonged to the department concerned, though in fact legislation generally confers powers on the minister in charge of a department. The text thus refers to delegated legislation as being made by the DETR, though it is strictly speaking made by the Minister responsible for the Department, the Secretary of State for the Environment, Transport and the Regions. 1-55

As a result of the Government of Wales Act 1998, Wales now has a degree of devolved government, and the powers which in England are exercised by government departments are in Wales exercised by the Welsh Assembly. Other changes to the operation of the law have also been made. For the sake of simplicity, the difference is not pointed out in the text on every occasion. 1-56

See, for example, 2-49 for the different meaning of "local authority" under the 1960 Act.

Local government in England and Wales is generally made up of different bodies, including County Councils and District Councils. As a general rule, the text merely refers to "the local authority". 1-57

Legislation, when it refers to people, generally uses "he" and "him", relying on the Interpretation Act 1978 for the rule that masculine references include feminine. In giving examples, however, this book follows the modern convention of using "he" and "him" on some occasions and "she" and "her" on others. 1-58

Layout of the book

Chapters 2 deals with site licensing under the Caravan Sites and Control of Development Act 1960 Act, and is followed in chapter 3 by an explanation of planning law, since this is related to the subject of site licensing. Chapters 4 and 5 then deal with the Caravan Sites Act 1968 and the Mobile Homes Act 1983. 1-59

Chapter 6 deals with the special position of gipsies under the legislation on caravan sites and planning. Chapter 7 goes into general questions concerned with legal arrangements for stationing a caravan on land, both where this is a contract and where it is a lease. The final three chapters summarise some aspects of the general law, which may be relevant on caravan sites. The headings are only broad indications of what these chapters cover: the law cannot in practice be divided neatly into these categories. At the end of most chapters is an Assessment which tries to bring out what is of practical importance. 1-60

1-61 An Appendix sets out the text of the Acts which deal specifically with caravan sites, some delegated legislation, and some DETR Circulars and Policy Planning Guidance Notes (or extracts from them) relating to caravan sites.

How use the book

1-62 Both the detailed Table of Contents and the Index can be used to find the relevant part of the book. But the answer to a legal problem is unlikely to be found in a single place. The cross-references are designed to help users of the book move around the text, and to understand how separate passages relate to each other. These have been placed in the margins to make it easier for the eye to move from the text to the cross-reference and back again.

1-63 References to legal sources will be found in footnotes throughout the book, and gathered together in a Table of Authorities at the end of the book; and these are designed to help users who wish to carry out further legal research.

How to use the Internet site

1-64 Whilst the book is complete in itself, additional material will be found on the Internet, in "Notes and Queries" pages which are cross-referenced to the paragraph numbers in the printed text. These:

- Update the text when changes in the law occur.
- Provide links to others sites containing information about the law.
- Set out extra comments on, and clarification of, the printed text, often in response to users of the book who wish to know more about a particular point.

1-65 To find to the Notes and Queries pages for the book, go to http://www.barsby.com, then click on the Notes and Queries icon under *Caravan Sites*. (Alternatively, go direct to http://www.barsby.com/cs2web/output/cs2contents.html.) Then click on a chapter heading to go to the Notes and Queries pages for that chapter. Alternatively, to see whether there is any extra material on a particular point, go to the Index for the Notes and Queries pages—this is at http://www.barsby.com/cs2web/Output/cs2-1IOM2.html.

Subjects not covered

A number of subjects are outside the scope of this work. While the book summarises some aspects of the general law, subjects not covered include: 1-66

- VAT and other tax issues.
- Litigation.
- Conveyancing (transferring land).
- Insurance.

Law reform

At any given moment, many areas of law are under review, to see whether reform is needed. The law on caravan sites and mobile home parks is no exception. In 2000 the DETR published a Report of the Park Homes Working Party[1]. The Working Party was set up in 1998, and is made up of representatives from different sides of the industry. 1-67

The Working Party's recommendations include a number of changes to the law, but further action has been deferred pending a report by consultants into the economics of mobile home parks. 1-68

Glossary

The following notes summarise the way in which "caravan", and other words and phrases particularly relevant to caravan sites, are used in this book. Some are defined in the legislation; others are in common use but do not appear in the legislation. Other words and phrases which have a special legal meaning are identified in the Index. 1-69

Camping The term is generally used to mean staying in tents, but is used in the Criminal Justice and Public Order Act 1994 to mean living in vehicles (including caravans).* The law regulates the use of land for camping and caravanning separately—camping under the 1-70

* See 6-17 onwards.

1. DETR Housing Research Summary No. 121.

Public Health Act 1936, caravanning under the Caravan Sites and Control of Development Act 1960.

1-71 *Caravan* This word is defined in the Caravan Sites and Control of Development 1960 Act, together with *caravan site* and these terms have a wide meaning. The same definition is used in the Caravan Sites Act 1968, and in planning legislation. In this book, "caravan"and "caravan site" are used as general terms, to include what are usually referred to as mobile homes and mobile home parks; but in dealing with the 1983 Act the text follows the Act and refers to mobile homes and mobile home parks.

See 2-9 onwards.

See 4-5 and 3-2.

1-72 *Caravan site* See *caravan*.

1-73 *Court* The word is used in the general sense to mean whatever court has power to deal with the matter in question. In relation to civil matters, Part I of the Caravan Sites Act 1968 provides that "the court" means the appropriate County Court; and in the Mobile Homes Act 1983 it means the County Court *or* an arbitrator. For criminal matters generally, less serious offences are dealt with by magistrates' courts, and more serious ones by the Crown Court.

See 4-1 and 5-18.

1-74 *Curtilage* The area surrounding a house; an important concept in planning law and also relevant to caravans. The meaning of the word is not given in legislation but has been developed by the courts.

See 2-31 and 3-14.

1-75 *DETR* The Department of the Environment, Transport and the Regions, which has overall responsibility for the planning system and the regulation of caravan sites.

1-76 *Gipsy* This word is defined in s. 24 of the Caravan Sites and Control of Development Act 1960, as meaning "persons of nomadic habit of life, whatever their race or origin", but not including members of an organised group of travelling showmen. The text standardises on "gipsy", which is how the word is spelled in legislation, though official documents sometimes spell the word "gypsy".

See 6-2 onwards.

1-77 *Holiday site* This expression is not found in the legislation, but it is a common term and is used (for example) in DETR guidance. It is used to mean sites which, because of the terms of their planning permission or site licence, cannot open all year round (though caravans may remain on the site throughout the year). These sites are therefore not "protected sites" for the purposes of the 1968 Act.

See 4-7 for protected sites under the 1968 Act.

Licence In the legal sense, this is a general word which means permission. When a landowner gives permission for someone to come on to the land he is said to give them a "licence" to do so. Many sorts of official permission are also known as "licences", for example the licences which allow people to drive cars or use TVs, and a site licence—meaning permission from the local authority to use land as a caravan site—is in this category. 1-78

Local authority In a general sense the term is used to mean the appropriate part of local government, whether a District Council, County Council, or part of an urban authority. However the term has special, narrower meaning in the 1960 Act. 1-79

See 2-49.

Mobile home This term defined in s. 5(1) of the Mobile Homes Act 1983, and its legal meaning is the same as *caravan*. As noted above, the law does not distinguish between caravans and mobile homes according to their appearance. 1-80

See 5-11.

Mobile home park is not used in the legislation. This book generally uses the terms *caravan* and *caravan site*. However in dealing specifically with sites to which the Mobile Homes Acts apply (i.e. permanent residential sites) it follows the language of the Acts in using *mobile home* and also uses *mobile home park*. 1-81

Occupier Both the Caravan Sites Act 1968 and the Mobile Homes Act 1983 use the word "occupier" to refer to a person living in a caravan. But see *site owner*, below. The text generally uses "resident" to refer to someone living in a mobile home. 1-82

Park home This term is not found in the legislation, and is not generally used in the text, though this is now a common way of referring to a mobile home. 1-83

Pitch The legislation does not use this word, but it is in common use and is used in this book to describe an area of land on a caravan site on which a caravan is stationed. 1-84

Pitch agreement See *pitch*. 1-85

Protected site This is an important term, defined in the Caravan Sites Act 1968 to mean (with some exceptions) land requiring a site licence. The same phrase is also used in the Mobile Homes Act 1983, where its meaning is very slightly different. Where a site is a 1-86

See 4-7 and 5-6.

"protected site", residents have a degree of protection under these Acts.

1-87 *Residential contract* A term used in the 1968 Act to mean a contract or licence allowing a person to station a caravan on a protected site, or to occupy a caravan stationed on a protected site.

See 4-3.

1-88 *Security of tenure* This phrase is used to mean rights (though often limited ones) which protect a person's position as a tenant or as the resident of a caravan. The 1968 Act gives some security of tenure, since notice must be given to end a residential contract, and after it has been ended an eviction order can be suspended. The Mobile Homes Act gives a higher degree of security.

1-89 *Site owner* The book generally uses the expression "site owner", to refer to the person occupying land as a caravan site or mobile home park, and hence responsible for it—such a person will in most cases be the owner of the land. This is consistent with the Caravan Sites Act 1968, which defines "owner" in relation a caravan site, and with the Mobile Homes Act 1983, which contains a similar definition. However the Caravan Sites and Control of Development Act 1960 uses "occupier" to mean the person who is using land as a caravan site.

See 4-5 and 5-5.

1-90 *Site licence* See *Licence.*

1-91 *Stationing a caravan* "Stationing" a caravan means putting it on land. The term appears in all of the three main Acts, the point of using it being to make clear that this is something different from attaching a caravan permanently to the land, and so making it part of the land.

See 1-11.

1-92 *Touring site* This term is not to be found in the legislation, but is in common use and the text adopts it in order to describe sites on which people touring with caravans stay temporarily.

Touring unit Used in DETR Planning Policy Guidance Note 21: *Tourism* to refer to a pitch on a site which may be occupied either by a holiday caravan or a touring caravan.

See A-108 for an extract from the text.

1-93 *Twin-unit caravan* A particular sort of caravan, defined in Part III of the 1968 Act.

See 2-19.

Chapter 2—Site licensing

Introduction

2-0 This chapter is concerned with site licensing, under Part I of the Caravan Sites and Control of Development Act 1960. Subject to various exceptions, a licence must be obtained from the local authority by a person who wishes to use land as a caravan, and using land as a caravan site without a licence is an offence. The Act allows local authorities to attach conditions to a licence: repeated breaches of the conditions can lead to the revocation of the licence. Planning permission, as well as a site licence, is usually required in order for land to be used as a caravan site.

The text of the Act is set out at A-0 onwards.

See chapter 3 for planning law.

2-1 The Act also deals with some additional matters, including:

- Caravans on commons (s. 23).
- Local authorities' power to set up caravan sites (s. 24).

See 8-43.

See 2-79.

2-2 Sites which already existed when the 1960 Act came into force were the subject of sections 13 to 20 of the Act. These sections are no longer relevant, and have been repealed[1].

When is a site licence required?

2-3 Section 1(1) of the 1960 Act provides that:

> "Subject to the provisions of this Part of this Act, no occupier of land shall after the commencement of this Act cause or permit any part of the land to be used as a caravan site unless he is the holder of a site licence (that is to say, a licence under this Part of this Act authorising the use of the land as a caravan site) for the time being in force as respects the land so used."

2-4 Any "occupier" who "causes or permits" land to be used as a caravan site without a site licence commits an offence and is liable to be fined by a magistrates' court. The maximum fine is level 4 on the standard scale (s. 1(2)).

See 1-48 for the standard scale of fines.

---

1. By the Statute Law Revision Act 1993.

2-5 The different terms used in s. 1(1) need to be explained in order for the meaning to be clear. Some are defined in the Act itself; others have been considered and clarified by the courts.

"Occupier"

2-6 This word is defined by s. 1(3) of the Act, and means:

> "...the person who, by virtue of an estate or interest [in land] held by him is entitled to possession thereof or would be so entitled but for the rights of any other person under any licence granted in respect of the land..."

2-7 The effect of these words is that anyone is an occupier, for the purposes of the 1960 Act, if they are entitled to the use of the land, provided they do so because they are the owner, or have a lease or some other "estate or interest" in the land (meaning a right in the land itself). A person who has only a licence (i.e. permission from the owner) to use the land is not included; nor is a trespasser[1]. So a person who is entitled to the use of the land, because he has a right in the land, does not cease to be the occupier because he gives someone else permission to use it. If A owns land, but gives B permission to use it, A remains the occupier, and is liable to be prosecuted if he causes or permits the land to be used as a caravan site without a site licence. But if A leases the land to B, it is B who is the occupier, because he has an interest in the land.

• The definition overrides the usual meaning of occupier: see 1-43.

• See 1-15 for licences.

2-8 This is not the end of the matter, however. The Act goes on to say, in s. 1(3), that where there is a lease of land amounting to not more than 400 square yards, with a view to its use as a caravan site, the landlord remains the occupier. This is an anti-avoidance measure: otherwise, a landowner could escape responsibility for an unlicensed site by granting leases of individual pitches. He would then not be the occupier of the pitches, and would not commit an offence if the land was used as a caravan site—though the people who occupied the individual pitches would do so. As it is, the Act only allows an owner of land to avoid responsibility by not being the occupier if he leases out areas of more than 400 square yards at a time.

---

1. *Hereford City Council v Edmunds* (1985) 274 EG 1032.

"Caravan site"

By s. 1(4) of the 1960 Act: 2-9

> "... the expression "caravan site" means land on which a caravan is stationed for the purposes of human habitation and land which is used in conjunction with land on which a caravan is so stationed."

2-10 The definition (which depends upon the meaning of "caravan") includes not just the land on which one or more caravans are actually stationed, but land around individual caravans which is used for amenity purposes, roads or communal recreation areas, and land used for parking and services[1].

See 2-12.

2-11 Land on which a caravan is stationed for some other purpose—for example to store it, or so that it can act as office space, or a shop—cannot be a "caravan site" for the purposes of the 1960 Act. But if a caravan is stationed on land for the purposes of being lived in, the fact that no-one is living in it does not of itself prevent the Act from applying. Unless an exemption applies, temporary stationing requires a licence just as much as permanent stationing. One caravan is enough to form a "caravan site"; though as is explained below there is a range of exemptions from the Act, some of which can apply to single caravans. Where an exemption applies, there is no need for a licence.

See 2-30 onwards.

"Caravan"

The definition of a "caravan" is in s. 29(1) of the 1960 Act: 2-12

See also 2-19 for twin-unit caravans.

> "'caravan' means any structure designed or adapted for human habitation which is capable of being moved from one place to another (whether by being towed, or by being transported on a motor vehicle or trailer) and any motor vehicle so designed or adapted, but does not include—
>
> (a) any railway rolling stock which is for the time being on rails forming part of a railway system, or
>
> (b) any tent."

2-13 The definition is not confined to things which look like caravans in the everyday sense of the word, though the different types of these—including horse-drawn caravans—are of course included. The presence or absence of wheels, for example, is not conclusive. The

---

1. *R v Axbridge Rural District Council, ex parte Wormald* [1964] 1 WLR 442; [1964] 1 All ER 571.

definition includes any portable building or other structure which has been designed or adapted for human habitation and which is capable of being moved in the way described in the Act. .

2-14 Buildings are not caravans, because they are regarded for legal purposes as forming part of the land itself. Nor are "moveable dwellings", which are regulated under the Public Health Act 1936.

See 1-9 and 1-26 onwards.

2-15 The definition in the 1960 Act is concerned with two main questions:

- Whether a structure is "designed or adapted for human habitation".
- Whether it is movable.

2-16 Caravans (using the word in its ordinary sense) are certainly "designed" for human habitation, as are Dormobiles, motorhomes and other vehicles with features such as beds and cookers. What does "adapted" mean? The question was considered by the court in *Backer v. Secretary of State for the Environment*[1], a case involving a Commer van. The van had been on a site for at least two years. It was lived in, and contained a bed and other furniture, including some stoves. But the court decided that "adapted" meant physically altered in some way for the purpose of human habitation. The Commer van had not been physically altered and was therefore not a "caravan".

2-17 A "caravan" must be capable of being moved from one place to another, whether by being towed or transported. The wording of the definition in s. 29(1) seems to require that a caravan must be capable of being moved in one piece: if it has to be dismantled, it is no longer capable of being moved as a single "structure". Section 29(1) has been generally understood to mean that it must be possible for the caravan to be towed or carried lawfully on public roads—in other words, that a caravan must not exceed the maximum dimensions for being towed or carried. If that were not so, the definition would depend upon what was possible, as a hypothetical feat of engineering. Some very large structures would then be "caravans" if they were capable of being moved in one piece by specialised equipment, but this is evidently not the intended meaning of the 1960 Act.

See 9-33 for caravans on the road.

2-18 Questions may arise if a static caravan has been fitted with a porch or other extension. It seems that it is a question of fact and degree whether the extension has become part of the caravan. If so, the extension must be included in considering whether the caravan passes the test of being lawful movable on the highway[2].

---

1. [1983] 1 WLR 1485; [1983] 2 All ER 1021.

Twin-unit caravans

The definition of "caravan" in the 1960 Act has been modified by s. 13 of the Caravan Sites Act 1968, which deals with "twin-unit" caravans. Firstly, s. 13(1) provides that: 2-19

> "A structure designed or adapted for human habitation which—
>
> (a) is composed of not more than two sections separately constructed and designed to be assembled on a site by means of bolts, clamps or other devices; and
>
> (b) is, when assembled, physically capable of being moved by road from one place to another (whether by being towed, or by being transported on motor vehicle or trailer),
>
> shall not be treated as not being (or not having been) a caravan within the meaning of Part I of the Caravan Sites and Control of Development Act 1960 by reason only that it cannot lawfully be moved on a highway when assembled".

Provided they comply in other respects with the definition in s. 29(1) of the 1960 Act, twin-unit caravans come within it, even though they cannot be moved lawfully on a highway when assembled, *provided* that they can still be moved from one place to another when assembled and do not consist of more than two sections. 2-20

Section 13(2) goes on to set maximum dimensions for twin-unit caravans: 2-21

> "For the purposes of Part I of the Caravan Sites and Control of Development Act 1960, the expression "caravan" shall not include a structure designed or adapted for human habitation which falls within paragraphs (a) and (b) of the foregoing subsection if its dimensions when assembled exceed any of the following limits, namely—
>
> (a) length (exclusive of any drawbar): 60 feet (18.288 metres);
>
> (b) width: 20 feet (6.096 metres);
>
> (c) overall height of living accommodation (measured internally from the floor at the lowest level to the ceiling at the highest level: 10 feet (3.048 metres)[1]."

---

2. See *Charlton v Howard* Canterbury County Court, 20 June 2001, in which the County Court decided that a porch extension measuring about 12′ by 6′ had not become part of the caravan.

1. The DETR has the power to amend these dimensions, by delegated legislation, but the power has not yet been exercised.

2-22 Since s. 13(1) says that a twin-unit caravan must not consist of more than two sections, it might be thought that something consisting of more than two sections could not be a caravan for the purposes of the 1960 Act. However this was not entirely clear. The meaning of s. 13 has been considered by the courts in several cases[1], most recently in *Byrne v Secretary of State for the Environment and Arun District Council*[2] in which the court was concerned with a log cabin. The owner of the land had been served with an enforcement notice, requiring him to remove it. The notice made the assumption that the log cabin was technically a twin-unit caravan, so that stationing it on the land was a change of use, and the period for enforcement action was 10 years. But the planning inspector considered that the cabin was not in fact a twin-unit caravan. Erecting it therefore amounted to a "building operation", and the period for enforcement was only four years.

See 3-40 onwards for enforcement of planning control.

2-23 The court agreed that the log cabin could not be a twin-unit caravan, since it did not consist of only two sections, separately constructed. For something to be a twin-unit caravan, it was necessary for the caravan to consist of separately-constructed units, which were designed to be assembled on site by means of bolts, clamps, etc. Because the log cabin was not technically a twin-unit caravan, its erection involved building operations and the period for enforcement was four years.

2-24 To summarise, something is a "caravan" for the purposes of the 1960 Act (and later legislation) if it is designed or adapted for human habitation, and either:

- It can be lawfully moved, in one piece, on the highway. Or:
- It can be moved by road in one piece, even if it cannot lawfully be moved on the highway, provided that it is not composed of more than two sections, separately constructed, and does not exceed the specified dimensions.

2-25 The fact that a structure is outside the definition of "caravan" in the 1960 Act means that the legislation on caravans and caravan sites will not apply to it. Other legislation may apply, however: planning law may apply if there is "development"; and "moveable dwellings" are regulated under s. 269 of the Public Health Act 1936.

See chapter 3.

1. See *Carter v Secretary of State for the Environment and Carrick District Council* [1994] 1 WLR 1212, and *Tyler v Woodspring District Council and Secretary of State for the Environment* [1991] JPL 727.
2. [1997] 74 P&CR 420.

"Causing" and "permitting"

The offence under s. 1 of the 1960 Act can be committed either by "causing" or by "permitting" land to be used as a caravan site. Where an occupier uses the land himself, he will be "causing"; where he allows someone else to use the land as a caravan site he will be "permitting". 2-26

As explained above, a person who grants a lease of 400 square yards or less, or a licence, remains the "occupier" of the land. What does "permitting" mean in this situation? An occupier who knowingly allows someone to use his land to station a caravan is permitting that use. However, s. 1(1) of the Act widens the meaning of "permitting", by making it a condition of any such tenancy or licence that it may be terminated if the tenant or licensee does anything which would be an offence under the Act. Section 12(2) goes on to say that, in deciding whether an occupier has permitted the land to be used as an unlicensed caravan site, his power to act under s. 12(1) shall be taken into account. 2-27

See 2-8.

In other words, if the occupier does not end a tenancy or licence when he is entitled to, he may be regarded as permitting the use of the land as an unlicensed caravan site. Whether the occupier commits an offence will depend upon the circumstances. If A owns a field, which he gives B permission to use, and B stations a caravan in the field, A has the right under s. 12(1) to end B's use of the field. If, however, the field is a long way from where A lives, and he does not know what B has done, the right conclusion would seem to be that A has not "permitted" the unlawful use of the field by B and so has not committed an offence. 2-28

Section 12 does not apply if trespassers use land as a caravan site. In this situation an occupier who makes reasonable efforts to persuade the trespassers to leave, even if he does not take legal action or use physical force, is not likely to be regarded as "permitting" the land to be used[1]. 2-29

Exemptions from the requirement to have a licence

The use of land as a caravan site does not need a site licence if it comes within one of the exemptions set out in the First Schedule to the 1960 Act. These exemptions may be summarised as follows. The paragraphs are numbered in the same way as those in the Schedule. In 2-30

See A-21 for the full text of the Schedule.

1. *Bromsgrove District Council v Carthy and Another* (1975) 30 P&CR 34.

some cases the DETR has power to alter the exemptions in certain ways.

2-31 1. The use of land within the "curtilage" of a dwelling house if the use is incidental to the enjoyment of the dwelling. This involves two questions. Firstly what is the curtilage of a dwelling house? This is an important concept in planning law, and is also relevant here. The question of what is included in the curtilage of a house has been considered on various occasions by the courts. It is an area of land which "goes with" a house, and would typically include front and back gardens and perhaps a driveway and a garage, and other outbuildings, but not paddocks, orchards and other additional areas of land[1]. In *Skerritts of Nottingham Ltd v Secretary of State for the Environment, Transport and the Regions*[2] the court explained that the extent of a dwelling's curtilage must depend upon the facts: often it would be a small area, but for a large country house it could larger. Furthermore, land could only form part of the curtilage of one house at a time.

Secondly, when is the use "incidental to the enjoyment of the dwelling"? There must be a connection with the use of the house itself: if the occupants of the caravan formed an independent household, the necessary connection would not be there. Subject to that, the use would generally be regarded as incidental if, for example, the caravan was used to accommodate relatives or lodgers.

2-32 2. The use of land by a person travelling with a caravan, who stays for not more than two nights, provided that during the stay no other caravans are stationed on the land for human habitation, or on adjoining land in the same occupation, and provided that during the 12 months up to the time of the stay the number of days on which a caravan was stationed anywhere on the land for human habitation did not exceed 28. In short, then, the exemption allows occasional stays, for one or two nights, but only for one caravan at a time. This exemption would be of use to a landowner who wished to provide occasional accommodation for touring caravans.

2-33 3. The use of land of not more than five acres, for up to three caravans, provided that in the previous 12 months there were

1. *Snowdonia Park Authority v Porter* (2000) 97 (05) LSG 36; for an earlier case see *Dyer v Dorset County Council* [1988] 3 WLR 213.
2. [2000] 3 WLR 511.

caravans on the land (including adjoining land in the same occupation) for no more than 28 days[1]. The exemption is similar to the last one, but covers up to three caravans in a smaller area; it would also allow limited use for touring caravans.

4. The use of land by an organisation which has been granted a certificate of exemption by the DETR under paragraph 12 of the Schedule. The land must be occupied by the organisation. The use must be for the purposes of recreation and must be supervised by the organisation. 2-34

See 2-43.

5. The use of land for up to five caravans by an organisation exempted under paragraph 12 of the Schedule. The organisation must issue a certificate to the occupier of the land in question, and send details to the DETR. The maximum period of use permitted is a year. 2-35

See 2-43.

6. The use of land as a caravan site if the use is for a meeting, lasting not more than five days, by the members of an organisation exempted under paragraph 12 and under its supervision. 2-36

See 2-43.

7. The use of agricultural land as a caravan site to accommodate workers on the land. This exemption applies to accommodation "during a particular season". The courts have decided[2] that the exemption does not apply where caravans on a farm were used throughout the year—the exemption is for situations where there is a seasonal influx of workers for some purpose, such as picking fruit. 2-37

8. The same as 7, but in relation to forestry. 2-38

9. The use of land which forms part of, or adjoins, a building site, to accommodate people employed in connection with the work. This exemption applies provided planning permission for the work has been granted, if it is required. 2-39

10. The use of land as a caravan site for travelling showpeople. The exemption is confined to members of organisations of travelling showpeople which hold certificates issued by the DETR. 2-40

---

1. The DETR has power (not yet exercised) to reduce the area of land to which the exemption applies, and to add a condition that the 28 days' use takes place between specified dates.
2. *North v Brown* (1974) 231 EG 737; *Vale of White Horse District Council v Mirmalek-Sani and Mirmalek-Sani* (1993) 25 HLR 387.

The DETR may grant a certificate to any organisation which confines its membership to genuine travelling showpeople. The exemption covers showpeople while they are travelling and while occupying winter quarters between the beginning of October and the end of the following March. In other words, the exemption cannot be used to allow showpeople to occupy a site permanently[1].

2-41 11. The use of land as a caravan site if it is occupied by the local authority. A local authority occupying land in its own area and wishing to use it as a caravan site can thus do so without issuing a site licence to itself.

2-42 11A. The use of land occupied by a county council (or in Scotland a regional council) as a caravan site providing accommodation for gipsies.

See 2-79 for local authorities' power to provide sites, and chapter 6 for gipsies.

2-43 Paragraph 12 of the Schedule allows the DETR to grant certificates of exemption for the purposes of paragraphs 4, 5 and 6. The DETR can grant certificates to any organisation if satisfied that "its objects include the encouragement or promotion of recreational activities". The organisation can then use land as a caravan site itself (paragraph 4) or approve sites for use by up to five caravans (paragraph 5) or supervise meetings which involve use of land for up to five days as a caravan site (paragraph 6). Organisations granted a certificate include the Caravan Club, the Boy Scouts Association and the Girl Guides Association.

2-44 Paragraph 13 gives the DETR another power, which is to make an order that the exemptions in paragraphs 2 to 10 shall not apply in particular areas. The DETR can do this only on the application of the local authority for the area in question. The power could be used, for example, for areas where the local authority considered that there was a particular need to protect the amenity of the land.

Exemptions and planning permission

2-45 The fact that an exemption applies, so that there is no need for a site licence, does not by itself mean that planning permission is not required. However, planning law also contains exemptions, almost all of which run parallel to the exemptions from site licensing requirements. These are dealt with in chapter 3. The result is usually

See 3-13 onwards.

1. *Holmes v. Cooper* [1985] 1 WLR 1060; [1985] 3 All ER 114.

that both exemptions apply together, so that a site needs neither a site licence nor planning permission.

Site licences and planning permission

The issue of site licences is linked, by s. 3(3) of the Caravan Sites and Control of Development Act 1960, to the existence of planning permission for the use of the land as a caravan site. A site licence can only be issued by a local authority if the applicant has planning permission to use the land as a caravan site. Planning permission must come from a specific grant: permission which comes from a development order (i.e. delegated legislation from the DETR which grants planning permission automatically) does not count for these purposes. 2-46

Furthermore, if planning permission has been specifically granted, the local authority *must* issue a site licence (s. 3(4)). The grant of a licence is not a mere formality, however, because the local authority may attach conditions to the licence. There is only one situation in which a licence must be refused, even though planning permission has been granted, and that is where the applicant has held a licence which has been revoked during the past three years (s. 3(6)). 2-47

Making an application

Applications must be made in writing to the local authority, by the occupier of the land in question. The application must specify the land in respect of which the application is made (s. 3(2)). The application must contain such information as the local authority may reasonably require[1]. 2-48

See 2-6 for the meaning of "occupier".

"Local authority" is defined by s. 29(1), and means a District Council, a London Borough Council, the Common Council of the City of London, and the Council of the Isles of Scilly. In Wales, however, it means the council of a Welsh county or a county borough. The local authority must issue a site licence within two months unless the applicant agrees that the period should be longer. If the local authority 2-49

1. Section 3(2) originally said that the DETR could make delegated legislation dealing with the contents of applications. The Caravan Sites (Licence Applications) Order 1960, SI 1960 No. 1474 was duly made by the Department. Section 3(2) has since been amended, and although the 1960 Order has not been revoked, it no longer has to be complied with.

fails to issue a licence, no offence can be committed between the date when the licence should have been issued and the date when it is issued, if the applicant uses the land as a caravan site (s. 6)[1]. The applicant is thus protected during this period; though once a licence is issued, he may commit an offence by breaching a condition of the licence.

2-50 Often the local authority responsible for granting planning permission will be the same body as the local authority for site licensing. But if they are different there is a duty on the planning authority to consult the site licensing authority before granting planning permission[2].

2-51 A person can apply simultaneously for planning permission and for a site licence. They must be the occupier of the land in order to apply for a site licence; though this is not necessary in order to apply for planning permission.

Duration of site licences

2-52 A site licence cannot normally be granted for a fixed period only: it must be expressed to run indefinitely. But if the planning permission associated with the site licence has been granted for a fixed period, the site licence will expire at the end of that period—and must say so (s. 4(1) of the 1960 Act). It may happen that, after the site licence has been issued, there is an appeal relating to the planning permission and the terms of the planning permission are altered—for example, the period allowed for use of the land as a caravan site may be increased. In this situation the local authority must amend the terms of the licence so that it matches the planning permission (s. 4(2)).

The power to attach conditions to site licences

2-53 Because a site licence cannot normally be refused, the importance of a site licence lies in the conditions which the local authority can attach to it. Section 5(1) of the 1960 Act both gives local authorities a general power to impose conditions and gives particular examples of what the conditions may do:

---

1. *Hereford City Council v Edmunds* (1985) 274 EG 1032.
2. See s. 71 of the Town and Country Planning Act 1990.

"A site licence issued by a local authority in respect of any land may be so issued subject to such conditions as the authority may think it necessary or desirable to impose on the occupier of the land in the interests of persons dwelling thereon in caravans, or of any class of persons, or of the public at large; and in particular, but without prejudice to the generality of the foregoing, a site licence may be issued subject to conditions—

(a) for restricting the occasions when caravans are stationed on the land for the purposes of human habitation, or the total numbers of caravans which are so stationed at any one time;

(b) for controlling (whether by reference to their size, the state of their repair or, subject to subsection (2) of this section, any other feature) the types of caravan which are stationed on the land;

(c) for regulating the positions in which caravans are stationed on the land for the purposes of human habitation and for prohibiting, restricting, or otherwise regulating, the placing or erection on the land, at any time when caravans are so stationed, of structures and vehicles of any description whatsoever and of tents;

(d) for securing the taking of any steps for preserving or enhancing the amenity of the land, including the planting and replanting thereof with trees and bushes;

(e) for securing that, at all times when caravans are stationed on the land, proper measures are taken for preventing and detecting the outbreak of fire and adequate means of fighting fire are provided and maintained;

(f) for securing that adequate sanitary facilities, and other facilities, services or equipment as may be specified, are provided for the use of persons dwelling on the land in caravans and that, at all times, when caravans are stationed thereon for the purposes of human habitation, any facilities and equipment so provided are properly maintained."

See also 2-76 on conditions relating to fire precautions.

Subsection (2), referred to in s. 5(1)(b), says that conditions may not control the stationing of caravans by reference to the materials used in their construction. A local authority thus cannot, for example, impose a condition that only wooden caravans may be stationed on a site. However it would seem to be open to the local authority to specify the colour of paint to be used, on the basis that paint is a matter of finish, not construction. 2-54

Further clarification of the local authority's powers is provided by s. 5(4) of the 1960 Act, which says that if a condition requires work to be carried out, it may also prohibit or restrict the bringing of caravans on to the site until the local authority has certified in writing that they 2-55 are satisfied with the work. If the work is not done, the local authority may do it themselves and recover the cost from the licence-holder (s. 9(3)). And, by s. 5(5), a condition is valid even if the site owner is required to carry out work which she has no right to carry out. This provision would be relevant if, for example, a condition required the site owner to arrange for access to the site over neighbouring land: whether this could be done would depend upon whether the neighbouring landowner would give permission. But the condition would still be valid.

See 2-73 for model standards.

2-56 Under s. 5(6), the DETR can specify "model standards" for caravan sites, and, where model standards have been specified, local authorities must take them into account in imposing conditions. Model standards do not have to be followed precisely, however, and local authorities are entitled to depart from the model standards in laying down conditions[1].

Alteration of site licences

2-57 By s. 8(1) of the 1960 Act, a local authority may at any time alter a site licence, by changing or cancelling the existing conditions, or by adding new ones, or a combination of all three. Before doing so they must allow the holder of the licence the opportunity of making representations. The local authority must have regard to any model standards, and must, under s. 8(4), consult with the "fire authority" before altering a condition under s. 5(1)(e).

See 2-77 for fire precautions.

2-58 The holder of the licence may himself apply to the local authority for the conditions to be changed (s. 8(2)). Alterations do not take effect until the licence holder has been informed in writing; and if the alteration means that work has to be done, the alteration does not take effect until the end of the period allowed for appealing, and if there is an appeal, until the end of the appeal proceedings (s. 8(3)). The local authority may require a licence-holder to surrender the licence, so that it can be altered—failure to do so is an offence, the maximum fine being level 1 on the standard scale (s. 11)

1. *Clyde Caravans (Langbank) Ltd v Renfrew County Council* [1962] SLT 20, a Scottish case.

Challenging decisions of the local authority

The 1960 Act allows the licence holder to appeal to a magistrates' court against conditions attached to a licence when it is issued, and against any alteration of a licence. If the licence holder is "aggrieved" by the conditions attached to the licence, she has 28 days from the issue of the licence in which to appeal. The appeal is made to the magistrates' court, and the court, if satisfied that the condition is "unduly burdensome," may cancel or vary it (s. 7(1)). Whether a condition is unduly burdensome is a question of fact for the magistrates to decide. 2-59

There is a special rule for conditions which require work to be done on the land: these have no effect during the 28-day period, nor, if the licence-holder appeals, while the appeal is pending (s. 7(2)). Furthermore, the condition that a copy of the site licence be displayed cannot be the subject of an appeal (s. 7(1)). The fact that a site owner cannot comply with a condition, and will have to stop using the land as a caravan site, is not enough by itself to justify its cancellation by the magistrates' court. 2-60

Where the local authority wish to alter the conditions attached to a licence, they must tell the licence holder about the proposed alteration and allow her the opportunity to make representations. If the local authority then decide to alter the licence, the licence holder can appeal to the magistrates' court against the alteration. She has 28 days in which to do so, from the date when she received notification of the alterations. 2-61

Since the licence holder can always apply to the local authority for a variation of the conditions, and can appeal to the magistrates' court if this is refused, the 28-day limit which applies when the local authority alters the conditions is not of great importance in practice[1]. 2-62

Breaches of conditions in site licences

By s. 9(1) of the 1960 Act, failure to comply with the conditions attached to a site licence is an offence, the maximum fine being level 4 on the standard scale. 2-63

On a third or subsequent conviction for breach of site licence conditions, the local authority may apply to a magistrates' court to revoke the site licence, and the magistrates may make an order revoking the licence at the end of a specified period. The revocation 2-64

1. *Peters v Yiewsley and West Drayton Urban District Council* [1963] 2 WLR 702; [1963] 1 All ER 843.

must not take effect before the end of the period in which the holder can appeal (there is a right of appeal to the Crown Court against conviction or sentence) and the period can be extended (s. 9(2)).

2-65 Once a licence has been revoked, the site owner cannot obtain a new one for three years (s. 3(6)).

Site licence conditions and planning conditions

2-66 Conditions can be attached to planning permission, just as they can be attached to site licences[1]. The site owner may thus be subject both to planning conditions and site licence conditions. Questions may arise about the relationship between the two sorts of condition.

See 3-22 for planning conditions generally.

2-67 The courts have taken the view that where planning permission restricts the use of the land, the site licence cannot have conditions which are less restrictive—though it can have conditions which are more restrictive. If, for example, planning permission limits the number of caravans allowed, the site licence can have a condition allowing fewer caravans, but not more[2].

2-68 Conditions which by their nature relate to planning matters cannot be imposed under the 1960 Act. It may often be difficult to tell the difference between conditions which can be imposed under the 1960 Act, and those which cannot, even though the local authority's power is wide[3]. There may be some overlap between the two categories[4]. However the courts have, for example, disallowed as site licence conditions:

- Conditions relating to security of tenure, rent, site rules and other matters[5].

See *Glossary* for the meaning of "security of tenure".

- Conditions requiring caravans to be removed from the site, for part of the year, in the interests of the visual amenity of neighbouring land[6].

---

1. Under s. 72 of the Town and Country Planning Act 1990.
2. *R v Kent Justices, ex parte Crittenden* [1963] 2 WLR 1124; [1963] 2 All ER 245.
3. *Babbage v North Norfolk District Council* (1990) 59 P&CR 248.
4. *Esdell Caravan Parks Ltd v Hemel Hempstead Rural District Council* [1965] 3 WLR 1238; [1965] 3 All ER 737.
5. *Chertsey Urban District Council v Mixnam's Properties Ltd* [1965] 2 WLR 1210; [1964] 2 All ER 627.
6. *Babbage v North Norfolk District Council*—see above.

◆ Conditions designed to ensure that caravans could be removed swiftly from a site liable to flooding[1]: the court said that in this case the magistrates (dealing with the case under s. 7 of the 1960 Act) had not considered whether the same result could be achieved in a way less burdensome to the site owner.

Display of site licences

Section 5(3) of the 1960 Act imposes an important practical requirement. Unless a site licence restricts the site to three caravans or fewer, there must be a condition in the licence requiring that a copy of the licence is displayed on the site "in some conspicuous place". 2-69

Register of licences

The local authority must keep a register of site licences, and the register must be open to the public "at all reasonable times" (s. 25(1) of the 1960 Act). When a licence is transferred, the details of names and dates must be recorded in the register (s. 25(2)). 2-70

Transfer of licences

Where a person with a site licence ceases to be the occupier of the land in question, which will often be because he sells the site, the licence may be transferred to the new occupier with the consent of the local authority (s. 10(1)). The name of the new holder, and the date of transfer, must be endorsed on the licence by the local authority (s. 10(2)). Alternatively, a prospective occupier may, after an application for transfer consent has been made, take the initiative by applying for a fresh licence in his own name. If the local authority grant him a new licence, they need not proceed with the transfer of the existing licence (s. 10(3)). 2-71

Some transfers of property take place by "operation of law", the most common being the transfer of a person's property on death. When this happens to a licensed site, the person to whom the site is 2-72

1. *Goodwin v Stratford-upon-Avon District Council* (1996) 73 P&CR 524.

transferred is treated as having become the holder of the licence (s. 10(4)). If the transfer of the licence was subject to local authority consent, the person concerned would be guilty of running an unlicensed site as soon as ownership of the site passed to her—hence the different rule. Again, the licence must be amended, to show the name of the new holder.

Model standards

See 2-53.

2-73 As noted above, the DETR has a power, given by s. 5(6) of the 1960 Act, to specify "model standards" for caravan sites, and the Act says that in deciding what (if any) conditions to attach to a site licence, the local authority shall have regard to the model standards which have been specified. The model standards do not have to be followed rigidly by local authorities: they can be omitted or adjusted, as the local authority thinks fit.

2-74 Model standards for touring sites were published in 1983. There are also sets of model standards for holiday sites and permanent residential sites: the latest versions were published together in 1989[1] The model standards for permanent residential sites and holiday sites do not apply to other types of site such as gipsy sites and touring sites.

The text of the model standards is set out at A-117 and A-154.

2-75 Model standards deal with a wide range of matters, such as:

- Layout of sites (density, spacing of caravans, parking, recreation space, roads and paths).
- Fire precautions and storage of liquefied petroleum gas.
- Services (electrical installations, water supply, sewerage and washing facilities, refuse disposal).
- Incidental matters such as signs and notices.

1. Model Standards: Permanent Residential Caravan Sites ISBN 011 7522171; and Model Standards: Holiday Caravan Sites ISBN 011 752218X. These are contained in DETR Circulars 23/83 and 14/89.

Fire precautions

Section 5(3A) of the 1960 Act lays down a special procedure for licence conditions which relate to fire precautions. The "fire authority"[1] must be consulted about the extent to which model standards on fire precautions are appropriate. If there are no model standards for the type of site in question, or the view of the fire authority differs from the model standards about what is required for the site, the views of the fire authority prevail, and the local authority must take them into account (s. 5(3B)). The last word thus rests with the fire authority about what conditions a site licence should contain in relation to fire precautions. 2-76

Powers of entry for authorities

Local authority staff are given, by s. 26(1) of the 1960 Act, power to enter land which is being used as a caravan site, or the subject of an application for a licence, for specific purposes. They may enter, for example, to see whether conditions should be imposed, or whether there has been a breach of the Act. Twenty four hours' notice must be given before there is a right to enter, and written authorisation by the local authority must be produced. 2-77

There is a reserve power, enabling the local authority to enter without giving notice, for use where entry to land is refused, or the occupier is temporarily absent, or it would defeat the object of the entry to give notice. The local authority may obtain a warrant from a magistrate, authorising entry. They may thus, if they need to do so, obtain entry by force and without notice (s. 26(2)). It is an offence to obstruct a person acting in accordance with the provisions of this section, the maximum punishment being level 1 on the standard scale (s. 26(5)). 2-78

Local authority sites

Section 24 of the Caravan Sites and Control of Development Act 1960 gives local authorities the power to set up caravan sites (s. 24(1)). (Without this power, it would be doubtful whether local authorities 2-79

1. Usually the County Council—see the Fire Services Act 1947 as amended by the Local Government (Miscellaneous Provisions) Act 1982 s. 8(2).

could lawfully do so.) They may acquire land in order to set up a site; and they may run sites and provide facilities for residents (s. 24(2)). The power applies to temporary and permanent sites. It includes gipsies, and is not restricted to people who normally live in the local authority's area (s. 24(2) and (4). Reasonable charges can be made for the use of sites and facilities; but local authorities may not provide caravans (s. 24(3) and (7)).

Assessment

2-80 In most cases, a licence will be needed for a commercial caravan site, though the range of exemptions means that many non-commercial sites will be free of this requirement.

2-81 Whether the local authority should allow a caravan site to be established is primarily a planning question: if planning permission is granted for a site, then a site licence under the 1960 Act must generally follow. The important issue then is the conditions attached to the licence. These will normally be based on the DETR's model standards, but there is also room for the local authority to exercise its discretion and to impose other and different conditions where these appear appropriate. Breach of a site licence condition is an offence for which the site owner may be prosecuted; but some flexibility is built into the system in that site owners are able to approach the local authority and ask for conditions to be varied if they appear unduly onerous.

See chapter 3 for planning.

Chapter 3—Planning

Introduction

Planning law is a large and complex subject in its own right, and the aim of this chapter is not to give a full explanation of it, but to present an overview, and to show how planning law affects caravan sites and mobile home parks, both when they are set up and afterwards, when development takes places. 3-0

The chapter also deals briefly with the laws which apply for the protection of trees, and of special areas such as conservation areas, and with the control of advertisements. Here there are separate sets of rules, though they come within the overall system of planning law. Planning policy on gipsies, however, is considered separately, in chapter 6. 3-1

The meaning of "caravan site" in the 1990 Act and in the General Permitted Development Order are the same as in the Caravan Sites and Control of Development Act 1960[1]. The courts have decided that where "caravan" is used in a grant of planning permission, the word should be understood in the same way as in the 1960 Act[2]. So there is some common ground between planning legislation and site licensing legislation. 3-2

The planning system generally

The main Act dealing with planning law is now the Town and Country Planning Act 1990, which will be referred to as "the 1990 Act". Other Acts were also passed in 1990 to deal with specific aspects of planning law[3]. The 1990 Act has been amended in some important respects by the Planning and Compensation Act 1991 ("the 1991 Act"). In particular, the provisions on enforcement of planning control have been strengthened. Delegated legislation is also important in the 3-3

See 1-0 on delegated legislation.

1. See s. 336(1) of the Act, and article 1(2) of the Order. The General Permitted Development Order also adopts the definition of "caravan" in the 1960 Act.
2. *Wyre Forest District Council v Secretary of State for the Environment* [1990] 2 WLR 517; [1990] 1 All ER 780.
3. The Planning (Listed Buildings and Conservation Areas) Act 1990, the Planning (Hazardous Substances) Act 1990 and the Planning (Consequential Provisions) Act 1990.

field of planning, since it contains more detailed rules, which supplement the Acts themselves.

3-4 Planning permission is required in order to carry out "development". Usually, planning permission is obtained by applying to the local authority, who can grant it with or without conditions. But the legislation contains several different ways of short-circuiting that process. Of particular importance is the General Permitted Development Order ("GPDO")[1]. This is a piece of delegated legislation which grants permission automatically in some circumstances. Where it applies, there is thus no need to apply to the local authority for planning permission.

See 3-7 onwards for the meaning of "development".

3-5 While the day-to-day administration of the system is in the hands of local authorities, central government (the DETR) has overall responsibility for the legislation, arranges appeals, and also issues documents giving guidance on planning issues. The most important are:

- Planning Policy Guidance Notes (or "PPGs"), which lay down broad lines of planning policy.
- Circulars. These are addressed to local authorities and give guidance on the handling of a range of planning issues.

3-6 Under the planning system, special protection can be given to particular areas of land, and these include:

- Conservation areas.
- National Parks.
- Areas of outstanding natural beauty.

See 3-36.

See 3-38.

See 3-38.

The result is that in these areas stricter planning controls apply.

Meaning of "development"

3-7 This key concept is defined in s. 55 of the 1990 Act, as amended by s. 13 of the 1991 Act. The first part of the section reads as follows:

---

1. Its full title is The Town and Country Planning (General Permitted Development) Order 1995, SI 1995/418.

"(1) Subject to the following provisions of this section, in this Act, except where the context otherwise requires, "development" means the carrying out of building, engineering, mining or other operations in, on, over or under land, or the making of any material change in the use of any buildings or other land.

(1A) For the purposes of this Act "building operations" includes—

(a) demolition of buildings;

(b) rebuilding;

(c) structural alterations of or additions to buildings; and

(d) other operations normally undertaken by a person carrying on business as a builder."

The 1990 Act provides that "'building' includes any structure or erection, and any part of a building, as so defined, but does not include plant or machinery comprised in a building" (s. 336(1)). The courts have laid down some tests for deciding whether something is a "building" for the purposes of planning law. They consider: 3-8

- Size, and the question of whether the structure was built on the site or brought there ready made.
- Whether it is attached to the land.
- Its degree of permanence.
- Whether it can be moved (something may be a "building" even though it can be moved to a certain extent)[1].

There are thus two main sorts of development—"operations" of various kinds (sometimes referred to as "operational development") and material changes of use[2]. 3-9

Section 55 of the 1990 Act goes on to provide that some operations or uses of land do not constitute development, so planning permission is not required. Three examples may be mentioned: 3-10

---

1. *Barvis Ltd v Secretary of State for the Environment* (1971) 22 P&CR 710. See also *Skerritts of Nottingham Ltd v Secretary of State for the Environment, Transport and the Regions* (No 2) [2000] EGCS 43.
2. The Town and Country Planning (Use Classes) Order 1987, SI 1987/764, defines "use classes". A change within the same use class does not involve development—for example a change from a hairdresser's shop to a travel agency, both uses being within class A1.

◆ Carrying out works "for the maintenance, improvement or other alteration of any building" which affect only the interior of the building, or which do not materially affect the exterior (s. 55(2)(a)).

◆ "The use of buildings or other land within the curtilage of a dwellinghouse for any purpose incidental to the enjoyment of the dwellinghouse as such" (s. 55(2)(d)).

See 2-31 for the meaning of "curtilage".

◆ "The demolition of any description of building specified in a direction given by the [DETR] to local planning authorities generally or to a particular local planning authority" (s.55(2)(g))[1].

3-11 In these cases the effect of the legislation is that it is not necessary to apply for planning permission. The same result follows, but by a different route, under the GPDO, which provides that planning permission is granted automatically.

The General Permitted Development Order

3-12 The GPDO grants planning permission for various classes of development. These are set out in Schedule 2 to the Order, which contains 31 separate parts. Most are subject to conditions, and there are some circumstances in which the automatic permission does not apply. The classes mentioned below are those which are most relevant to caravan sites.

See particularly 3-39 onwards.

3-13 Part 5 of Schedule 2 applies specifically to caravan sites. Permission is granted for two sorts of development. Firstly, land can be used as a caravan site when an exemption from the need for a site licence applies. However the GPDO makes one exception: there is no automatic planning permission for the use of land as winter quarters for travelling showpeople. Secondly, Part 5 grants permission automatically for any development required by the conditions of a site licence. It is a condition of the grant of planning permission by the GPDO that use must be discontinued when the relevant exemption ceases to apply, and all caravans must be removed from the site as soon as practicable.

See 2-30 onwards. The exemptions are set out in paragraphs 2 to 10 of Schedule 1 to the 1960 Act

See 2-53 for conditions in site licences.

1. The Town and Country Planning (Demolition—Description of Buildings) Direction 1995 mentions most buildings other than houses, and walls, fences and gates (except in conservation areas). Part 31 of Schedule 2 to the GPDO grants permission for the demolition of buildings, but subject to some conditions.

Part 1 of Schedule 2 grants permission for some sorts of development within the curtilage of a dwellinghouse. This includes permission for a limited amount of operational development, including the provision of buildings "incidental to the enjoyment of the dwellinghouse as such". Such things as containers for the storage of oil for heating, and satellite dishes, are also permitted subject to conditions; and there is automatic permission for the provision of a hard surface for any purpose incidental to the enjoyment of the dwelling house as such. The latter would allow a hardstanding to be laid down for a caravan. 3-14

Part 2 of Schedule 2 grants permission for some "minor operations", which include the erection, improvement and maintenance of fences, gates, and other means of enclosure, provided that they are not more than two metres high, or one metre if adjoining a highway, or (for existing fences, etc) not more than their former height. 3-15

In some circumstances temporary use of land is permitted, by Part 4 of Schedule 2. Temporary buildings and other structures required for building and other operations are allowed. Permission is also granted for use for up to 28 days in each year; but this does not apply to caravan sites—no doubt because of the provisions of Part 5 of Schedule 2, and the fact that exemptions under the Caravan Sites and Control of Development Act 1960 allow for temporary use of land as a caravan site. 3-16

Part 9 grants permission for works required for the maintenance or improvement of an "unadopted street or private way". A road or path is "adopted" when the local authority takes it over and assumes responsibility for its maintenance, at which point it becomes a highway, open to the public at large to use. Part 9 allows private roads and paths on caravan sites to be repaired and maintained without the need for planning permission to cover any operational development required. 3-17

Development and caravan sites

How do the rules described above apply to caravans and caravan sites? Planning permission will generally be required in order for land to be used as a caravan site, since the change will be a "material change of use", and so development. In some cases, however, the courts have decided that the stationing of a caravan on land was not a material change of use, because it was ancillary to the existing use of the land. In the case of *Borough of Restormel v Secretary of State for the* 3-18

Environment[1] the court decided that putting a caravan within the curtilage of an hotel, to provide sleeping accommodation for two waitresses during the holiday season, did not amount to a material change of use. And in *Wealden District Council v Secretary of State for the Environment and Colin Day*[2] the court considered that stationing a caravan on farm land to provide a weatherproof place to mix cattle feed, did not constitute a material change of use. Planning permission was therefore not required in these cases.

3-19 Permission will also be required for any operational development such as landscaping, or the construction of buildings, unless required as a condition of the site licence, in which case permission is automatically granted by the GPDO. Permission may be required for any later development involved in the improvement or expansion of the site.

See 3-12.

3-20 A caravan will not usually be a "dwelling house". This word is generally understood, in the context of planning law, to mean a building containing the facilities for day-to-day domestic existence[3]; and a caravan is unlikely to be a "building". This will mean, for example, that the special grant of permission in the GPDO for satellite dishes does not apply to caravans and mobile homes in the same way that it does to houses; but equally that permission is not required, since the fitting of a satellite dish is unlikely to be regarded as operational development on land. But other parts of the GPDO will apply, for example the grant of permission for "minor operations" such as the erection of fences. The construction of an extension or porch may require planning permission, if attached to the land, since the work will then amount to operational development.

3-21 The use of land within the curtilage of a dwellinghouse, for purposes incidental to the enjoyment of the dwellinghouse as a dwellinghouse, does not amount to development. This allows caravans to be kept in the driveways or gardens of houses. In view of the exemption from the site licensing requirements in this situation, such caravans can also be used as living accommodation, provided that the occupiers of the caravan do not form an independent household. If the occupiers of the caravan did form an independent household, the use of the caravan would not be "incidental to the enjoyment of the dwelling house as such".

See 3-10.

See 2-31.

1. [1982] JPL 785.
2. (1987) 56 P&CR 268.
3. *Gravesham Borough Council v Secretary of State for the Environment* [1983] JPL 307, where the court decided that a small holiday chalet was a "dwellinghouse", even though it had no bathroom or lavatory.

Conditions

Under s. 70(1) of the 1990 Act, local authorities have a wide general power to impose conditions in granting planning permission. If the conditions are not complied with, there is a breach of planning control and enforcement action can be taken. Section 72 deals with various specific points relating to conditions, and makes clear that permission can be granted for a limited period only. Planning permission is deemed, by s. 91, to be subject to the condition that the work be started within five years (though the local authority can specify a longer or shorter period). In practice local authorities almost always add other conditions in granting planning permission. 3-22

See 3-40 onwards for enforcement.

Circular 11/95 gives guidance to local authorities on planning conditions. It summarises the law developed by the courts in considering whether conditions in particular cases were valid by saying that conditions must be necessary, relevant to planning, relevant to the development being permitted, enforceable, precise and reasonable in all other respects. 3-23

Where a planning condition is invalid, the question arises of whether the planning permission itself remains valid, without the condition. The answer will depend upon whether the condition is one of fundamental importance, without which the permission would not have been granted, or whether it concerns some minor, incidental matter. In the case of *Fisher v Wychavon District Council*[1], planning permission had been given for use of land as a caravan site, but with a condition intended to make the consent temporary. The condition, however, was unclear. The court decided that the permission was of no effect: it was not possible to delete the condition and regard the consent as permanent consent for a caravan site. 3-24

Planning policy and caravan sites

There is no single document laying down central government policy on caravan sites. The DETR has published a range of Circulars and PPGs which deal with aspects of planning policy in relation to caravan sites. The following paragraphs summarise policy relating to the establishment of new sites, and related decisions of the courts. 3-25

See 3-5 on the significance of this DETR material.

Policy on gipsy sites is dealt with separately in chapter 6: see 6-20 onwards.

Caravan sites and mobile home parks generally DETR Circular 12/78[2] followed a review of the rôle of mobile homes, and a related study of mobile home living. It made the following points: 3-26

1. *The Times* 22 November 2000

◆ Local authorities should pay attention to the demand for mobile home sites, which could help meet the demand for housing generally.

◆ Planning permission granted for mobile home sites should not generally be temporary.

◆ Further protection for residents was required.

See chapter 5 for the Mobile Homes Act 1983.

◆ Local authority sites were sometimes poor and could be improved.

◆ Local authorities should consider leasehold or freehold pitches for mobile homes.

See chapter 7 for the implications of leasing land for a caravan.

3-27 PPG 3 *Housing* recognises the rôle of mobile home parks in providing low-cost accommodation for small households, and suggests that planning conditions, together with the DETR's model standards, should be used to minimise the impact of a site on its surroundings and to control conditions on the site itself.

An extract from PPG 3 is set out at A-98.

3-28 *Caravans in the countryside* PPG 2: *Green Belts* lays down a general presumption against inappropriate development in Green Belts. PPG 7: *The Countryside—Environmental Quality and Economic and Social Development* has a wider application, since it applies to the countryside generally. Annex I deals with cases in which it is essential for agricultural workers to be accommodated close to where they work, so that it may be right to grant permission for a new permanent dwelling, whether a house or a mobile home or caravan. The farm or other agricultural business must be financially viable in order for permission to be granted.

See 3-13 and 2-37 on caravans for *seasonal* work.

See A-101 for an extract from Annex I of PPG 7.

3-29 The courts have considered this rule in a number of cases. Difficulties sometimes arise as to whether the farm is financially viable[1]. However, the purpose of PPG 7 is to give guidance, not to impose a rigid rule[2]. In some cases it may be appropriate to grant planning consent temporarily, to test the viability of an agricultural operation[3].

3-30 *Tourism* PPG 21: *Tourism* urges local authorities to consider the need both for touring and for static holiday sites. Both sorts of site are

2. Welsh Office Circular 9/78.
1. See *South Buckinghamshire District Council v Secretary of State for the Environment, Transport and the Regions* (1999) 78 P&CR 255.
2. See *Petter v Secretary of State for the Environment, Transport and the Regions* (2000) 79 P&CR 214.
3. See *Brightwell v Secretary of State for the Environment* [1996] EGCS 170.

expected to remain an important part of the holiday sector. The PPG points out that permission may be sought for flexible arrangements, so that a touring site can accommodate both caravans and tents, in "touring units", underlining the fact that licences will be required both under the 1960 Act and the Public Health Act 1936. New sites should be screened. They should be set back from the seaside; and there may be a case for dividing larger sites into smaller ones, to lessen the environmental impact.

See 1-26 onwards for the regulation of camping.

See A-108 for an extract from PPG21.

The development plan

As part of the planning process, local authorities must draw up plans for their area, to show how they consider the land should be used in the coming years. In most areas there are two sorts of plan—a structure plan, drawn up by the County Council, and a local plan drawn up by the District. The local plan is much more detailed. 3-31

Developments plan should reflect guidance from the DETR. In turn, they are very important when the local authority considers an application for planning permission. The 1990 Act makes it a specific requirement that the decision should be made in accordance with the development plan "unless material considerations indicate otherwise" (s. 54A). In relation to caravan sites and mobile home parks, as with any other sort of planning application, the local authority must decide in accordance with what is in the development plan, unless there are good reasons for reaching a different decision[1]. 3-32

Environmental Impact Assessments

European legislation[2] requires that before certain major development takes place, there should be an assessment of the environmental impact of the proposal. In England and Wales the law is set out in the Town and Country Planning (Environmental Impact Assessment) Regulations 1999[3] 3-33

---

1. For cases on s. 54A see *Delaney v Secretary of State for the Environment, Transport and the Regions* [2000] *PLCR 40, R v Secretary of State for the Environment, Transport and the Regions, ex part Richmondshire District Council* [1999] EGCS 148, *R v Secretary of State for the Environment, Transport and the Regions, ex parte Smith* [1999] JPL 371.
2. Directive 85/337/EEC, as amended by 97/11/EC.
3. SI 1999/293.

3-34 Under these Regulations some projects, listed in Schedule 1, must always be given an environmental impact assessment. Caravan sites are not listed in Schedule 1. However, permanent camp sites and caravan sites are listed in Schedule 2, and an environmental impact assessment is required if the site is to exceed 1 hectare, or if it will be in a "sensitive area", including National Parks, the Norfolk Broads, and areas of outstanding natural beauty. The Regulations set out the procedure for handling planning applications which come within Schedule 2.

Special areas

3-35 Land can be given extra protection against inappropriate development by designating it as a conservation area, a National Park, or an area of outstanding natural beauty. The following paragraphs deal with some of the special rules which apply in these areas.

3-36 *Conservation areas* Local authorities must consider whether land in their area is "of special architectural or historical interest, the character or appearance of which it is desirable to preserve or enhance". If so, they must designate it as a conservation area (ss. 69 and 70 of the Planning (Listed Buildings and Conservation Areas) Act 1990).

3-37 Once land has been designated as a conservation area, the local authority must, in dealing with planning decisions, pay special attention to "the desirability of preserving or enhancing the character or appearance" of the area (s.72). And it is generally an offence to fell or lop a tree in a conservation area without the consent of the local authority (s. 211 of the 1990 Act).

3-38 *National Parks* and *Areas of Outstanding Natural Beauty* Under the National Parks and Access to the Countryside Act 1949[1], a body known as the Countryside Agency may designate areas of countryside as National Parks, or as Areas of Outstanding Natural Beauty.

3-39 In all of the above areas, the planning permission which is automatically granted by the GPDO is more limited; and in conservation areas local authorities can also give a direction withdrawing some of the automatic grants of planning permission—for example, where land fronts a highway, waterway or an open space, the automatic permission relating to fences, gates and satellite aerials.

1. As amended by later legislation.

Enforcement

Local authorities have a range of powers to deal with breaches of planning control (that is, unauthorised development, or failure to comply with conditions attached to planning permission). These are to be found in the 1990 Act, as amended by the 1991 Act. They are of course additional to those under the Caravan Sites and Control of Development Act 1960. 3-40

See particularly 2-4 and 2-63 for powers under the 1960 Act.

As a first step in dealing with a breach of planning control, the local authority may serve a "planning contravention notice", under s. 171C of the 1990 Act, on anyone who is the owner or occupier of land, or carrying out operations on it, or using it. The notice may require the person to give information about when the operations or use started, and about anyone having an interest in the land. It can suggest a meeting with the local authority, at which the person concerned may offer to apply for planning permission or to stop the unlawful development. The notice must warn the person of the further enforcement action which may be taken by the local authority. Failure to comply with a planning contravention notice (i.e. give the required information) is an offence, the maximum fine being level 5 on the standard scale. 3-41

See 1-48 for the standard scale of fines.

However, the main way in which a local authority can deal with a breach of development control is to serve an "enforcement notice", under s. 72. The notice must be served on the owner and occupier of the land, and anyone else who appears to have an interest in it. It must specify the breaches of planning control complained of, the steps to be taken to put matters right, and the time allowed for them[1]. 3-42

A person served with an enforcement notice can appeal against it, under s. 174, on the grounds that permission for the development should be granted, or (as the case may be) that the condition should be removed; or that there has been no breach of planning control. Appeals are dealt with by the DETR—usually, a planning inspector is appointed to deal with the appeal. A public hearing may take place, or if the parties wish the appeal can be dealt with on the papers. Planning permission may be granted, the enforcement notice may be varied, or it may be upheld. Failure to comply with an enforcement notice is an offence punishable in the magistrates' court with a fine of up to £20,000, or in the Crown Court with an unlimited fine. 3-43

An additional measure, which can be used with an enforcement notice, is a "stop notice" under s. 183(1) of the 1990 Act. This requires the person concerned to stop the unauthorised development at once. 3-44

1. In *Smith v Secretary of State for Wales* (1999) JPL Sept. B172, a period of 10 months was not considered to be too short, when there was no evidence about how long would be reasonable.

Failure to comply is an offence, under s. 187, the maximum punishment being the same as for an enforcement notice. There is a catch for the local authority, in that if the enforcement notice is set aside on appeal, the local authority may have to pay compensation for loss or damage caused by the notice. But no compensation is payable in respect of an activity which is a breach of planning control, or where the person concerned was served with a planning enforcement notice and failed to comply (s. 186(5)).

3-45 Local authorities can also, by s. 187B of the 1990 Act, apply for an injunction to stop a breach of planning control. An injunction is an order from the court to do or stop doing something. Breach of an injunction is a contempt of court, for which the maximum punishment is imprisonment for up to two years. In practice, this power is for use where the other ways of dealing with a breach of planning control have failed to stop the unlawful development.

3-46 In addition, local authorities' powers of entry on to land, for the purposes of enforcing planning control, are enhanced by ss. 196A to 196C of the 1990 Act.

3-47 Enforcement of planning control is subject to time limits. There is a four-year time limit for operational development, and for the change of use of any building to a single dwellinghouse; after four years, the local authority can no longer take enforcement action. For any other breach of planning control, there is a 10-year limit (s. 171B).

3-48 This distinction is important to caravan sites. If the stationing of a caravan involves development, this will usually be a material change of use, and the period will be 10 years. But if the caravan has been permanently attached to the land, the period will be four years. In the case of *Measor v Secretary of State for the Environment, Transport and the Regions*[1] there was an appeal against a refusal by the local authority to grant a certificate of established use, for some land on which there were 18 caravans. The planning inspector considered that the development involved was a change of use, to which the 10-year period applied, and that since the caravans had not been on the land for that length of time it was not too late to take enforcement action. A certificate of established use therefore could not be issued. The High Court agreed with this approach, and agreed that the caravans were not buildings: the four-year period did not apply. [2]

---

1. [1999] JPL 182. See also *Jarmain v Secretary of State for the Environment, Transport and the Regions, The Times* 13 April 2000, in which the subject of the enforcement notice was a caravan which had been transformed into a single-storey building.
2. See also *Lynch v Secretary of State for the Environment, Transport and the Regions* [1999] JPL 354, in which the landowner was unable to show that a mobile home had been on his land for 10 years before the use of the land changed to a mixed use.

Trees and tree preservation orders

The 1990 Act places a special duty on local authorities to impose conditions relating to the preservation of trees, whenever that is appropriate, in granting planning permission (s. 197). 3-49

See also 2-53 for local authorities' powers to attach conditions to site licences.

Local authorities also have the power to make tree preservation orders, the law being contained in ss. 198–210 of the 1990 Act, if they think it is desirable in the interests of amenity. An order can cover a single tree, or a group of trees, or an area of woodland. The Act gives no definition of what is a tree, and so common sense must be used in order to decide whether a given plant is a tree or not. 3-50

See 8-39 for the meaning of "amenity".

When an order is made, it is effectively provisional: it takes effect at once, but notice must be served on the owner of the land in question, and he has 28 days in which to make objections. The authority must consider any objections before deciding whether to confirm the order. 3-51

The order must follow the form laid down in regulations[1]. The effect of a tree preservation order is that the tree(s) in question must not be lopped, felled or damaged in any way without the consent of the local authority. By s. 210 of the 1990 Act, the maximum fine is £20,000 in the magistrates' court; and the Crown Court can impose an unlimited fine and up to 2 years' imprisonment. It is also open to the local authority to obtain an injunction to prevent breach of a tree preservation order, under s. 214A. If consent for felling is granted, it may be subject to the condition that the owner of the land replants with trees in accordance with the authority's directions. 3-52

By s. 198(6), however, no tree preservation order can apply to "the cutting down, uprooting, topping or lopping" of trees which are "dying or dead or have become dangerous", or to taking action which is necessary in order to abate a nuisance. "Dangerous" can include a tree which is perfectly healthy but which is dangerous because, for example, it is obstructing the view at a bend in a road. 3-53

See 10-7 for abating a nuisance.

In the absence of a tree preservation order trees can be lopped or felled as the owner wishes[2], *except* in a conservation area where a special rule applies. 3-54

See 3-37.

Advertisements

"Advertisement" is defined by s. 336(1) of the 1990 Act: 3-55

---

1. The Town and Country Planning (Trees) Regulations 1999, SI 1999 /1892.
2. Special controls apply to commercial forestry, but the subject is outside the scope of this book.

'"advertisement"' means any word, letter, model, sign, placard, board, notice, device or representation, whether illuminated or not, in the nature of and employed wholly or partly for the purposes of advertisement, announcement or direction, and (without prejudice to the previous provisions of this definition) includes any hoarding or similar structure used or designed, or adapted for use.... for the display of advertisements".

3-56 The detailed rules which govern the display of advertisements are contained in regulations, the Town and Country Planning (Control of Advertisements) Regulations 1992[1]. The Act itself, in s. 222, says that where an advertisement is displayed in accordance with the Regulations, planning permission is granted automatically for the advertisement.

3-57 Some classes of advertisements may be displayed without the consent of the local authority, because they are exempt. These classes are listed in Schedule 2 to the Regulations, and include advertisements on enclosed land which are not readily visible from outside the land, or any part of it to which the public have access, and advertisements on vehicles (provided the vehicle is not used primarily for the display of advertisements) (classes B and C). Directions signs on a caravan site will often come within this exemption, provided they are not readily visible from outside the site. However, these advertisements must comply with five standard conditions, for example that the owner of the land has consented to the display of the advertisement, and that any hoarding used is kept in a safe condition (Schedule 1 to the Regulations).

3-58 Some other advertisements do not need local authority consent because consent is granted automatically by the Regulations. These are listed in Schedule 3, and include signs identifying buildings or giving warnings or directions about land or buildings, and temporary advertisements. The five standard conditions apply to all of these classes, and special conditions also apply. Some advertisements on a caravan site which were not within Schedule 2, might qualify for automatic consent under Schedule 3, for example signs which were visible from outside the site.

3-59 The consent of the local authority is required for the display of other advertisements. Consent must be subject to five standard conditions, and must be for a fixed period—five years, unless the authority decide on a shorter or longer period. There is a right of appeal to the DETR against refusal.

3-60 A breach of advertising control is an offence, which is punishable with a fine of up to level 3, and a tenth of that amount for each day the

1. SI 1992/666.

offence continues after conviction (s. 224). Local authorities are also given special powers, in s. 225, to remove flyposting advertisements.

Hedgerows

The Hedgerows Regulations 1997[1] are not strictly a part of planning law, but are included here for the sake of convenience. They apply to hedgerows which are at least 20 metres long (or which join other hedgerows) and which are in, or adjacent to: 3-61

- Common land.
- A nature reserve under s. 21 of the National Parks and Access to the Countryside Act 1949, or a site of special scientific importance.
- Land used for agriculture or forestry, or for breeding horses, ponies or donkeys.

Depending on the land to which it was adjacent, a caravan site with a hedgerow on its boundary might be subject to the Regulations.

The Regulations do not apply to a hedge which forms the boundary 3-62
of a dwelling-house. Where they do apply, the owner of the land who wishes to remove a hedgerow must give notice to the local authority. They can either grant permission, or in some circumstances serve a "hedgerow retention notice". This can be done if the hedgerow is "important" according to various tests set out in the Regulations, which relate either to archaeology and history, or to wildlife and the landscape.

A landowner can appeal to the DETR against a hedgerow retention 3-63
notice. But removing a hedgerow in breach of a notice is an offence punishable with the statutory maximum fine in the magistrates' court or an unlimited fine in the Crown Court. There are also powers which allow the local authority to require a hedgerow to be replaced. Records must be kept, open to the public, of notices under the Regulations.

1. SI 1997/1160.

Assessment

3-64 Planning will often be relevant when a caravan site is established, and may be relevant at a later date if there is to be building on the site, or a material change in its use. Local authorities must follow the policy laid down by the DETR in drawing up their development plans. Whether permission is given for a new site will depend in most cases on what is in the development plan, taken together with any specific arguments for and against the proposal.

3-65 The best approach to planning is often a discussion with local authority staff, who can give guidance on whether planning permission is required, and if so whether an application is likely to be successful.

Chapter 4—The 1968 Act

Introduction

This chapter deals with the protection given by Part I of the Caravan Sites Act 1968 to most people living in caravans on "protected sites"—in effect residential sites, not touring or holiday sites. 4-0

See 4-7 for "protected site".

When it applies, Part I of the 1968 Act has three main effects. First, it protects occupiers from being unlawfully evicted, and from being harassed. The Act makes it an offence to evict an occupier without obtaining an eviction order from the court, and to harass an occupier. Secondly, the court is given power in most cases to suspend an eviction order, thus allowing the occupier to remain in the caravan. (The Act, in s. 5, defines "the court" as meaning the County Court.) Finally, Part I of the 1968 Act also requires that a minimum of four weeks' notice be given, in some cases, if the site owner wishes to make an occupier of a caravan leave. 4-1

The Act thus gives some basic protection to occupiers of caravans against losing their homes. It does not give complete security of tenure, but in many cases the occupier who behaves reasonably will be able to resist attempts to move her. Apart from the question of notice, the protection given by Part I of the 1968 Act does not extend to the terms of the agreement between the occupier and the site owner: the Act does not have anything to say about what these will be. As will be seen in chapter 5, the Mobile Homes Acts have since extended the protection in this respect, to some though not to all of those who live in caravans on protected sites. 4-2

See 1-88 for "security of tenure".

When does the 1968 Act apply?

By s. 1(1) of the Act: 4-3

> "This Part of this Act applies in relation to any licence or contract (whether made before or after the passing of this Act) under which a person is entitled to station a caravan on a protected site (as defined by subsection (2) below) and occupy it as his residence, or to occupy as his residence a caravan stationed on any such site; and any such licence or contract is in this Part referred to as a residential contract, and the person so entitled as an occupier."

4-4 "Occupier" in the Act has a special meaning, since it covers only the person who is entitled to live in the caravan under the licence or contract, not all the people who in fact occupy the caravan. However, the licence or contract could extend to more than one person so that, for example, a husband and wife could both be "occupiers" for the purposes of the Act.

4-5 The Act goes on to say (in s. 16) that "caravan" has the same meaning as in the 1960 Act, subject to the amendments made by the 1968 Act in respect of caravans. The meaning of "caravan" has already been explained. The "owner" of a protected site is the person who is entitled to the possession of the land.

See 2-12 onwards.

See 1-43 onwards for "possessing" land.

4-6 The 1968 Act covers two sorts of situation. Firstly it applies where a person has the right to station a caravan on the site—in other words, where the person concerned owns the caravan. Secondly it applies where the site owner supplies the caravan, and the person concerned merely lives in it.

4-7 The 1968 Act applies only to a "protected site". This is an important concept. A protected site is (by s. 1(2)), any land for which a site licence is required under Part I of the Caravan Sites and Control of Development Act 1960, or would be required but for the exemption in paragraph 11 of Schedule 1 to that Act, *except* land for which planning permission or a site licence:

See 2-41.

- "Is expressed be granted for holiday use only". Or—
- "Is otherwise expressed or subject to such conditions that there are times of the year when no caravan may be stationed on the land for human habitation".

4-8 This definition is simple when applied to privately-run sites, since it is only necessary to ask whether a licence is required, and, if so, whether full-time occupation is permitted. If these conditions are satisfied, the site is protected.

4-9 In relation to local authority sites, the position is more complicated. For bodies which are "local authorities" for the purposes of s. 29(1) of the 1960 Act —typically, English District Councils—a licence is not actually required, but would be but for the exemption in paragraph 11 of the Schedule. So such sites are protected. Bodies which are *not* "local authorities"—typically, English County Councils—*do* generally require a licence, and so their sites which are for full-time occupation are protected. Sites are thus usually protected whether or not the site owner is a "local authority".

See 2-49.

But see also 6-9 on gipsy sites.

4-10 If there is no planning permission, and land is being used as a site in breach of planning law, it cannot be a protected site[1]. But if there is planning permission, the absence of a site licence does not prevent the site from being "protected"—the test laid down in the Act is whether a licence is "required" for the site, not whether one has been obtained.[1] The explanation for this rule may be that if planning permission has been granted a site licence must be granted too, on the application of the site owner, and the occupier of a caravan should not be prejudiced by the lack of a site licence.

But see 4-34: this *does* prevent the court from suspending an eviction order.

4-11 There must be a "licence or contract" by which a person is entitled to station a caravan on the protected site. "Licence" here means permission from the site owner to station the caravan on the site. The legal meaning of "contract" is an agreement which the parties intend to be binding and which is a bargain, in the sense that each gives the other something of value, whether money or money's worth. Someone with no licence or contract (in particular, a trespasser) does not qualify for protection under the 1968 Act. An occupier who is a tenant under a lease is covered by the Act in the same way as an occupier who has a licence (because a tenancy agreement is a contract). As can be seen from s. 1(1), the Act uses the phrase "residential contract" to cover both permission and agreement.

See 1-78 for "licence".

See chapter 7 for contracts generally.

It would be unusual for a site owner to grant a lease of land so that the land can be used for stationing a caravan. See 1-14.

4-12 The Act says that it applies "in relation to any licence or contract .... *under which* a person is entitled to station a caravan on a protected site.... and occupy it as his residence...." The effect of the words emphasised is probably that if the licence or contract says nothing about what the occupier may do, he does have the right to occupy the caravan as his residence, and the Act applies. If, however, there is an agreement or permission restricting the use to (say) an office or shop, the Act cannot apply. Whether the occupier actually lives in the caravan is not relevant: for the Act to apply, the question is whether he has the right to live there.

Though it is relevant to whether the site owner has a defence if prosecuted for harassment or unlawful eviction; and it could be relevant also to the question of whether an eviction order should be suspended. See 4-28.

4-13 The "licence or contract" does not have to be in writing. It does not have to give a permanent or indefinite right to station a caravan on the site: a temporary right could be within the definition. The agreement may be one to which the Mobile Homes Acts apply—the occupier will then have both sorts of protection.

See chapter 5 for the Mobile Homes Acts.

Scope of Part I in practice

4-14 Part I of the 1968 Act will apply quite widely, covering many situations where a person has an agreement, or permission, which allows her to

---

1. *Adams v Brown, The Times* 22 November 1989, which dealt with two earlier inconsistent decisions, *Hooper v Eaglestone* (1977) 76 LGR 308 and *Balthasar v Mullane* (1985) 84 LGR 55.

live in a caravan on a protected site. It is perhaps easier to be specific about the circumstances in which the Act will *not* apply. The main ones will be:

- Where no site licence is required, because of an exemption: the site cannot then be a protected site (unless the site owner is a local authority exempt under paragraph 11).

- Where the site should have planning permission, but does not do so.

- Where planning permission or the site licence is limited to holiday use, or otherwise has the effect that there are times during the year when caravans cannot be lived in on the site.

- Where there is an agreement or licence which says that the caravan is not to be used as a residence.

- Where the occupier has no permission or agreement from the site owner—in particular, where the occupier is a trespasser.

Ending a residential contract: notice

4-15 Section 2 of the 1968 Act provides that:

> "In any case where a residential contract is determinable by notice given by either party to the other, a notice so given shall be of no effect unless it is given not less than four weeks before the date upon which it is to take effect."

4-16 Not all residential contracts are "determinable by notice"—that is, capable of being brought to an end by the giving of notice. An agreement for a fixed period might *not* be determinable by notice, especially if the period is short: the agreement will then simply end when the period runs out. However an agreement will be determinable by notice if it specifically says so. There might be a term allowing the agreement to be ended at various points (for example, a five-year agreement might provide for the agreement to be determined at the end of each year) or a term allowing the agreement to be ended for breach of site rules or non-payment of rent. If there is a periodic agreement, under which a pitch fee is payable, say, every month or every year, that period is likely to be the period of notice required. A licence not granted by a contract can always be brought to an end by the giving of notice.

4-17 If the occupier or the site owner can end the residential contract by giving notice (s. 2 applies equally to both) a minimum of four weeks' notice must be given. The minimum period will be longer in the case of an agreement which lays down a longer period, but it cannot be shorter. The notice does not have to be in writing; though in practice that is preferable, in order to avoid disputes about what was said.

4-18 A special situation in which the site owner can end a residential contract is that dealt with in s. 12 of the 1960 Act. The site owner can always end a licence if the person with the licence does anything which would be an offence under s. 1 of the Act (i.e. unlicensed use of land as a caravan site). There is a similar right to end a lease of land of less than 400 square yards. The 1968 Act makes clear in s. 5(4) that where the site owner is ending a residential contract under s. 12 of the 1960 Act, the requirement for notice applies.

See 2-27.

4-19 If the requirements of the Act are not complied with, the notice has no effect, and the residential contract is not ended by it.

Protection against eviction and harassment

4-20 The relevant part of s. 3 is as follows:

"(1) Subject to the provisions of this section, a person shall be guilty of an offence under this section—

(a) if, during the subsistence of a residential contract, he unlawfully deprives the occupier of his occupation on the protected site of any caravan which the occupier is entitled by the contract to station and occupy, or to occupy, as his residence, thereon;

(b) if, after the expiration or determination of a residential contract, he enforces, otherwise than by proceedings in the court, any right to exclude the occupier from the protected site or from any such caravan, or to remove or exclude any such caravan from the site;

(c) if, whether during the subsistence or after the expiration or determination of a residential contract, with intent to cause the occupier—

(i) to abandon the occupation of the caravan or remove it from the site, or

(ii) to refrain from exercising any right or pursuing any remedy in respect thereof, he does acts calculated to interfere with the peace or comfort of the occupier or persons residing with him, or persistently withdraws or withholds services or facilities reasonably required for the occupation of the caravan as a residence on the site."

4-21 The maximum punishment for an offence is a level 5 fine, or six months' imprisonment (s. 3(3)). Where an offence under the 1968 Act is committed by a company, with the consent or connivance of, or through the neglect of, any director or manager or secretary (i.e. company secretary) of the company, that person is also guilty of the offence (s. 14(1)).

See 1-48 for the standard scale of fines.

Analysis of section 3

4-22 Section 3 lays down three separate ways of committing an offence, in paragraphs *(a)*, *(b)* and *(c)*. The first paragraph, *(a)*, applies while a "residential contract", as explained above, is in force. Its effect is that any person—the site owner or anyone else—who prevents an occupier from occupying the caravan on the site commits an offence. Any method of doing so will be covered, for example refusing to let the occupier come on to the site, or locking the caravan, or removing it from the site.

See 4-11.

4-23 Paragraph *(b)* applies after the end of a residential contract. When a residential contract has ended, the site owner will be legally entitled to remove or exclude the occupier from the site, because the occupier will be a trespasser, and (if the caravan is the occupier's) remove the caravan from the site, but he can enforce this right *only* by obtaining an order from the court—an eviction order—not by taking physical action himself.

4-24 Paragraph *(c)* applies both during the existence of a residential contract and after it has been ended. It is aimed at harassment which is designed to make the occupier leave the site, or refrain from exercising any rights relating to the occupation of his caravan. Any act designed to interfere with the peace or comfort of the occupier (or persons living with him) is covered, for example using or threatening violence, or subjecting the occupier to noise or other annoyances. The withholding of services or other facilities is also included, though it must be done persistently in order for an offence to be committed.

4-25 How do these provisions fit together?

- If a residential contract is still in effect, the occupier has the right to occupy the caravan on the site (since that is what the definition of "residential contract" means) and for the site owner to deprive the occupier of that right is unlawful, and so contrary to *(a)*. The site owner may be able to end the residential contract by giving notice; otherwise he must wait for it to end.

◆ When the residential contract has ended, *(b)* applies, and the site owner can enforce his right to evict the occupier only by obtaining an eviction order from the court.

◆ Whether or not the residential contract has ended, it is always an offence, under *(c)*, for the site owner to try to make the occupier leave by harassing him.

Defences

If a person is prosecuted for an offence under s. 3(1)*(a)* or *(b)* it is a defence under s. 3(4) for him to prove that he believed on reasonable grounds that the occupier had "ceased to reside on the site". This defence does not apply to *(c)*. Section 3(4) applies whether the occupier was living in the caravan on a full-time or only part-time basis. "Ceased to reside" seems to mean that the occupier has ceased permanently, not just temporarily, to live in the caravan. 4-26

Furthermore s. 3(5) says that the section does not apply to the exercise by any person of a right to take possession of a caravan of which he is the owner, provided the right does not arise under a residential contract. A right under a *separate* agreement—for example, a consumer credit agreement relating to a caravan—could be exercised despite s. 3, provided the right did not arise on the expiration of the residential contract. 4-27

But see also 4-38.

Suspending an eviction order

The court (the County Court) has power, under s. 4 of the 1968 Act, to suspend an eviction order. This means that the order is made by the court, but does not take effect for a specified period, which can be up to 12 months. 4-28

How does the court decide whether to suspend an eviction order? The fact that the court has been given the power indicates that it should be exercised in appropriate cases. The court is told by s. 4(4) to "have regard to all the circumstances", and this means that the court must 4-29 consider the interests of both the occupier and the site owner. Section 4(4) also tells the court to have regard to the following specific matters—

> "*(a)* whether the occupier of the caravan has failed, whether before or after the expiration or determination of the relevant residential contract, to observe any terms or conditions of that contract, any conditions of the site licence, or any reasonable rules made by the owner for the management and conduct of the site or the maintenance of the caravans thereon;
>
> *(b)* whether the occupier has unreasonably refused an offer by the owner to renew the residential contract or make another such contract for a reasonable period and on reasonable terms;
>
> *(c)* whether the occupier has failed to make reasonable efforts to obtain elsewhere other suitable accommodation for his caravan (or, as the case may be, another suitable caravan and accommodation for it)."

4-30 The court must take all these matters into account and arrive at a fair decision. By s. 4(2) the court may, if it decides to suspend an eviction order, impose:

> "such terms and conditions, including conditions as to the payment of rent or other periodical payments or of arrears of such rent or payments, as the court thinks reasonable".

4-31 Such conditions are likely to be appropriate if the site owner is seeking to evict the occupier for non-payment of pitch fees: by imposing conditions, the court can allow the occupier to remain in the caravan, provided he continues to pay the pitch fee.

4-32 Section 4(3) allows the occupier and the site owner to apply to the court to "extend, reduce or terminate" the period of suspension, or to vary any terms or conditions on which the eviction order was suspended. In particular, the occupier can, at or towards the end of the period of suspension, go back to the court and apply for the eviction order to be suspended for a further period of 12 months; and can make further applications, year by year, so as to remain in residence on the site. A site owner, if there has been a breach of a condition, for example as to the payment of the pitch fee, can ask the court to terminate the suspension and allow the eviction order to take effect.

4-33 The court has no power to reverse an eviction order (which would imply bringing back to life the contract or licence under which a caravan was stationed on land). Unless the site owner agrees to enter into a new contract, or give fresh permission, all the caravan occupier can do is to return to the court each year and ask for the suspension to be continued.

Situations in which there is no power to suspend

In two situations, the court is not able to suspend an eviction order (s. 4(6)). These are where: 4-34

- The proceedings are brought by a local authority within the meaning of the 1960 Act.

See 2-49.

- There is no site licence in force for the site. (The apparent reason for this provision is to avoid a conflict between the policies of the 1968 Act and the 1960 Act. The earlier Act says that land should not be used as a caravan site without a site licence. If the power to suspend existed here it would tend to lead to the continued use of the land as a caravan site.)

Furthermore, if the site licence has been granted for a limited period only, an eviction order cannot be suspended beyond the end of the site licence. If the site licence is due to expire in (say) six months' time, the eviction order may only be suspended until then (s. 4(6)). 4-35

Protection for relatives

If the occupier dies, then the provisions on eviction and harassment apply to anyone living with the occupier who is the occupier's widow or widower, or (in the absence of a widow or widower) any other member of the occupier's family living with the occupier at the time of his death (s. 3(2)). (The Act does not define who counts as a member of the occupier's family.) This will protect the survivor of a married couple if he or she was not party to the licence or contract. If both husband and wife were parties to the licence or contract, then both will be "occupiers" and entitled to the full protection of the 1968 Act. 4-36

Compare the 1983 Act: see 5-48.

Otherwise, the protection given by the 1968 Act cannot be passed on; though if the site owner enters a new residential contract with the person living in the caravan, that person will of course become an occupier for the purposes of the 1968 Act, and will enjoy the protection given by the Act. 4-37

When the 1968 Act does not apply

4-38 Suppose that the 1968 Act does not apply, and that an occupier's agreement with the site owner has come to an end, so that by remaining on the site he is trespassing. Does this mean that he can be physically removed by the site owner? The law does give landowners the right to take action themselves to remove trespassers, but this right must be exercised with great care[1].

4-39 Two further points should be made. Firstly, a person who is physically present on premises enjoys protection under the criminal law. Secondly, there are other Acts which give protection to certain classes of people living in caravans. These are dealt with in chapter 7.

See 9-2 onwards.

Assessment

4-40 The 1968 Act is limited in scope, because it does not apply to all caravan sites—in particular, it does not apply where there is no need for a site licence, because an exemption applies, or where the site requires planning permission but does not have it.

4-41 The protection given by the 1968 Act is also limited. Perhaps the most important right given by the Act is the right to resist eviction by the site owner. But this does not apply in all circumstances, and the suspension of an eviction order is in any event a matter for the County Court's discretion.

4-42 Site owners and residents should be aware of whether the 1968 Act applies to their agreement. If it does, then the resident is likely to be able to stay on, even if the agreement is ended; and this should influence their relationship. If there are disputes, and the Court is asked to evict the resident, the Court will have to bear in mind that an eviction order will deprive the resident of her home, and will have to consider whether that is fair and reasonable in the circumstances.

4-43 Other aspects of the law should not be forgotten. The Mobile Homes Act 1983 may apply, in which case the resident has the grater protection given by that Act. Or there may in some cases be a lease, rather than a licence for stationing a caravan, and this will have an important effect on the law which applies.

1. *Burton v Winters* [1993] 1 WLR 1077

Chapter 5—The Mobile Homes Act 1983

Introduction

5-0 Part I of the Caravan Sites Act 1968 Act gives some protection to occupiers of caravans. The Mobile Homes Acts 1975 and 1983 were passed to provide a greater degree of protection. The 1975 Act is now relevant only because it contains a power by which the DETR can lay down minimum standards for sites containing mobile homes. The power has not yet been exercised. If it were exercised, the standards would have to be met—they would not be merely guides to the site licence conditions which local authorities should set. Meanwhile, the model standards set out in 1989 under the 1960 Act for permanent residential sites will apply.

The text of the 1975 Act is set out at A-51 and the 1983 Act at A-54.

See 2-73 for model standards.

5-1 The Mobile Homes Act 1983 Act adds to the Caravan Sites 1968 Act; it is not a substitute for it. However the 1983 Act applies less widely, in two ways:

- It protects only owner-occupiers of mobile homes.
- It applies only where the occupier has an agreement with the site owner.

Some occupiers of caravans will thus have the protection of the 1968 Act, and a smaller class will have the protection of both Acts.

5-2 The 1983 Act is concerned with regulating agreements for stationing mobile homes on land. The Act lays down what the main terms of an agreement must be, and says that there must be a written statement setting out those terms. The 1983 Act also contains provisions dealing with the transfer of agreements. It gives the court (the County Court, or an arbitrator) the power to amend agreements in certain ways and to deal with disputes about agreements.

See 1-8 for "stationing".

See 5-18 for "the court".

5-3 The Mobile Homes Act 1983 is not the only source of law relevant to agreements concerning caravans, since the law of contract generally also applies.

See chapter 7 for contracts generally.

Definitions

5-4 To understand the 1983 Act it is necessary to start by considering the words which determine its scope. By s. 1(1):

> "This Act applies to any agreement under which a person ("the occupier") is entitled—
>
> *(a)* to station a mobile home on land forming part of a protected site; and
>
> *(b)* to occupy the mobile home as his only or main residence."

The words and phrases which are relevant to the meaning must be considered in turn. Some of them are defined in s. 5(1) of the Act.

"Owner"

5-5 The definition of "owner" in s. 5(1) of the 1983 Act is very similar to the definition of "occupier" in s. 1(3) of the Caravan Sites and Control of Development Act 1960. The owner of the site is the person who is entitled to possession as a result of an interest in the land (disregarding the rights of mobile homes owners to station mobile homes on the site). In practice, the question of who is the owner of the site is unlikely to give rise to difficulties.

See 2-6 for the definition in the 1960 Act.

See 1-43 for "possession".

See 5-60 for what happens when ownership of the site changes hands.

"Protected site"

5-6 This term means, subject to one difference, the same here as it does in Part 1 of the 1968 Act. The difference is a technical one. A caravan site for gipsies which is run by "local authorities" for the purposes of the 1960 Act—in particular, English District Councils—is not a protected site under the 1983 Act.

See 4-7 onwards.

See further 6-10 onwards for gipsies and protected sites.

"Agreement"

5-7 The agreement between the occupier and the site owner does not have to be written: it can be oral, or partly written and partly oral. It must be an agreement under which the occupier is entitled to station a mobile home on the site and occupy it as her only or main residence. The agreement does not have to say expressly that the occupier can occupy the mobile home as her only or main residence: provided she is left free to do so, the Act will apply. To prevent the Act from applying, it would be necessary for the agreement to say, expressly or by implication, that the occupier was *not* to use the mobile home as a residence at all, or not as her only or main residence.

Because the agreement must be one under which the occupier is entitled to station a mobile home on the site, the protection of the Act is effectively confined to situations where the mobile home belongs to the occupier rather than the site owner. If the mobile home belonged to the site owner, it would be a matter for him where he stationed it, not a matter for agreement with the occupier—his agreement with the occupier would merely be to let the occupier use the mobile home. In that case Part I of the 1960 Act might protect the occupier, but the 1983 Act would not apply. 5-8

By using the word "agreement", the 1983 Act requires a contract, not a licence on its own (a "bare" licence). In this respect it is narrower than the 1968 Act. But, like the 1968 Act, it extends to cases where the agreement takes the form of a lease or tenancy, since these are contracts too[1]. 5-9

See 7-7 onwards for contracts generally.

"Occupier"

This word is used to refer to the person who is entitled to station the mobile home on the site. There could be more than one occupier, and this would be the case where, for example, both husband and wife were party to the agreement with the site owner. 5-10

See 5-60 onwards as to the transfer of Mobile Homes Act agreements.

"Mobile home"

"Mobile home" is defined in s. 5(1) as having exactly the same meaning as "caravan" in Part I of the 1960 Act. The 1983 Act could simply have used the word "caravan"; but "mobile home" was a commonly-used term in this context, and the Act adopted it. If the subject of an agreement is not a caravan —for example, because it is too large to be transported by road, or because it is permanently attached to the ground—the 1983 Act cannot apply. 5-11

See 2-12 onwards.

Taking into the extension of the definition to include twin-unit caravans: see 2-19.

1. *West Lothian District Council v Morrison* (1987) SLT 361, a Scottish case.

"Only or main residence"

5-12 This expression is not defined in the Act, and it will thus be a question of fact in each case whether a mobile home is a person's only or main residence. The question is not particularly likely to arise in considering whether the Act applies. The reason is that unless there is some restriction in the agreement which prevents the occupier from using the mobile home as his only or main residence, he will be entitled to do so. But the expression is important in considering questions which arise under the Act, for example, whether an agreement can be ended by the site owner and whether it can passed on.

See 5-36 and 5-61 onwards.

Requirement to provide a written statement

5-13 By s. 1(2) of the Act, the owner of the site must, within three months of the agreement[1], give the occupier a written statement which, as the Act puts it:

> "(a) specifies the names and addresses of the parties and the date of commencement of the agreement;
>
> (b) includes particulars of the land on which the occupier is entitled to station the mobile home sufficient to identify it;
>
> (c) sets out the express terms of the agreement;
>
> (d) sets out the terms implied by section 2(1) below;
>
> (e) complies with such other requirements as may be prescribed by regulations made by the Secretary of State."

The written statement is thus a document which sets out the agreement between the occupier and the site owner.

5-14 Paragraphs (a) and (b) are self-explanatory. The "express terms" referred to in paragraph (c) are the terms which the occupier and site owner have actually agreed between themselves. The intention is that all the express terms must be set out in the agreement. The express terms may have been drawn up the occupier and the site owner, or they may be standard conditions, for example those prepared by the BH&HPA and NCC, or a mixture of the two.

5-15 The "terms implied", referred to in paragraph (d), are the terms set out in Part I of Schedule 1 to the Act. Section 2(1) provides that these terms are a part of every agreement and that the express terms of the

See 5-22 onwards.

1. Unless the agreement was made before the 1983 Act came into force (20 May 1983) in which case the written statement must be provided within six months of that date.

agreement cannot delete or amend any of them. They are thus automatically part of every agreement under the Mobile Homes Act. There is also the possibility of the court adding terms to deal with some other matters, these being listed in Part II of Schedule 1 to the Act.

See 5-54 onwards.

5-16 Also relevant is paragraph (e), since this allows the DETR, by means of delegated legislation, to add to the requirements relating to written statements. Using this power, the DETR has made some regulations, the Mobile Homes (Written Statement) Regulations 1983[1].

The Mobile Homes (Written Statement) Regulations 1983

5-17 These regulations provide that written agreements shall be "in the form prescribed in the Schedule to these Regulations or a form substantially to the like effect". The Schedule has four parts.

The text of the Regulations is set out at A-73 onwards.

- Part I contains spaces for the parties to fill in their names and addresses, and details of the land on which the mobile home is to be stationed. There is also space to record the fact, if this is the case, that the owner's interest in the site will come to an end, or that planning permission for the site will expire, on a given date. In this case, the agreement must end at that point too.

See 5-30.

- Part II gives an explanation of the occupier's rights under the agreement.
- Part III sets out the terms implied by the Act.
- Part IV details any express terms agreed by the parties.

The court

5-18 As explained above, the court has power over agreements under the Mobile Homes Act 1983. "The court", by s. 5(1) of the Act, means the County Court, the appropriate court being the one in whose area the mobile home in question is situated[2].

See 5-2.

1. SI 1983/749.
2. *Faulkner v Love (trading as W Love & Son)* [1977] 2 WLR 477; [1977] 1 All ER 791.

5-19 "The court" also includes an arbitrator, if the parties have agreed in writing to refer disputes to an arbitrator (s. 5(1))[1]. No special qualification is required for a person to act as an arbitrator. An arbitrator has the same powers as the court to add to and vary the agreement. An arbitrator cannot punish the owner for failing to comply with an order to supply a proper agreement; but there is a procedure by which the County Court can enforce an arbitrator's decision[2].

Failure to provide a statement

5-20 If the owner fails to provide a written statement within three months, or provides one which does not comply with the Act, the occupier has the right to apply to the court (s. 1(5)). There is no time limit for making an application. The court can then order the owner to provide the statement. The significance of this is that disobedience to the court's order amounts to a contempt of court, for which the owner can be punished by a fine or imprisonment.

See 1-45 for contempt of court.

5-21 On the other hand, if the owner provides a statement voluntarily but does so after the end of the three months allowed, this is still a statement within the meaning of the Mobile Homes Act[3]. The Act applies in the same way as it does to a statement provided during the three-month period, and the provisions of the Act which deal with the addition of terms apply.

Implying, varying and deleting terms

5-22 An agreement will automatically include the implied terms set out in Part I of Schedule 1 to the Act; and the court can be asked to add terms dealing with the matters set out in Part II of the Schedule. The parties are also likely to have decided some terms for themselves (the "express" terms), for example terms dealing with the payment of the pitch fee, and compliance with site rules.

5-23 Within six months of the date when the written statement is given, either the occupier of the mobile home or the site owner can make an

1. The standard conditions drawn up by the BH&HPA and NCC for mobile home sites do not commit the occupier or the site owner to arbitration.
2. Arbitration Act 1996, s. 66(1).
3. *Barton v Care* (1992) 24 HLR 684.

application to the court for an order that further terms, dealing with certain "matters", be part of the agreement (s. 2(2)). The matters are set out in Part II of Schedule 1: they indicate the nature of the terms which can be implied, but it is for the court to decide precisely what terms (if any) should be implied.

Within the same period, either party can apply to the court to vary 5-24
or delete any of the express terms of the agreement—that is, the terms they have agreed themselves (s. 2(3)). Section 2(3) does not allow the court to *add* a term to the agreement; but s. 2(2) will in most cases allow the court to do this.

Where the court is dealing with an application, whether to imply a 5-25
term, or to vary or delete an express term, it must "make such provision as [it] considers just and equitable" (s. 2(4)). In other words, the court must aim for fairness.

The court has no power to extend the six-month limit. However, 5-26
the Mobile Homes (Written Statement) Regulations make sure that the occupier knows about the time limit, because this is included in the explanation which the written statement must contain. There seems no reason why there should not be more than one application during the six-month period; but it appears that the court cannot act if an application is made after the six months.

Section 2 is concerned only with applications to imply terms, or to 5-27
vary or delete express terms, and does not prevent either the occupier or the site owner from taking legal action for breach of contract. It seems that additions under Part II of Schedule 1, and variations and deletions, can take effect only from the date of the court's decision.

The following paragraphs deal first with the provisions of Part I of 5-28
Schedule 1, following the headings used in the Schedule itself, then with Part II, and the terms which can be implied.

Length of agreement (paragraphs 1 and 2 of Part I)

Paragraph 1 says that an agreement shall continue in force until ended 5-29
in accordance with paragraphs 3, 4, 5 and 6. None of these paragraphs allows an agreement to run for a fixed period only. All Mobile Homes Act agreements, therefore, must be capable of running indefinitely.

However, this general rule is subject to several points dealt with in 5-30
paragraph 2. If the site owner has only a limited interest in the site—for example, a lease lasting for a certain number of years—the agreement ends with the site owner's interest, if it has not ended before then. The same is true if planning permission for the site has been

5-41 If the mobile home is shown to be having a detrimental effect on the amenity of the site, the agreement can be terminated at the end of the current five-year period. Suppose the site owner can only show that the mobile home is likely to have a detrimental effect before the end of the *next* five-year period? The wording of the Act appears to indicate that the agreement can then be terminated at the end of the *current* period. An agreement might thus be determined at the end of the first 10 years on the ground that before another five years have passed the caravan will have a detrimental effect.

5-42 Whether a mobile home is having a detrimental effect on the amenity of the site (that is, its pleasantness and attractiveness) will depend upon its own age and condition and the age and condition of the other mobile homes on the site. This provision of the Mobile Homes Act is limited to the age and condition of the mobile home itself. It does not apply to the behaviour of the occupier, or to the condition of land around the mobile home. If the owner wants to be able to end the agreement on these grounds, he must include an express term in the agreement to allow him to do so; and he can then take action for breach of the term, as explained above.

See 8-39 for "amenity" in relation to planning law.

5-43 If the occupier has paid his pitch fee for a given period, but the agreement is terminated before the end of that period, paragraph 7 provides that the appropriate amount must be refunded.

Sale and gift (paragraphs 8 and 9 of Part I)

5-44 The Mobile Homes Act 1983 contains some provisions about the transfer of agreements. Section 3(2) provides that a lawful assignment (i.e. transfer) to another person will be effective, and the person concerned will thus take over the agreement with the site owner. Section 3(2) covers both selling and giving a mobile home agreement.

5-45 A transfer will be lawful if it is in accordance with the terms in Part I of Schedule 1, or the express terms of the agreement. The latter, as explained above, can give the occupier rights which are wider than the terms in Part I, but not rights which are narrower.

5-46 Part I deals firstly with the sale of the mobile home (paragraph 8). The occupier is entitled to sell the mobile home, and transfer the agreement, to a person approved by the site owner. The site owner's approval must not be unreasonably withheld. In practice, the site owner will have to give his approval unless he has a good reason for withholding it. If there is a dispute about whether the site owner has broken the agreement by unreasonably refusing consent, this can be resolved by the court.

See 5-2.

Part I of Schedule 1 also says that when the home is sold and the agreement transferred, the owner is entitled to a commission at a rate not exceeding that laid down by the DETR. The DETR has laid down that the maximum rate is 10%[1]. It is thus open to the occupier and site owner, in the agreement, to fix a lower figure, but not a higher one. It appears that the 10% can be charged on the total sale price, covering both the mobile home and the transfer of the agreement. 5-47

The occupier is also entitled to give the mobile home to a member of his family approved by the site owner (paragraph 9). Who does this include? Section 5(3) of the Act answers this question specifically: parents, grandparents, children and grandchildren are included, as are brothers, sisters, aunts, nephews and nieces, and the husband or wife of the occupier, or someone living with the occupier as a husband or wife. Illegitimate children are treated as legitimate; relationships by marriage are treated as blood relationships; half-blood relationships are also treated as blood relationships, and stepchildren are treated as children. The 1983 Act thus gives detailed rules for determining who can take over an agreement on the death of the occupier of a mobile home. 5-48

Again, the site owner's approval cannot be unreasonably withheld. Commission cannot be charged in this situation. There is no requirement that the person to whom the agreement is transferred should have been living with the occupier. 5-49

Re-siting of mobile home (paragraph 10 of Part I)

If the express terms of the agreement give the site owner the right to require the occupier to move to land in another part of the site[2] paragraph 10 of Part I imposes two conditions: 5-50

> "(a) that other land shall be broadly comparable to the land on which the occupier was originally entitled to station the mobile home; and
>
> (b) all costs and expenses incurred in consequence of the requirement shall be paid by the owner".

This will not apply, of course, if the express terms of the agreement do not allow the site owner to require a move. In that case, any move 5-51

1. The Mobile Homes (Commission) Order 1983, SI 1983/748.
2. The BH&HPA and NCC standard conditions for mobile home parks give the site owner this right in order to carry out essential work on the pitch or the park as a whole.

will be a matter for discussion and agreement between the occupier and the site owner.

5-52 The requirement in paragraph 10 would appear to apply both to temporary and permanent moves. What is "broadly comparable" will be matter of fact in each case, taking into account size of pitch, amenity, and other factors.

Part I of Schedule 1 generally

5-53 In some respects—for example the rules dealing with what happens on the death of the occupier—the Act is compulsory. But in other respects, the Act is in effect setting minimum rights for occupiers, and (to a lesser extent) owners: a Mobile Homes Act agreement can contain other terms which are more generous to the occupier than those set out in Part I of Schedule 1. An occupier could thus be given the right to transfer an agreement without the approval of the site owner: this would not conflict with the requirements of the Mobile Homes Act.

Part II of Schedule 1: terms which may be implied

5-54 Part II of Schedule 1 lists the following "matters", as an indication of the terms which the court can add to a Mobile Homes Act agreement:

> "1. The right of the occupier to quiet enjoyment ..... of the mobile home.
>
> 2. The sums payable by the occupier in pursuance of the agreement and the times at which they are to be paid.
>
> 3. The review at yearly intervals of the sums so payable.
>
> 4. The provision or improvement of services available on the protected site, and the use by the occupier of such services.
>
> 5. The preservation of the amenity of the protected site.
>
> 6. The maintenance and repair of the protected site by the owner, and the maintenance and repair of the mobile home by the occupier.
>
> 7. Access by the owner to the land on which the occupier is entitled to station the mobile home."

5-55 As explained above, the court can only add terms on these matters if there is an application, within six months of the date of the agreement, by the occupier or the site owner.

See 5-22 onwards.

5-56 Any terms added by the court become part of the agreement. The Act does not require them to be added to the written statement which the site owner has to provide, but the form of agreement laid down by the Mobile Homes (Written Statement) Regulations 1983 contains a reference to the court's power to add terms, and any new term will be set out in the order of the court, so that the occupier and site owner will have a record of it.

Other terms

5-57 In addition to terms under Parts I and II of Schedule 1 to the 1983 Act, an agreement may contain express terms. Express terms are those which the site owner and occupier have agreed on themselves, in contrast to those laid down by the Act or inserted by the court. They may be standard terms, or terms which the site owner and occupier have devised for themselves. Finally, the agreement may contain some implied terms; that is terms which the general law says shall be part of the agreement.

See chapter 7, and in particular 7-11.

Death of the occupier

5-58 Section 3 of the Mobile Homes Act 1983 lays down what is to happen if the occupier of the mobile home dies. Provided that the mobile home is the occupier's only or main residence at the time of death, the agreement does not come to an end but continues, and applies to any person who was living with the occupier at that time, and who is the occupier's widow or widower, or, if there is no such person, any other member of the occupier's family who was living with him (s. 3(3)(a)).

See 5-48 for who counts as a member of the occupier's family.

5-59 If there is no such person to take over the agreement, some of the benefit of the agreement can be passed on under the occupier's will or under the law relating to intestacy (s. 3(3)(b))[1]. In this situation, not all of the terms of the agreement apply: the person to whom the mobile home is left does not have the right to live in the mobile home herself, the agreement cannot be ended on the ground that the mobile home is

1. See *Berkeley Leisure Group Ltd v Scott and the Spastics Society* (1993) CLY 4135.

not her only or main residence, and she cannot give the mobile home and transfer the agreement to a member of her family (s. 3(4)). But she is entitled to sell the mobile home, and transfer the agreement, to someone else. The consent of the site owner is required, but this cannot be unreasonably withheld: unless the site owner has a good reason to object to the new occupier, he must agree to the transfer[1].

Change of site owner

5-60 What happens to a Mobile Homes Act agreement if the ownership of the site changes? Section 3(1) of the 1983 Act deals with this by saying that the agreement continues in force and applies to the new owner of the site: the new owner is bound by the mobile home agreement just as the old one was, including implied and express terms.

Transfer summarised

5-61 A summary of the position under the Act as a whole may be helpful:

- If the occupier dies, the agreement can pass to a member of his family who was living with him, and that person will be entitled to the full benefit of the agreement.

- If the occupier dies, the agreement can pass to someone other than a member of his family who was *not* living with him, and that person will be subject to most but not all the terms of the agreement. The person concerned will not be entitled to live in the mobile home[2]. Consequently, the agreement cannot be ended on the ground he is not using it as his only or main residence. He will not have the right to transfer the agreement to a member of his family. However he can sell the mobile home, and transfer the agreement, with the site owner's approval.

- The occupier can transfer the agreement, and *sell* the mobile home, to a person approved by the site owner (subject to the payment of commission of up to 10%) and that person will then have the full benefit of the agreement.

---

1. See *Lee v Berkeley Leisure Group Ltd* (1997) P&CR 493.
2. Unless the site owner enters a new Mobile Homes Act agreement allowing them to do so.

◈ The occupier can transfer the agreement, and *give* the mobile home, to a member of her family approved by the site owner, and that person will then have the full benefit of the agreement.

Assessment

The 1983 Act provides much fuller protection than the 1968 Act for residents who are owner-occupiers on protected sites. In essence, they are given the right to remain indefinitely, provided their mobile home is their only or main residence, and they abide by the terms of their agreement with the site owner and keep the mobile home in good condition. 5-62

The scheme laid down by the Act is not a rigid one: it still allows some freedom to site owners and occupiers to decide on the terms of agreements. But any terms agreed between the parties—including site rules, if these are made part of the agreement—can be altered or deleted by the Court, and there is thus a degree of control here too. 5-63

An agreement under the Mobile Homes Act will in most cases be subject to the general law of contract, which contains rules about unfair terms and other matters. 5-64

See chapter 7.

Chapter 6—Gipsies

Introduction

6-0 In many respects caravans belonging to gipsies, and sites used by gipsies, are treated by the law no differently from other caravans and sites. However there are some differences. For example, the protection given by the Caravan Sites Act 1968 and the Mobile Homes Act 1983 is different; and planning law and policy contain rules which reflect the special position of gipsies.

6-1 This chapter deals with the position of gipsies under the legislation on caravan sites and planning, as well as policy guidance and human rights issues. It also sets out the law on unauthorised camping, now contained in the Criminal Justice and Public Order Act 1994—though this applies to others as well as to gipsies.

Meaning of "gipsy"

6-2 According to s. 24(8) of the Caravan Sites and Control of Development Act 1960 and also s. 16 of the Caravan Sites Act 1968:

> "'Gipsies' means persons of nomadic habit of life, whatever their race or origin, but does not include members of an organised group of travelling showmen, or of persons engaged in travelling circuses, travelling together as such."[1]

6-3 The definition is thus not restricted to persons of a particular origin or racial group, but embraces anyone who adopts a "nomadic [i.e. wandering] habit of life". For the purposes of the legislation, any person can become a gipsy by adopting a nomadic habit of life, or stop being a gipsy by giving it up. The fact that a person leads a nomadic life for only part of the year, returning to the same site for the rest of the year, does not prevent them from a being a gipsy[2].

6-4 However, the courts have clarified the meaning of the word "gipsy" by deciding that it covers only people whose nomadic habit of life is connected to their work. A person who pursues a nomadic way of life for some other reason is not a gipsy so far as the law is

1. For a criticism of the definition, see Lord Millett writing at (1999) 20 Stat LR 109.
2. *Greenwich London Borough Council v Powell* [1989] 2 WLR 7.

concerned[1]. A "New Age Traveller" would not be a gipsy if her travelling was not connected with her work.

6-5 The courts have also had to consider the time when a person's status as a gipsy is determined. In the case of *Hearne v National Assembly for Wales*[2], the question was whether Mr Hearne was a gipsy for the purposes of planning law—if so, his application for permission to change the use of land to a caravan site would be treated more favourably. He was a gipsy when he came to the land where he wanted to live, but then gave up his nomadic way of life. The court decided that Mr Hearne's status has to be determined at the point when the relevant decision (here an appeal against an enforcement notice) was taken. By this time he was no longer a gipsy, and so was not entitled to the more favourable treatment.

See 3-42 for enforcement notices.

History of legislation

6-6 The Caravan Sites and Control of Development Act 1960, s. 24, gives local authorities the power to set up caravan sites, and this includes, in relation to gipsies, the power to provide working space and other facilities. "Local authority" here includes English County Councils (s. 24(8)), which are thus able to set up gipsy sites. There was, however, no specific duty on local authorities under the 1960 Act to set up caravan sites, whether for gipsies or others.

See 2-79 for this power.

6-7 Part II of the 1968 Act placed a duty on local authorities to set up sites for gipsies: councils had to use their power under s. 24 of the 1960 Act to provide "adequate accommodation for gipsies residing in or resorting to their area", though there was no duty, but only a power, to provide working space and other facilities (s. 6 of the 1968 Act). Other provisions in Part II included:

- A power by which the DETR could direct local authorities to provide sites if the DETR considered that they had not done enough to carry out their duty (s. 9).

- An offence of camping in "designated areas", i.e. areas designed by the DETR. The power to designate areas could be used where it was considered that there were adequate sites for

---

1. See *R v South Hams District Council, ex parte Gibb, The Times* 8 June 1994, [1994] 3 WLR 1151.
2. Unreported, 22 October 1999. See also the earlier case of *Runnymede Borough Council v Secretary of State for the Environment and Smith* [1992] JPL 178.

gipsies, so that there was no need for unauthorised camping (s. 10).

◆ A power by which a magistrates' court could make an order requiring a caravan stationed on land to be removed (s. 11).

6-8 Part II was repealed by s. 80(1) of the Criminal Justice and Public Order Act 1994, so there is now no longer a duty to provide sites for gipsies. However, many local authority gipsy sites remain in existence[1].

Current position

6-9 Privately-run sites for gipsies follow the same rules as for other sites, and these are explained in other chapters.

See particularly chapter 4 for the 1968 Act, chapter 5 for the 1983 Act, and chapter 7 for contracts generally.

6-10 In relation to gipsy sites run by local government bodies, the position is more complicated. The main question is whether such sites are "protected" under the 1968 and 1983 Acts. Under the 1968 Act, a site is protected if a licence is required, or would be required but for the exemption in paragraph 11 of the First Schedule to the 1960 Act. This exemption covers English District Councils and Welsh County Councils[2], which are "local authorities" as defined in s. 29(1) of the 1960 Act. Their sites are thus protected generally under the 1968 Act, for gipsies and others. Gipsy sites run by English County Councils are *not* protected. A licence is not required for such sites, but neither are they exempt under paragraph 11: they have a different exemption, under paragraph 11A. This was the conclusion reached by the courts in *Stoke on Trent City Council v Frost & Frost*[3]. (It follows that English County Council sites which are not for gipsies are protected, because a licence is required.)

See 2-41 and A-31 for this exemption.

See 4-9 and 5-6 for protected sites generally.

See 2-42 for the exemption.

6-11 Under the 1983 Act, the position is slightly different: land occupied by a "local authority" as a site for gipsies cannot be a protected site, which means that the protection given by the Mobile Homes Act 1983 does not apply (s. 5(1)). "Local authority" has the same meaning as in the 1960 Act, so includes English District Councils and Welsh County Councils. Otherwise the position is the same as under the 1968 Act,

See 2-49.

1. At the beginning of 2000, according to the DETR, there were 319 local authority gipsy sites in England, with room for about 5,000 caravans, this being about half the total number of gipsy caravans.
2. Local government in Wales is unitary, County Councils exercising the functions of District Councils.
3. (1991) 24 HLR 290.

and English County Council gipsy sites are not protected, for the reason given above.

It may be helpful at this point to summarise the position in relation to protected sites generally. 6-12

Table 2: Protected sites generally

	PROTECTED		UNPROTECTED
1968 Act	Sites requiring licence under 1960 Act.	"Local authority" sites exempt under para. 11 (including English DCs, Welsh CCs).	Sites exempt under other provisions (including particularly para. 11A for English CC gipsy sites).
1983 Act	As above.	As above, *less* local authority gipsy sites.	As above, *plus* local authority gipsy sites.

In other words, in relation to sites run by local government bodies for gipsies: 6-13

- Bodies which are "local authorities" for the purposes of the 1968 Act (in particular, English District Councils and Welsh County Councils): the site is a protected site under the 1968 Act, but not under the 1983 Act.

- English County Councils: the site is not protected under either Act.

—assuming, in each case, that the site is not limited to holiday use, or otherwise restricted so that it cannot be occupied throughout the year.

The fact that, on a site provided by a local authority for gipsies, some settle down and become permanent residents, does not mean that the site ceases to be a gipsy site and can therefore become protected[1]. 6-14

1. *Greenwich London Borough Council v Powell*: see above.

Closing gipsy sites

6-15 Given that local authorities no longer have a duty to provide sites for gipsies, the question arises of whether they can lawfully close gipsy sites. In *R v Wrexham Borough Council, ex parte Hall*[1] the local authority decided to close a site occupied by gipsies, and to develop another site. The authority therefore withdrew an application for further temporary planning permission for the site. The decision was challenged, on the basis that the local authority had failed to take account of government guidance in the form of DETR Circulars.

6-16 The court's view was that the decision by the local authority was not a planning decision, so there was no duty to take account of the Circulars. Nor was there a duty to consult residents on the site, though the local authority had in fact carried out some consultation. Gipsies living on the site could themselves have applied for planning permission for the site to continue if they had wished. There was no legal reason why the local authority could not close the site.

Unauthorised camping

6-17 The offence of camping in designated areas, created by Part II of the 1968 Act, has now been replaced by a procedure set out in s. 77 of the Criminal Justice and Public Order Act 1994. This applies not just to gipsies but to people generally.

6-18 If it appears to a local authority that persons are residing in vehicles, on the highway, or on unoccupied land, or on occupied land without the consent of the owner, they may give a direction requiring them to leave. A direction does not have to refer to the persons concerned, unless there is only one person. Failing to leave as directed, or to remove a vehicle from the land, is an offence for which the maximum fine is level 3 on the standard scale. It is a defence for a person to show that the failure was due to ill-health, mechanical breakdown, or other "immediate emergency".

See 1-43 for occupying land.

See 1-48 for the standard scale.

6-19 For the purposes of s. 77, "vehicle" includes caravans, but is not limited to them: it includes any vehicle, whether or not fit for use on the roads, and anything which is attached to or part of a vehicle. Before giving a direction, a local authority should consider the effect on the person who will be required to leave, and this will include the effect on children of school age and anyone who may be in poor health[2]. Once a person has left land, in accordance with a direction from the

1. [2000] 1 PLR 32.

local authority, they must not re-enter for a period of three months—doing so is also an offence.

See 6-31 onwards on enforcement generally in relation to gipsies.

Policy on gipsy sites

6-20 Caravan sites in general have received only limited attention in central government policy documents. Gipsy sites, on the other hand, have been the subject of a number of guidance documents.

6-21 *Circular No. 1/94: Gypsy sites and planning* This applies both to local authority sites and to privately-run sites, whether set up by gipsies themselves or others. The Circular emphasises the need for the local authority to discuss gipsies' needs, and to show in development plans the provision they have made for gipsy sites—both under the duty in the 1968 Act, when it was in force, and since then. Sites should generally not be in areas of outstanding natural beauty and other sensitive areas; they should if possible allow mixed residential and business use. Three main types of site may be needed:

See A-248 for the text of the Circular.

- For settled occupation.
- For temporary stopping places.
- Transit sites.

Local authorities should not refuse private applications just because they feel that there are enough public sites in the area.[1]

6-22 The Circular also deals with the use of planning conditions, and enforcement. It outlines the circumstances in which planning permission for a caravan site may not be required, or development may be permitted under the GPDO.

See 3-12 onwards for the GPDO.

6-23 In the case of *Rexworthy v Secretary of State for the Environment*[2] a planning inspector refused to grant further temporary permission for a site for gipsies. His decision was based on Circular 1/94, which he regarded as laying down the rule that only factors relating to the use of the land could be relevant—not the shortage of sites for gipsies. The

2. See *R v Wolverhampton Metropolitan Borough Council, ex part Dunne* (1997) 29 HLR 745.
1. But the absence of other sites is not a good reason for allowing a gipsy site, if there are strong objections to the application: see *Mendip District Council v Secretary of State for the Environment, Transport and the Regions* [2000] JPL Jan. B7
2. [1998] JPL 864.

court decided that this was wrong. The first sentence of paragraph 22 of the Circular (said the court) was badly worded. Weight should have been given to the shortage of sites for travellers, as the last sentence of the paragraph made clear.

See A-107 for an extract from PPG12.

6-24 A duty to show gipsy sites in developments plans is also laid down by *PPG 12: Development Plans and Regional Planning Guidance.*

See A-285 for the text of the Circular.

6-25 *Circular No. 18/94: Gypsy sites policy and unauthorised camping* The Circular gives guidance on the application of ss. 77–80 of the Criminal Justice and Public Order Act 1994. It explains how local authorities may use their powers, but also indicates that they should apply a policy of tolerating unauthorised gipsy camping for short periods if the gipsies are not causing a level of nuisance which cannot be effectively controlled. When a local authority is considering whether to evict gipsies from land where they have no right to be, the authority should carry out, before proceeding, an assessment of the humanitarian needs of the gipsies[1].

6-26 Local authorities should consider providing basic services at such sites. The Circular reminds local authorities of the duty they have in the fields of education and housing, the latter under Part III of the Housing Act 1985.

6-27 Local authorities should generally follow the procedure in Circular 18/94, and so should generally make investigations before taking enforcement action under the Criminal Justice and Public Order Act 1994. But the Circular is only a guide: failure to follow it does not render a local authority's actions unlawful[2].

6-28 In October 1998 the DETR and the Home Office together published *Good Practice Guidance on Managing Unauthorised Camping*. This gives guidance to local authorities on how to approach unauthorised camping, and gives examples of codes drawn up by County Councils which explain the standards of behaviour expected and the circumstances in which the Council will refrain from taking eviction action.

Broader planning issues concerning gipsies

6-29 *Granting and refusing consent for gipsy sites* Local authorities dealing with planning applications relating to caravan sites for gipsies (and planning inspectors and the courts, when there are appeals) must take into account the planning policies mentioned above and also more

1. See *R v Leeds City Council, ex parte Maloney (No. 1)* (1999) 31 HLR 552.
2. *R v Hillingdon London Borough Council ex parte McDonagh* [1999] EHLR 169, (1999) 31 HLR 531.

general policies, including some which are concerned with caravan sites generally and some which have a broad relevance, such as:

See 3-25 onwards.

- PPG2: *Green Belts.*
- PPG3: *Housing*
- PPG7: *The Countryside—Environmental Quality and Social and Economic Development*

Applicants seeking planning permission for gipsy sites in the Green Belt often face considerable difficulties[1]. (By contrast, in one case, the courts considered that an Inspector's decision to grant permission for a gipsy site was perverse and unjustified.[2]) 6-30

Enforcement An enforcement notice can be issued, under s. 172 of the Town and Country Planning Act 1990, to deal with a breach of planning control. The notice must explain what the breach of planning control is, what must be done to put matters right, and the period allowed for this to be done (s. 173). If a person fails to comply with an enforcement notice, he commits an offence under s. 179(1) of the Town and Country Planning Act 1990. But it is a defence for a person to show that he did everything he could be expected to do to ensure that the notice was complied with. 6-31

See 3-40 onwards.

In one case[3] a gipsy had installed a mobile home on some land without planning permission. The period given for compliance with the enforcement notice was 10 months. He argued that this was not long enough for him to find alternative accommodation; but the court disagreed, saying that it was for the person concerned to show that the period given for compliance was unreasonably short, and he had failed to do so. 6-32

In *R v Beard*[4] the court had to consider the defence in relation to a gipsy. The gipsy said that there was only one other gipsy site in the area, but he could not go there because he was afraid of being assaulted. The court decided that this was not sufficient to provide a defence. But in *R v Wood*[5], Mr Wood had done nothing to comply with the enforcement notice, but wished to argue that for family reasons he 6-33

---

1. See e.g. *Delaney v Secretary of State for the Environment, Transport and the Regions* [2000] PLCR 40 and *R v Secretary of State for the Environment, Transport and the Regions, ex parte Smith [1999] JPL 371.*
2. *Powys County Council v National Assembly for Wales* [2000] PLCR 385.
3. *Edwin Smith v Secretary of State for Wales and Rhondda Cynon Taff County Borough Council* [1999] JPL B172, following *Smith v King* (1970) 21 P&CR 560.
4. 10 May 1996, unreported.
5. 25 May 2001, unreported.

could not move. At his trial the judge ruled that he had no defence. The Court of Appeal allowed his appeal and ordered a retrial.

Administrative law

6-34 Local authorities, like other public bodies, have a legal duty to behave reasonably and fairly when they carry out their functions. If they do not do so, their decisions can be challenged by the legal procedure known as judicial review. These principles affect the way in which they carry out their functions.

6-35 Local authorities have a broad measure of discretion. In *McPhee v North Lanarkshire Council*[1] the local authority wanted to modernise a site. Mrs McPhee agreed to move, on the understanding that she would be offered a pitch on the modernised site. The court decided that, despite this understanding, it was not unreasonable for the local authority to refuse her application for a pitch on the modernised site, bearing in mind information which had by then come to light. And in *R v Essex County Council, ex parte Curtis*[2] the local authority operated a non-harassment policy but started legal proceedings to remove gipsies from a lay-by, in view of complaints about rubbish, noise and obstruction. The court decided that it was not unreasonable to start proceedings.

Human rights issues

6-36 The Human Rights Act 1998 came into force in England and Wales on 2 October 2000. The Act makes human rights, as set out in the European Convention on Human Rights ("ECHR") a part of the law in England and Wales and lays down how the courts are to enforce those rights.

6-37 Even though the ECHR was not part of the law of England and Wales until October 2000, it was possible for those who considered that their human rights had been infringed to apply to the European Court of Human Rights. And it was also the case that the courts took the ECHR into account in considering whether the actions of public bodies were lawful. For example, in the *Tandridge District Council v Delaney*[3]

1. 1998 SLT 1317—a Scottish case.
2. [1991] COD 9.
3. [2000] 1 PLR 11.

an injunction was issued, but was held by the court not to be disproportionate and so in conflict with the ECHR.

The European Court of Justice has, in the case of *Chapman v United Kingdom*[1] considered complaints by five different gipsy families about their treatment. In each case they had bought land to use as a caravan site, in the green belt or other rural areas, but had not been able to obtain planning permission or a site licence. They had been subjected to enforcement action—either prosecution under the Caravan Sites and Control of Development Act 1960 or action under the planning legislation to prevent breaches of planning control. 6-38

See 3-40 onwards for enforcement of planning control.

The main complaint made to the European Court was that there had been a lack of respect for family and private life, in breach of Article 8 of the ECHR. However, the court found that the action taken against the gipsies was in accordance with the law and was legitimate given the strong environmental reasons for not allowing the land to be used for stationing caravans. It was not accepted that the lack of pitches on authorised gipsy sites entitled the gipsies to station caravans on other land without a site licence or planning permission; nor did the court consider that there was an obligation on the United Kingdom under Article 8 to provide suitable gipsy sites. 6-39

Other complaints were also made to the European Court in this case. The court decided that there was no discrimination contrary to Article 14 of the ECHR against the gipsies; that there were adequate procedures under the law for challenging the official decisions to take action against the gipsies (Article 6); that their property had not been wrongly interfered with, since the official action struck a fair balance between the use of private property and the public interest (Article 1 of the First Protocol); and that—in the case of some of the gipsies—there was no deprivation of the right to education for their children (Article 2 of the First Protocol to the ECHR). 6-40

The decision of the European Court of Human Rights does not mean that a gipsy's human rights could never be infringed by enforcement action relating to a caravan; but it does suggest that if the procedures are applied carefully and responsibly there should be no infringement of human rights. 6-41

While the European Court was concerned with complaints from gipsies, similar complaints could be made by a person other than a gipsy who bought land and sought to use it as a caravan site without a site licence and without planning permission. For the reasons given by 6-42

1. *The Times,* 30 January 2001. In another case, reported on the same day, the government settled complaints under the ECHR by paying compensation and legal costs: see *Varey v United Kingdom, The Times* 30 January 2001. An earlier case on the treatment of gipsies, involving complaints under Articles 8 and 14 of the ECHR, was *Buckley v United Kingdom* (1997) 23 EHRR 103.

the court, enforcement action should not involve any infringement of human rights.

Assessment

6-43 The definition of "gipsy" for the purposes of the legislation is perhaps a rather unexpected and artificial one, since it is concerned purely with a person's way of life and not with ethnic origin or family history or tradition. Careful note needs to be taken of the way in which the courts have clarified and explained the definition.

6-44 Local authorities are no longer under a duty to provide sites for gipsies; but they are encouraged to make allowance for gipsies by adopting a policy of tolerance and restraint in enforcing the law on unauthorised camping. This is particularly relevant to land owned by the local authority itself, including highways and lay-bys. Where land is privately-owned, the owner can take action herself against trespassing.

6-45 Cases on human rights issues suggest that the law in England and Wales is not at odds with the European Convention on Human Rights in relation to the treatment of gipsies. However, the Human Rights Act 1998 has not been in force for very long, and it may be that further decisions will establish rights for gipsies which override some areas of planning law and policy.

Chapter 7—Licences, contracts, leases

Introduction

An arrangement for stationing a caravan or mobile home on land will in most cases involve a licence, which will usually be part of a contract between a site owner and a caravan resident. Occasionally, a lease may be granted by the owner of land so that a caravan can be stationed there. This chapter looks more closely at these legal concepts—licences, contracts and leases—and explains how they relate to the provisions of the Caravan Sites Act 1968 and the Mobile Homes Act 1983. 7-0

See 1-14 onwards for licences and leases generally.

Licences

Generally A person going on to land without a licence (or some other form of legal authority) is a trespasser. A licence makes the person's presence on land lawful. When caravans are stationed on land under a licence, this could be: 7-1

There are many different ways in which the right to go on to land can be given. See for example 2-77 onwards for local authorities' rights of entry on to land.

- A "bare" licence—permission given on its own, not as part of a contract.
- A contract which has been drawn up specially by the site owner and the resident.
- A contract which is based on the standard forms for mobile home parks and holiday sites issued by the BH&HPA and the NCC.

Writing is not necessary as a matter of general law, in order to create a licence to go on to land (though a Mobile Homes Act agreement must be in writing). Nonetheless it will be sensible and businesslike for a licence to be recorded in writing, so that it is clear to those involved how long the licence lasts, how it may be ended, and what its terms are. 7-2

Ending a licence If a licence has been granted as a part of a contract, the contract may lay down when and how it can be ended. 7-3

Alternatively, although nothing is said in the contract, it may be possible to infer from the circumstances that the licence will come to an end at a particular point. For example, if a landowner wants to carry out building work on the land, and as part of his agreement with a builder allows the builder to station a caravan on the land, to accommodate workers, it will probably be an implied term of the contract, if it is not expressly set out in an agreement, that the caravan is to be removed when the work is finished.

7-4 When a bare licence is granted by the owner of land, the owner is in principle free to revoke it whenever he wishes. But there may be circumstances in which the immediate ending of a licence would cause hardship to the person using the land, and the courts may insist that reasonable notice is given before the person has to leave the land.

7-5 The above principles have been modified by the legislation on caravan sites. In particular, the Caravan Sites Act 1968 requires that at least four weeks' notice be given before a "residential contract" (which includes a licence) can be ended. And the Mobile Homes Act 1983 limits the circumstances in which an agreement can be ended.

See chapter 4 generally and in particular 4-15 onwards.

See chapter 5 generally and in particular 5-28 onwards.

7-6 If a licence ends, or the person exceeds its terms—for example by going on to land for some purpose not covered by the licence—then he is a trespasser. The owner of the land can bring legal proceedings against a trespasser. If the trespasser remains on the land, and is in control of it, the right legal remedy is an order for possession, requiring the person to leave the land. Otherwise, the court can be asked to grant an injunction, which is an order forbidding the person to come on to the land again. Breach of an order of the courts can be punished with a fine or imprisonment.

See 1-43 for possession of land.

Contracts

7-7 *Generally* The essence of a contract, legally speaking, is that it is a bargain, in which two or more people each agree to give something to the other(s), in money or money's worth, and to be legally bound by what has been agreed. Not every agreement is a contract, because many are informal arrangements, for example between the members of a family, or between friends, about what is to be done[1]. If there is an intention to make a legally binding agreement, the fact that the bargain

1. The rules of a society or other organisation may not amount to a contract between the members. In *Anderton & Rowland v Rowland, The Times* 5 November 1999, the court decided that a breach of the rules of the Showmen's Guild did not give a member the right to compensation.

is a bad one for one of the parties does not prevent the resulting contract from being enforced by the courts.

But see 7-23 for the law on unfair terms in contracts.

7-8 *Contracts for stationing caravans on land* A contract for stationing a caravan on land does not generally have to be in writing. The contract will consist of whatever is agreed between the site owner and the resident, including any amendments to the original agreement.

7-9 What may be included in the agreement? Site owners may have site rules, which residents are required to abide by. These will only be part of the contract between a caravan occupier and the site owner if the contract says so. The BH&HPA and NCC standard form agreements for mobile home parks and holiday caravan sites both require compliance with site rules. It is now possible for a contract to give rights to people who are not party to it[1]. But this will only happen if a contract specifically says so. Normally, therefore, residents will not be able to take legal action against other residents for breach of site rules. Conditions attached to a site licence by the local authority will not be part of the contract between a resident and the site owner, so the resident cannot take action for breach of contract if the site owner breaches the conditions.

See 2-53 onwards for conditions and site licensing.

7-10 The law can, however, intervene in contracts, to lay down what the obligations of the parties shall be, and this is a feature of the legislation on caravan sites. The 1968 Act intervenes in one respect, namely by requiring notice. The 1983 Act intervenes extensively, by providing that certain terms are automatically included in an agreement, and others can be included if the court so orders.

See 5-22 onwards.

7-11 Apart from these Acts, the law is that terms may be implied into contracts where this is necessary in order to make them effective. In one case[2], the County Court considered that a site owner was able, as a result of an implied term in the contract, to exclude a resident from a holiday site for misbehaviour.

Contracts for selling and hiring caravans For contracts between a business and a consumer, the law implies terms into the contract in order to protect the consumer. Where the contract involves the sale of goods, the implied terms include a term to the effect that the goods are of satisfactory quality (s. 14 of the Sale of Goods Act 1979). This covers:

- Fitness for purpose.
- Appearance and finish.
- Freedom from minor defects.

1. Under the Contracts (Rights of Third Parties) Act 1999.
2. *Brookes v Iddon* [2000] 4 CL 431.

- Safety.

- Durability.

7-12 But there is no implied term in relation to defects which were drawn to the attention of the buyer, or, if the buyer inspected the goods, which would have been apparent on inspection. This rule is particularly important for a person buying a second-hand caravan or mobile home from a business: there can be no complaint about breach of contract in relation to defects which would have been discovered by an inspection.

7-13 The Supply of Goods and Services Act 1982, s. 9(2), takes a similar approach to goods which are hired from someone acting in the course of business: the goods must be of satisfactory quality. Here, however, the business cannot escape being liable in relation to defects which were drawn to the attention of the hirer or which would have been apparent on examination.

Pitch fee reviews

7-14 A contract between a site owner and a person wishing to station a caravan on the site may include a clause allowing the site owner to raise the pitch fee from time to time—a very important matter both for the site owner and for residents on the site. The standard conditions produced by the BH&HPA and the NCC do this, both for mobile home parks and holiday caravan sites, laying down that each year the pitch fee is to be reviewed. In fixing the new amount regard must be had under the conditions for mobile home parks[1] to:

- The Retail Price Index.

- Expenditure by the site owner which has benefited occupiers of caravans and mobile homes.

- Other factors which are relevant, including legislation which has increased the site owner's costs.

7-15 The Court of Appeal has considered the process of reviewing pitch fees in several cases concerning mobile homes. In *Stroud v Weir*

1. The agreement for holiday sites contains a slightly different formula.

Associates Ltd[1] the site owner wanted to raise the pitch fees for the site, and the factors he relied on included:

- An increase in the Retail Price Index.

- The Mobile Homes (Commissions) Order 1983. This Order limits the amount of commission which the site owner can charge when an agreement is transferred, and its effect was therefore to limit the site-owner's income.

- What would be a "fair market rent", or in other words what would pitch fees be on comparable sites.

See 5-47 for the effect of this Order, and A-71 for the text of the Order.

There was a dispute between the site owner and residents about the increase, and the case went to the County Court. There the judge decided that there should be an increase to reflect the rise in the Retail Price Index. The judge accepted that the Mobile Homes (Commissions) Order 1983 was a relevant factor, but concluded that the level of pitch fees on other sites was *not* a relevant factor. Mr Stroud, a resident, appealed. The Court of Appeal agreed on both these issues, though the Court said they would not decide whether the level of pitch fees for new residents on the site would be relevant. The Court added some general remarks about the procedure for reviewing pitch fees under the standard form agreement. First, "determining" the fee was not something which the site owner could do by himself: if there was no agreement between the site and owner and residents, the matter must be dealt with by the County Court. Secondly, two separate issues could arise: (1) whether something was a "relevant factor", and, if so, (2) what increase was appropriate as a result. The County Court could deal with both these questions. Finally, if it happened that there was a conflict between the change indicated by the Retail Price Index, and the change indicated by other factors, the judge must decide what weight to give to each factor. 7-16

See 5-18 for the powers of the County Court under the Mobile Homes Act 1983.

In *Walker v Badcock*[2] the site owner spent about £1,000 on surgery to some trees on the site, and sought to increase the pitch fee by 12p per week for each of the 33 pitches on the site, so as to raise an extra £200 per year, over five years. Mr Badcock, a resident, objected; the County Court decided that the expenditure on the trees could be taken into account in setting the pitch fee. Mr Badcock appealed. 7-17

The Court of Appeal said that provided there was a benefit to residents as a class, new or intermittent expenditure by the site owner 7-18

1. (1987) 19 HLR 151.
2. (1997) 42 EG 180.

could be taken into account. Pitch fees could be adjusted downwards as well as upwards, so there was no reason why they should be increased for a period of five years, to recover the cost of the tree surgery, then reduced again. The court said that it was not necessary for the site owner to consult residents before deciding to seek an increase in the pitch fee. But as had been said in the case of *Stroud v Weir Associates Ltd*, if residents did not agree with the proposed increase, it was for the County Court to settle the dispute.

7-19 The case of *Howard v Kinvena Homes Ltd*[1] concerned the supply of bottled gas to occupiers of mobile homes. The site owner sold gas at a profit to residents: he had a specially-constructed store for supplies of gas, and arranged for the delivery of bottles to mobile homes, and for a qualified fitter to be available 24 hours a day. There was no obligation to buy the gas from the site owner, but under the standard form agreement the site owner had a duty to do his best to maintain the facilities available to residents. Sale of the gas was an important and traditional source of additional income for the site owner. Some residents bought gas more cheaply from other suppliers, and there was a dispute about whether the pitch fee could be increased in order to compensate the site owner for the loss of income. The County Court decided that the loss of profit on the sale of gas was not a "relevant factor" and so could not be taken into account in fixing the pitch fees.

7-20 On appeal by the site owners, the Court of Appeal decided that the loss of profits was relevant. The fact that this reduced the site owner's income, rather than adding to his expenditure (as in *Walker v Badcock)* was not relevant. The Court of Appeal's decision was that where the site owner provided a service which it was under a duty to do its best to maintain, and which was traditionally an important source of income, then a loss of income from the service was a relevant factor, and could be taken into account for the purposes of the pitch fee review.

7-21 In a County Court case, *Oaktree Parks Ltd v Hughes*[2] the site owner wished to increase pitch fees, taking into account:

- The level of fees which would be charged to residents moving on to the site.
- Administrative costs, including the costs of running the company which owned the site.

---

1. (2000) 32 HLR 541. And see [1999] Conv. 374–5 for a forceful criticism of all three decisions.
2. Exeter County Court, 6 October 2000.

- Money spent on maintenance—which the site owner said should be added to the previous year's pitch fee.

- Return on capital.

The County Court decided that the leval of fees for new residents was only relevant if an increase was needed to pay for the running of the park, which was not the case here. Pitch fees included an element of "rent" and an element of "service charge", to pay for maintenance. The right approach was not to add maintenance costs to the previous year's pitch fees but to taken the cost into account in setting the current year's fees. Administrative costs could be taken into account, but the site owner's aspirations for return on his capital could not. The court increased the pitch fees by the rate of the Retail Price Index, but made a deduction because a launderette had been closed. 7-22

Unfair contracts

Several pieces of legislation have addressed the question of unfairness in contracts between people dealing in their private capacity and businesses. The Unfair Terms in Consumer Contracts Regulations 1999[1] are perhaps the most important; but an earlier Act, the Unfair Contract Terms Act 1977 is also relevant. The Consumer Credit Act 1974 deals with some situations in which a loan agreement imposes "grossly excessive" interest on a consumer. This is a general consumer protection measure, but can apply to loans which are used to buy caravans and mobile homes. 7-23

Unfair Terms in Consumer Contracts Regulations 1999 These Regulations were made in order to give effect to a European Directive. (An earlier version of the regulations, the Unfair Terms in Consumer Contracts Regulations 1994, was cancelled when the 1999 regulations were made.) 7-24

The 1999 Regulations apply to contracts made after 1 October 1999, between a consumer (a person acting outside his trade, business or profession) and a person acting in the course of business. While the Regulations have not yet been fully tested in the courts, they are understood to apply to licences and tenancies, so could apply to a pitch agreement or any other contract relating to the stationing of a caravan on land. 7-25

---

1. SI 1999/2083.

See 5-22 onwards.

7-26 The Regulations do not affect terms which are part of contracts as a result of some legal requirement, such as the terms implied by the Mobile Homes Act 1983. They also do not affect the main subject matter of the contract, or the price to be paid for it, provided these things are clearly stated in the contract. So if a pitch agreement gives the right to station a mobile home on a site, for a pitch fee of £500 per year, the size and position of the pitch, and the £500 fee, cannot be attacked under the Regulations for being unfair.

7-27 Otherwise, the Regulations apply to terms in a contract which have not been individually negotiated—in other words, standard-form terms, and terms which (although they are not in standard form) have been drafted in advance, and which the consumer does not have the chance to influence. Site rules which have been made part of a pitch agreement could also be subject to the Regulations. Such terms are unfair if they are "contrary to the requirement of good faith", and if they cause "a significant imbalance in the parties' rights and obligations arising under the contract, to the detriment of the consumer".

7-28 The Regulations do not say what exactly the requirement of good faith is; but this will involve looking to see how strong each party's bargaining position is, and other surrounding circumstances. It is easier to see whether there is a "significant imbalance" in rights and obligations. If there is, and the balance is against the interests of the consumer, then the contract is unfair. Schedule 2 to the Regulations gives examples of terms which may be considered unfair, and the list includes terms which:

- Limit the liability of the business for breaches of contract.
- Allow the business to forfeit money paid by the consumer.
- Allow the business to end the contract at its discretion, when the consumer does not have the same ability.
- Allow the business to alter the terms of the contract of its own accord, without a valid reason which is set out in the contract.

7-29 The consequence of unfairness is that the term in question is of no effect. The rest of the contract, however, continues, assuming that it makes sense without the unfair term. In addition, consumers can apply to the Office of Fair Trading and other "qualifying bodies" (including the weights and measures departments of local authorities) if they feel that a term in a contract is unfair. The OFT, or a qualifying body, can apply for an injunction against any business using the term in question.

The Unfair Contract Terms Act 1977 This Act restricts the ability of parties to a contract to include certain sorts of unfair terms. It applies only where one person is acting in the course of business, and using standard terms of contract, and the other is not (ss. 3, 12). The Act does not apply to all types of contract. Those not covered include contracts relating to an interest in land (Schedule 1). However, pitch agreements do not normally give the occupier of a caravan any interest in the land, and are therefore normally subject to the Unfair Contract Terms Act. 7-30

See 1-45 for injunctions.

The effect of the Act is that a person cannot exclude liability for breach of contract, or claim to be entitled to perform the contract in a different way (or not perform it at all) (s. 3). A site owner who tries to include such terms in a pitch agreement—for example, terms providing that he will not be liable to pay compensation even if he breaks the agreement—will find that they are of no effect, and the court will not enforce them. 7-31

See also 10-42 for the effect of the Act on warning notices.

The Consumer Credit Act 1974 This Act regulates consumer credit businesses (money lending, hire-purchase and similar businesses). It contains provisions which allow the County Court to help consumers who enter into credit agreements which have very high interest rates or are very unfavourable in some other way, whether or not the agreement is regulated by the Act. The Act could thus apply to an agreement for financing the purchase of a caravan or mobile home. Under s. 137, the court can act if a credit agreement: 7-32

> "(a) requires the debtor... to make payments...which are grossly exorbitant, or
>
> (b) otherwise grossly contravenes ordinary principles of fair dealing."

The court can take into account prevailing interest rates at the time the agreement was made and other factors including: 7-33

- The "age, experience, business capacity and state of health" of the borrower.
- The degree to which he was under financial pressure when making the agreement.

If the court is satisfied that the credit agreement is extortionate, the court can re-open and re-write the agreement, so as to produce what it considers a fair result.

Breach of contract

7-34 Where a caravan is stationed on land under a contract, breach of the contract by the resident or by the site owner may mean that one party has a claim to compensation, or can end the contract. In the case of an agreement under the Mobile Homes Act 1983, the breach may entitle the site owner to apply to the County Court to end the agreement. If there is no Mobile Homes Act agreement, the position will depend upon the terms of the contract. The contract may provide for what is to happen in the event of breach, and may allow for the contract to be ended; though this will be subject to the requirement for at least four weeks' notice if the site is a protected site.

See 5-32 onwards.

See 4-15 onwards.

7-35 In some circumstances, a contract can be ended prematurely even if there is no provision in the contract for this to happen. A person who has entered into a contract can end it at once if the other person commits a "fundamental breach" of the contract. A fundamental breach is a failure to carry out the main part of the contract. If, for example, there is a contract (not subject to the Mobile Homes Act) under which a person can occupy a caravan on a site for a year, paying £50 a month to the site owner, and the caravan occupier fails to pay the monthly fee, then the site owner would be able to end the contract at once. But the ending of the contract would not by itself allow the site owner to evict the caravan occupier: because of the 1968 Act it would be necessary to go the court and obtain an eviction order, which could be suspended.

See 4-23.

7-36 Breach of contract may also give rise to a right to compensation. A site owner can thus take legal action against a resident for failing to pay her pitch fee, or failing to abide by her contract in other respects, for example by refusing to co-operate if the site owner wishes to move her caravan to another pitch. As a general rule, the compensation which can be obtained is calculated by considering the sum needed to put the person concerned in the position he would be in if the contract had been performed properly. Sometimes this will be obvious, as where the pitch fee has not been paid. In other situations it may be less clear; in which case the courts do their best to assess the appropriate sum. In one important case[1] a swimming pool was constructed, but was not as deep as specified in the contract. The court decided that the compensation should not be the full amount needed to do the work again, bearing in mind that the value of the house, including the swimming pool, was not significantly affected by the mistake.

7-37 The courts do not generally award compensation for the annoyance and disappointment which a breach of contract can cause. As an

1. *Ruxley Electronics v Forsyth* [1996] AC 344.

exception, where the contract is specifically intended to provide a pleasurable experience, the typical example being a contract for a holiday, then compensation for disappointment can be awarded if the contract is broken. On the other hand, compensation can be awarded where a breach of contract causes inconvenience[1]. Such compensation is usually modest.

Tenancies

An arrangement for stationing a caravan on land can take the form either of a licence (permission) or a tenancy. (The words "tenancy" and "lease" mean the same thing, though "tenancy" tends to be used for short-term arrangements and "lease" for longer-term ones.) The difference between a licence and a tenancy or lease is legally very significant, and it is thus important to be able to tell the difference. 7-38

See 1-15.

In considering whether an arrangement is a licence or a tenancy, the courts pay little attention to how it is described by the parties: the key question is whether there is an intention to give the person concerned "exclusive possession" of the land; in other words, the sole right to use the land[2]. If so, the arrangement will be a tenancy; if not, it will be a licence. A lease for less than three years does not have to be made by deed, or even in writing, contrary to the usual rules for creating and transferring interests in land[3]. 7-39

In practice a site owner will rarely wish to create a tenancy of land in order for a caravan to be stationed on it[4]. In particular, on an organised site, the site owner will wish to have the ability to move caravans from one pitch to another, if need be, and to gain access to the pitch. So the appropriate arrangement will be a licence, not a lease. 7-40

There may occasionally be cases in which a caravan is treated as being separate from the land, and capable of being sold separately, or the subject of a Mobile Homes Act agreement, when it is in fact permanently attached to the land. Such arrangements will probably be of no effect, because of the mistake about the status of the caravan[5]. 7-41

---

1. See *Watts v Morrow* [1991] 1 WLR 1421, and *Farley v Skinner (No. 2)* [2000] PNLR 441.
2. See *Bruton v London & Quadrant Housing* [1999] 3 WLR 150. A landlord will often reserve the right to go on to the land at certain times to inspect it, but this does not prevent an arrangement from being a lease.
3. Law of Property Act 1925, s. 52(2) and 54(2).
4. According to Sarah Credland, however, writing in the *Advisor* for March/April 2000, pp. 8–10, about 10% of mobile home residents are tenants.
5. See *Nutt v Read, The Times* 3 December 1999, where there was an agreement to sell a chalet, and also an assured tenancy agreement relating to the pitch.

Protection for tenants

7-42 *When is there a residential tenancy?* If a lease of a pitch is granted, and the pitch has a caravan on it, does this mean that there will be a tenancy which is protected under the landlord and tenant legislation? In a case[1] under the Rent Act 1977, there was a dispute about whether the Rent Officer could register a fair rent for a caravan. The question was whether the caravan was a "house" for the purposes of the Rent Act. The court decided that a caravan could be a "house", but only if it was permanently fixed in position, as a bungalow or a prefabricated dwelling would be. Rent officers (said the court) should be on their guard against landlords renting out caravans which were effectively immobile, but making superficial arrangements designed to show some mobility and avoid the Rent Act. Here, however, the caravan was attached to mains services but remained movable, and so could not be a "house". The Rent Act did not apply, and a fair rent should not have been registered.

7-43 The Rent Act has been replaced by the Housing Act 1988, which gives similar rights to residential tenants. The Housing Act applied where a "dwelling-house" is let as a separate dwelling. It seems likely that just as a caravan cannot be a "dwelling-house" under the Rent Act unless it is permanently attached to the ground, so also it cannot be a "dwelling-house" under the Housing Act.

7-44 If a caravan has the necessary degree of permanence, so that it is subject to the legislation on residential tenancies, these rules will apply instead of those in the caravan sites legislation. A tenancy which started before 15 January 1989 may be subject to the Rent Act 1977. Between that date and 28 February 1997, the Housing Act 1988 applied, and tenants were "assured tenants". For tenancies starting since 28 February 1997, tenants will generally be an "assured shorthold tenants", unless one of the exceptions apply—these include business tenancies, student lettings, holiday lettings, and cases where the landlord is a public body, such as a local authority. The following paragraphs deal only with assured shorthold tenancies under the Housing Act.

7-45 *Security of tenure* The landlord can be sure of regaining possession if she gives at least two months' notice, and the tenancy has come to an end; however she cannot regain possession for six months from the start of the tenancy (s. 21 of the Housing Act 1988).

7-46 *Rent control* If the tenancy is for a fixed length of time, or is periodic (running from week to week, or month to month etc.) and has

1. *R v Rent Officer for the Nottinghamshire Registration Area, ex parte Allen* [1985] 2 EGLR 153. See also *Elitestone Ltd v Morris* [1997] 1 WLR 647, discussed at 1-10.

a clause providing for rent review, then the law does not interfere. But if the tenancy is periodic and has no review clause, there can be an application to the local Rent Assessment Committee, to review the rent (s. 22 of the Act).

Passing on a tenancy A periodic assured shorthold tenancy can be passed on by the tenant to his or her partner, and this can take place twice (s. 17 of the Act). 7-47

Under the Landlord and Tenant Act 1985, a weekly tenant has a right to a rent book, which sets out the terms of the tenancy (s. 4). This Act also gives a tenant other rights, including the right to know who the landlord is, if he is dealing with the landlord's agent. 7-48

Protection from Eviction Act 1977

The Caravan Sites Act 1968 has provisions dealing with harassment and unlawful eviction, which apply to caravans stationed on protected sites. Similar provisions, whose main purpose is to give protection against harassment and unlawful eviction for tenants, are to be found in the Protection from Eviction Act 1977. By s. 5(5) of the 1968 Act, the 1977 Act does not apply to caravans stationed on protected sites, and this prevents the two sets of provisions from overlapping. 7-49 7-50

See 4-20 onwards.

Section 1 of the 1977 Act is concerned with "residential occupiers". The definition in s. 1(1) of the Act includes licensees as well as tenants, and it seems that it can include situations in which a person has an agreement under which she occupies a caravan: even though the caravan is not attached to the land, it can be regarded, together with the land on which it stands, as "premises" for the purposes of the 1977 Act[1]. 7-51

It is an offence for any person to deprive a residential occupier of her occupation of the premises (i.e. evict her) unless he has reasonable cause to believe that the person had ceased to live there (s. 1(5)). It is also an offence for any person, with intent to make a residential occupier leave the premises, or not exercise a right she may have, to interfere with her peace or comfort or persistently withhold services (i.e. harass her)(s. 1(3)). The landlord of a residential occupier also commits an offence if he does the things mentioned in s. 1(3) and has reasonable cause to believe that they are likely to make the occupier leave or refrain from exercising her rights (s. 1(3A) and (3B). The 7-52

1. *Norton v Knowles* [1968] 3 WLR 183, [1967] 3 All ER 1061, a case on the similarly-worded s. 30 of the Rent Act 1965.

maximum punishment for these offences in the Crown Court is two years' imprisonment or an unlimited fine or both (s. 1(4)).

7-53 When a tenancy or licence comes to an end, s. 3 of the 1977 Act applies. This provides that the owner of the premises may only obtain possession by obtaining an order from the court. Physical action is thus forbidden, unless it takes place under the authority of an order from the court. In some circumstances residential occupiers do not have the benefit of this rule, however, including holiday lettings, and lettings where the tenancy or licence is not granted for money or money's worth (s. 3A).

7-54 The 1977 Act also lays down requirements on notices to quit (s. 5). At least four weeks' notice must be given, and the notice must be in writing and given in the form laid down by regulations, the Notices to Quit (Prescribed Information) Regulations 1988[1]. This rule applies to "premises let...as a dwelling" (s. 5(1)) which may be less wide than the term "residential occupier". In relation to caravans, it may apply only to those attached to land with a degree of permanence. The requirements do not apply to the arrangements mentioned in s. 3A.

7-55 Section 27 of the Housing Act 1988 allows a tenant who has been unlawfully evicted to obtain compensation, the amount being the difference between the landlord's interest in the land with and without the tenant (s. 28). Only the landlord himself can be required to pay compensation[2].

Application of legislation

7-56 The following table illustrates the way in which the legislation explained in this book protects residents of caravans and mobile homes in different situations. The table does not show the effect of the Criminal Law Act 1977, but this provides an important form of basic protection, since it in most cases prevents anybody from entering a caravan by force against the wishes of the occupier.

See 9-2.

7-57 In the first example, the farmer, A, is taking advantage of an exemption in the Caravan Sites and Control of Development Act 1960, so that he can accommodate touring caravans occasionally. There is thus no need for a site licence and the site is not protected. Because the site is not protected, neither the Caravan Sites Act 1968 nor the Mobile Homes Act 1983 applies.

1. SI 1988/2201
2. See *Sampson v Wilson* [1996] Ch 39.

Table 1: Protection for occupiers of caravans

Arrangement	Caravan Sites Act 1968	Mobile Homes Act 1988	Housing Act 1988	Protection from Eviction Act 1977
1. A, a farmer, uses part of a field to accommodate touring caravans. B stays for three nights, paying £10 per night.	No	No	No	No
2. C runs a holiday site, it being a condition of the site licence that the site is closed during the winter. D keeps a caravan there, paying an annual fee.	No	No	No	No
3. E owns a large house. In the grounds is a mobile home which is occupied by F as a permanent residence. F pays a weekly sum.	Yes	No	No	No
4. G runs an "adventure centre". He installs a mobile home on the site, fixing it permanently in position. It is occupied by H, the manager of the site.	No	No	Yes	Yes (ss. 1, 3 and 5)
5. I owns a permanent residential site. On one pitch is a mobile home belonging to her, which she lets J occupy as his permanent residence.	Yes	No	No	No
6. K owns a permanent residential site. L has a pitch agreement entitling her (L) to station her mobile home on the site.	Yes	Yes	No	No
7. M, a District Council, runs a caravan site. N has a caravan on the site.	Yes	Yes, unless a gipsy site	No	No
8. O owns a fruit farm, and has caravans in which he accommodates seasonal workers, including P, who pays a weekly rent which is deducted from his wages. P and other workers eat at O's house.	No	No	No	Yes (s. 1 only)

The second example is of a holiday site, which is not protected because it is required to close during the winter. The position is the same; though it would probably be different if the caravan was C's, and D occupied it, since it D would then be a "residential occupier", entitled to protection under the Protection from Eviction Act 1977. 7-58

7-59 E, in the third example, cannot claim an exemption under the 1960 Act, so needs a licence. Whether or not she has one, the site is protected, and F has the benefit of the 1968 Act. But because the mobile home is supplied by E, the 1983 Act does not apply. Because the 1968 Act protects F, the Protection from Eviction Act 1977 does not apply. (If there was an exemption, and so no need for a site licence, the site could not be protected and the Protection from Eviction Act 1977 would apply.)

7-60 In the next example, G has fixed the mobile home in position, rather than stationing it on the land. The caravan sites legislation does not apply (though planning permission is likely to be needed). H may well be protected under the Housing Act, though there are provisions which will allow G to regain possession if H loses his job. The Protection from Eviction Act applies.

7-61 The site in example 5 is a protected site. The 1968 Act applies. But because J is not an owner-occupier, the 1983 Act does not apply. The Protection from Eviction Act does not apply, because the 1968 Act gives protection.

7-62 Example 6 is the same, except that L, the resident, is an owner-occupier, so that the Mobile Homes Act applies as well as the 1968 Act.

7-63 In example 7, a District Council is the site owner. This means that the site is protected under the 1968 Act and under the 1983 Act except where it is a site for gipsies.

7-64 Finally, in example 8, the site owner does not need a site licence because there is an exemption for caravans occupied by seasonal workers. The 1968 Act and the 1983 Act therefore do not apply. The Protection from Eviction Act 1977 applies, but P only has the benefit of s. 1 (protection from harassment). Sections 3 and 5, which would give protection against unlawful eviction and require a minimum of four weeks' notice, do not apply because the agreement is excluded by s. 3A.

Timeshares

7-65 The essence of a timeshare agreement is that it gives the right to use property for a limited time each year, and is thus well-suited to holiday accommodation. Timeshare can apply to caravans and mobile homes as well as to cottages, flats and chalets. Although a timeshare can take the form of a lease, in practice the buyer of a timeshare almost always acquires only a licence to occupy the property.

7-66 Timeshares are regulated by the Timeshare Act 1992, and some regulations made under the Act, the Timeshare Regulations 1997[1]. When a timeshare is sold in the course of business, and the buyer is a consumer, the consumer has the right to cancel the agreement, and any related finance agreement. It is an offence for a person acting in the course of business to enter into a timeshare agreement without giving notice of the right to cancel.

Assessment

In the usual course of events, a caravan will be stationed on land as a result of a licence granted as part of a contract, and the important questions for the parties will be: 7-67

- Whether the site is a protected site, so that there will be protection under the 1968 Act. And if so—
- Whether the person living in the caravan is an owner-occupier, so that the Mobile Homes Act 1983 applies to the contract.

See chapter 5 for the Mobile Homes Act 1983.

The general law of contract will also apply, however; and this will be important if there is a dispute. There may be questions about whether the contract has implied terms, when it can be ended, and what compensation may be payable for breach of the contract. 7-68

A site owner may grant a lease of some land in order for a caravan to be stationed on it, but this is likely to be the exception rather than the rule. If the caravan is included in the lease, so that there is a residential tenancy, the law which governs the arrangement will be landlord and tenant law rather than the caravan sites legislation. 7-69

As the table above shows, the application of the law to different arrangements for stationing a caravan on land is complicated. In some cases there will be no special protection for a resident other than the protection given by the Criminal Law Act 1977. 7-70

See 9-2 onwards.

1. SI 1997/1081.

Chapter 8—Local authority matters

Introduction

8-0 Besides giving local authorities the power to license caravan sites and mobile home parks, the Caravan Sites and Control of Development Act 1960 gives them power to regulate what happens on sites in a number of ways. However the control is indirect: local authorities exercise it by setting and enforcing site licence conditions, which will generally be based on the DETR's Model Standards. Other powers are contained in the legislation on planning.

See 2-73 onwards for Model Standards.

See chapter 3 for planning law.

8-1 But these powers are only part of the wide range which allow local authorities to intervene in relation to what happens on land in their area, in the interests of the public at large. This chapter looks at a selection of other powers. Perhaps the most important are those relating to statutory nuisances, especially since most people living in caravans are legally at a disadvantage in relation to problems such as noise from neighbours. There are also powers which enable local authorities to deal with rubbish, dangerous trees and other matters.

See 10-8.

Statutory nuisances and caravan sites

"Nuisance", as a legal word, is used of things which cause annoyance or discomfort to people, or threaten their health. Some are listed in legislation (hence the term "statutory nuisance") and the local authority is given power to take action against them. Normally the law is concerned with nuisances coming from land and buildings.

See 10-5 for private nuisance.

8-2 However, there is a special rule in s. 268(1)) of the Public Health Act 1936 which allows all the provisions mentioned below to apply to caravans and caravan sites: "tents, vans, sheds and similar structures used for human habitation"—the latter phrase includes caravans—are treated as if they were houses or buildings; and provisions which refer to "premises" also apply to them. So a range of nuisances coming from caravans and mobile homes can be the subject of legal action by the local authority, as can nuisances from other parts of a caravan site.

Particular statutory nuisances

Not all the provisions on statutory nuisances are relevant to caravan sites; however the following types of nuisance may be mentioned: 8-3

Under the Public Health Act 1936 8-4

- Wells, tanks, cisterns or water-butts which are used for supplying water for domestic purposes and which are liable to contamination prejudicial to health (s. 141).

- Ponds, pools, ditches, gutters or watercourses which are prejudicial to health (s. 259).

- Any "tent, van, shed or similar structure used for human habitation" which is in such a state, or so overcrowded, as to be prejudicial to the health of anyone living there; or which, because of a lack of proper sanitary arrangements or otherwise, is prejudicial to health or a nuisance" (s. 268).

Caravans are no longer licensed under the 1936 Act: see 1-26.

Under the Environmental Protection Act 1990 These types of nuisance are all set out in s. 79 of the Act: 8-5

- Any premises in such a state as to be prejudicial to health or a nuisance (this includes things which interfere with people's comfort)[1].

- Smoke emitted from premises so as to be prejudicial to health or a nuisance—though this does not apply to "smoke emitted from a chimney of a private dwelling within a smoke control area"[2], and certain other situations.

- Fumes or gases emitted from premises so as to be prejudicial to health or a nuisance: this applies to dwellings only.

- Any accumulation or deposit which is prejudicial to health or a nuisance[3].

---

1. But this does not include nuisances arising from the *layout* of premises: see *Birmingham City Council v Oakley* [2000] 3 WLR 1936.
2. In smoke control areas, smoking chimneys are covered by the Clean Air Act 1993.
3. But see *Coventry City Council v Cartwright* [1975] 1 WLR 845, [1975] 2 All ER 99: inert matter such as earth, bricks and broken glass is not within this provision.

- Any animal kept in such a place or manner as to be prejudicial to health or a nuisance.

- Noise[1] emitted from premises so as to be prejudicial to health or a nuisance.

- Noise which is prejudicial to health or a nuisance and which is emitted from a vehicle, machinery or equipment in a street. Traffic noise is excluded. "Street" has a wide definition here, and could include roads on caravan sites if open to the public.

Taking action against statutory nuisances

8-6 Local authorities have a duty, under s. 79 of the Environmental Protection Act 1990, to inspect their areas from time to time, and also to investigate complaints about statutory nuisances.

8-7 Section 80 sets out the procedure to be followed by the local authority: if they are satisfied that a statutory nuisance exists, or is likely to occur or recur, they must serve a notice, known as an "abatement notice", on the person responsible for the nuisance. If that person cannot be found, the notice must be served on the owner or occupier of the premises which are the source of the nuisance. If the source was a caravan, the notice would normally be served on the occupier of the caravan. But it would also be possible to serve notice on the owner of the land—that is, the site owner.

See 1-43 for "occupying" land.

8-8 The notice must specify what is to be done in order to stop the nuisance. The person served with the notice may appeal to a magistrates' court, within 21 days. Otherwise she commits an offence if, without a reasonable excuse, she fails to comply with the notice (s. 80(5)). The maximum fine is level 5 on the standard scale—and if the offence continues after the conviction, the person concerned may also be fined one-tenth of the level 5 amount for each day it continues.

See 1-48 for the standard level of fines.

8-9 What is a "reasonable excuse" depends upon the facts of each case. It is also a defence in some circumstances to prove that the best practical means were used to prevent or to stop the nuisance (s. 80(7)). In one case[2], the local authority took action against a dog-breeding establishment in a residential area, on the ground that noise from the dogs was a statutory nuisance. When the case came before the magistrates' court, the magistrates considered that the owners of the

1. The 1990 Act lays down that "noise" includes vibration.
2. *Manley v New Forest District Council* [1999] 4 PLR 36.

establishment had not used the best practicable means to minimise the noise, since that would have meant moving the business. The owners appealed, and the higher court decided that it was not necessary to move the business elsewhere in order to show that the best practicable means had been used.

If an abatement notice is not complied with, the local authority has power, under s. 81(3), to do whatever is necessary to stop the nuisance, and may recover the cost of their actions from the person responsible for the nuisance. This power can be used whether or not the local authority prosecute anyone for failing to comply with the abatement notice. 8-10

Though the main purpose of the law is to enable local authorities to take legal action, it is also open to a private person who is "aggrieved" by the nuisance to do so, under s. 82 of the Environmental Protection Act 1990. The first step is to serve, on the person responsible[1], notice of the intention to bring proceedings. If the nuisance consists of noise, three days' notice must be given; otherwise, the period is 21 days (s. 82(7)). If the nuisance continues, the person concerned may apply to a magistrates' court. The court, if satisfied that there is a nuisance, has power to impose a fine (the maximum being level 5) and order compensation to be paid[2]. The court can make an order that the nuisance must stop, or (if it has stopped) that it must not start again; and the person responsible can be ordered to carry out any necessary work (s. 82(2)). Furthermore, the court may prohibit premises from being used for human habitation, if the nuisance makes them unfit for that purpose (s. 82(3)). If the person responsible for the nuisance cannot be found, and neither can the owner or occupier of the land, the magistrates' court can order the local authority to take action to end the nuisance (s. 82(13)). 8-11

The defences which can be used are the same as those which apply when the local authority brings proceedings. 8-12

See 8-9.

Byelaws

Local authorities have power, under s. 235 of the Local Government Act 1972, to make byelaws for various purposes, including the "prevention and suppression of nuisances". Byelaws cannot be made where legislation already covers the nuisance in question, but the 8-13

1. Or, where the person cannot be found, on the owner or occupier of the premises.
2. *Botross v Hammersmith and Fulham London Borough Council, The Times* 7 November 1994.

power enables local authorities to deal with nuisances particular to their area which are not already covered by the law.

8-14 Byelaws cannot come into force unless confirmed by the DETR. Once made they must be available for public inspection (s. 236). Breach of byelaws can be made an offence, the maximum permissible fine generally being level 2 on the standard scale; and there may be an additional fine of £5 for each day the nuisance continues after conviction (s. 237).

Noise

8-15 Apart from the provisions on statutory nuisance mentioned above, several other Acts deal with noise. Part III of the Control of Pollution Act 1974 is concerned with noise from two sources—noise from construction sites and noise from "streets".

8-16 In relation to construction sites, the local authority can take action in relation to a wide range of construction and demolition work, by imposing requirements about the way in which the work is carried out, in order to minimise noise (s. 60). The DETR has power, under s. 71 of the Act, to issues codes of practice giving guidance on how noise from construction sites can be minimised, and has issued a code entitled *Code of Practice on Noise Control on Construction Sites and Open Sites* and local authorities must take the Code into account when exercising their powers under s. 60.

8-17 Section 62 of the Act is concerned with the problem of loudspeakers in streets. A "street" means a highway and "any other road, footway, square or court which is for the time being open to the public". A road within a caravan site might thus be within the definition. The Act forbids the use of loudspeakers between the 9 p.m. and 8 a.m. for any purpose, and at any other time for advertising any entertainment, trade or business. There are exceptions, which include:

See 9-29 for roads to which the public have access.

- The emergency services.
- Car stereo systems, provided they do not give reasonable cause for annoyance to people in the area.
- Vehicles selling perishable food.

Waste

Separate sets of rules deal with different aspects of the problem of disposing of waste properly. 8-18

Rubbish Under s. 34 of the Public Health Act 1961, local authorities have a power to deal with rubbish: 8-19

> "(1) If it appears to a local authority that there is on any land in the open air in their area any rubbish which is seriously detrimental to amenities of the neighbourhood, the local authority may, subject to provisions of this section, take such steps for removing rubbish as they may consider necessary in the interests of amenity."

"Rubbish" here means "rubble, waste paper, crockery and metal, and any other kind of refuse (including organic matter)" (s. 35(5)). However, material accumulated for, or in the course of, any business is not included. The section only applies if the rubbish is "seriously detrimental to amenities". 8-20

See 8-39 on the meaning of "amenity".

The local authority must give at least 28 days' notice to the owner or occupier of the land in question. The owner or occupier can then, if he wishes, serve a counter-notice, saying that he will do the necessary work himself. Alternatively, he may appeal to a magistrates' court on the grounds that no action is justified, or that the steps proposed by the local authority are unreasonable. The matter is then determined by the court. 8-21

Litter The Environmental Protection Act 1990, Part IV, contains some provisions on litter. Section 90(1) allows the DETR to make delegated legislation describing sorts of land which may be designated as "litter control areas". The DETR has made the necessary regulations[1] which include, among many other sorts of land: 8-22

> "... land forming, or forming part of, a camping or caravan site (including a mobile home site) which is used for more than 28 days in one year."

The DETR, or a local authority, can therefore now designate particular caravan sites as litter control areas. Dropping litter is an offence under s. 87.

If land is designated as a litter control area, and is "defaced by litter or refuse", either the local authority or a private person can take action against the occupier of the land. Firstly, under s. 92, the local authority can serve a "litter abatement notice" on the occupier of the land, either requiring him to clear up the litter, or prohibiting him from allowing the land to become defaced by litter, or both. The occupier can appeal to a magistrates' court within 21 days, and can argue (apart from any 8-23

---

1. The Litter Control Areas Order 1991, SI 1991/1325

other ground) that he has complied with his duty under s. 89(1) to keep the land clear of litter. A person who fails to comply with a litter abatement notice commits an offence, the maximum fine being level 4 on the standard scale, and one-twentieth of that amount for each day the offence continues after conviction.

8-24 Secondly, a private person who is "aggrieved" by the fact that land is defaced by litter or refuse can take action under s. 91. He may (after giving five days' notice to the person responsible for the land) apply to a magistrates' court, and the court may make a "litter abatement order" against the person responsible, requiring him to clear up the litter. Failure to comply with a litter abatement order is an offence, the maximum fine being level 4 on the standard scale, with a further fine of one-twentieth of that level if the offence continues after conviction.

8-25 *Dumping* Section 2 of the Refuse Disposal (Amenity) Act 1978 deals with the dumping of cars and other things:

> "(1) Any person who, without lawful authority—
>
> (a) abandons on any land in the open air, or on any other land forming part of a highway, a motor vehicle or anything which formed part of a motor vehicle and was removed from it in the course of dismantling the vehicle on the land; or
>
> (b) abandons on any such land any thing other than a motor vehicle, being a thing which he has brought on to the land for the purpose of abandoning "

commits an offence. The maximum punishment is level 4 on the standard scale or three months' imprisonment.

8-26 Whether something has been abandoned is to be deduced from all the circumstances of the case, but the provision seems to be concerned with permanent rather than temporary abandonment: unauthorised parking would probably not amount to the offence of abandoning a motor vehicle. However, s. 2 provides that where circumstances suggest that something has been abandoned, the person responsible is deemed to have abandoned it, unless he proves the contrary.

8-27 Under s. 3 of the Act, local authorities have a duty to remove abandoned motor vehicles, and they have power to dispose of vehicles removed under this provision (s. 4). The local authority's expenses can
8-28 be recovered from the person responsible for the dumping (s. 5). The Act in s. 11 defines "motor vehicle" as including trailers, and it would appear that caravans are meant to be included, as being a type of trailer. The maximum punishment is 3 months' imprisonment or a level 4 fine.

8-29 Abandoned supermarket and luggage trolleys are sometimes a problem, and there are provisions in the Environmental Protection Act 1990 (s. 99 and Schedule 4) which local authorities can adopt to deal with the problem. If these provisions are adopted, local authorities can collect abandoned trolleys and return them to their owners, charging a fee for doing so.

Disposing of waste The Environmental Protection Act 1990 contains, in s. 33, a general offence of depositing, keeping or disposing of "controlled waste" in or on any land. This has a wide application. 8-30

"Controlled waste" includes "household waste", which in turn includes waste from a caravan usually situated on a caravan site (s. 75(4) and (5)). However the offence does not apply to household waste which is disposed of within the curtilage of a dwelling by the occupier, or with his consent (s. 33(2)). It seems likely that a caravan would be regarded as a dwelling, and its pitch as its curtilage. For the occupier of a caravan to keep or dispose of waste within his own pitch would not be an offence; but to do so elsewhere would be. 8-31

See 2-31 for the meaning of "curtilage".

The maximum punishment in a magistrates' court is six months' imprisonment, or a fine of up to £20,000, or both; and in the Crown Court two years' imprisonment or an unlimited fine, or both (s. 33(8)). 8-32

Powers under the Highways Act 1980

Local authorities have a responsibility for public roads, and the powers they need in order to discharge this responsibility are found mainly in the Highways Act 1980. 8-33

Roads within caravan sites are unlikely to be "highways", that is, roads over which the public have a right of way[1]; they are likely to be private roads. The powers in relation to this sort of private road[2] are relatively few. However, there are several powers which relate to roads and footpaths to which the public have access. Firstly, there is power to take action where a tree or shrub on that land is growing in such a way as to "endanger or obstruct the passage of vehicles or pedestrians, or obstruct or interfere with the view of drivers of vehicles or the light from a public lamp". Secondly, action can be taken if a tree or shrub is dead, diseased or damaged and is likely to cause damage by falling on the road or footpath. "Hedge, tree or shrub" is defined to include vegetation of any description, thus avoiding argument about what is a "tree or shrub" in this context (s. 154). 8-34

See 9-29 on public access.

1. There are essentially three classes of highway: footways (for pedestrians), bridleways (horses) and carriageways (vehicles). Bridleways include footways, and carriageways include both bridleways and footways.
2. For a fuller explanation of the difference between public and private roads, see *Private Roads: The Legal Framework (2nd ed.)*, A. W. & C. Barsby 1997.

8-35 The local authority can also require fences, shrubs, trees and other things to be removed if they obstruct the view of users of a highway maintainable at public expense at a junction with a road to which the public has access (s. 79).

Dangerous trees

8-36 Local authorities have a power which enables them to deal with dangerous trees. The power is contained in the Local Government (Miscellaneous Provisions) Act 1976, s. 23. The power applies to trees on "any land", thus including caravan sites. A local authority can take action if a tree appears likely to cause damage to persons or property.

8-37 A local authority can act in several different situations. The first is where it receives a request to make the tree safe from someone who is the owner or occupier of the land on which the tree is growing. The local authority can carry out the work and recover the cost from the person in question. The second situation is where the request comes from a person who is the owner or occupier of some other land. If the owner of the land on which the tree is growing cannot be found, the authority can proceed with the work and recover the cost from the person who made the request. But if the owner of the land can be found, the authority must (if they decide to take any action) proceed by serving a notice on that person requiring him to do the necessary work. The person concerned is entitled to appeal to the County Court against the notice, on one of four different grounds set out in s. 23. If he fails to carry out the work, the authority can do so instead, and can then recover the cost from him.

8-38 The final situation is where there is no request to make the tree safe but the tree is likely to damage persons or property on land owned by the authority itself. This would apply if a local authority owned a caravan site on which there was a dangerous tree, or if it owned adjoining land threatened by a dangerous tree.

Amenity

8-39 By the "amenity" of land the law means its general pleasantness and attractiveness. The idea is a vague but useful one, which is relevant to planning law and other areas of the law.* Local authorities have several powers which enable them to take action to protect the amenity of land.

* See e.g. 3-50.

By s. 215 of the Town and Country Planning Act 1990: 8-40

"(1) If it appears to the local planning authority that the amenity of a part of their area, or of an adjoining area, is adversely affected by the condition of land in their area, they may serve on the owner and occupier of the land a notice under this section."

This provision applies to all land. The authority's notice must set out the steps to be taken to remedy matters. There is a right of appeal against the notice, to the courts. But subject to that, failure to comply with the notice is an offence. The local authority can if necessary enter the land, and carry out the work themselves. The expense then falls on the owner. 8-41

There is a similar power in s. 89 of the National Parks and Access to the Countryside Act 1949. This applies to derelict land which in the opinion of the authority is "in any way unsightly". With the consent of anyone interested in the land the authority may plant trees or carry out other work for improving its appearance. However in this case the expense falls on the authority. Either power could be exercised in relation to a caravan site, if it was in a sufficiently poor state. 8-42

Caravans on commons

Under s. 23 of the Caravan Sites and Control of Development Act 1960, local authorities have a special power to prohibit the stationing of caravans on a common. The definition of a common for this purpose is complex, but includes areas of land which are commons in the ordinary meaning of the word, and town and village greens. The reason for giving them this power is that it might be difficult to tell who was the "occupier" of the land under the 1960 Act, and so impossible to enforce the 1960 Act. 8-43

The power can only be exercised if the local authority has not used powers in earlier legislation to regulate the use of the common. The Second Schedule to the 1960 Act lays down the detailed procedure for making an order. Once made, the order has to be publicised, so as to give people warning that caravans may not be stationed on the common. It is an offence to station a caravan on a common once an order has been made, the maximum fine being level 1 on the standard scale. 8-44

Assessment

8-45 Where behaviour on an organised caravan site gives rise to complaints, the first and probably best way of dealing with the matter will be to use procedures under the site rules.

8-46 Local authorities can, however, intervene to deal with problems if there is a need to do so. There is usually no obligation on local authorities to use their powers: instead, administrative law requires local authorities (and other public bodies) to act in a reasonable and rational way in exercising their powers. In practice, local authorities generally have a wide discretion about whether to use a particular power.

8-47 The law on statutory nuisance is an exception to this general rule, since local authorities have a *duty*, not just a power, to inspect their areas and to investigate complaints. Whether they take action by serving an enforcement notice is a matter for their discretion; but residents are perfectly entitled to ask the local authority to look into problems which come within the definition of statutory nuisances, if other ways of solving the problem are unsuccessful.

Chapter 9—Criminal law

Introduction

Some criminal offences have been considered in earlier chapters, including: 9-0

- Offences which reinforce the legislation on caravan sites.

See e.g. 2-4.

- The offence under planning law of failing to comply with an enforcement notice.

See 3-43.

- Offences under the Protection from Eviction Act 1977.

See 7-49.

This chapter is concerned with the criminal law more generally: it explains a selection of criminal offences which may be relevant on caravan sites and mobile home parks.

While the criminal law is there if needed, it may be possible to deal with antisocial behaviour in other ways, for example by relying on site rules, or applying a civil remedy. 9-1

See chapter 10 for civil law generally.

Offences concerned with residential premises

The Criminal Law Act 1977 created several offences concerned with the occupation of residential premises, punishing, in certain circumstances, both those who try to gain entry to premises by force, and trespassers who refuse to leave when called on to do so. For this purpose "premises" has a very wide definition, and includes "any movable structure, vehicle or vessel designed or adapted for use for any residential purpose" (s. 12(2)). Caravans and mobile homes are thus clearly within the definition of "premises". 9-2

"Premises" also includes land which is adjacent to a building (in the sense just explained) and used in connection with it. So the garden of a house and the pitch of a caravan would be included (s. 12(2)). 9-3

By s. 6 of the 1977 Act it is an offence to use or threaten violence, without lawful authority, in order to gain entry to any premises on which there is someone known to be present who opposes the entry. The Act makes it clear that the right to possession of the premises does not by itself constitute lawful authority (s. 6(2)). 9-4

See 1-43 for "possessing" land.

9-5 This is an important provision, because of the protection it gives to someone who is present on premises. Even if the person on the premises is a trespasser, it is still an offence for the owner (or anyone else) to use or threaten force to gain entry without sufficient lawful authority. An order from the court is sufficient authority for these purposes; and it is a defence for a person to show that he is (or is acting on behalf of) a "displaced residential occupier" or a "protected intending occupier" of the premises (s. 6(1A)). A "displaced residential occupier" is essentially any person who was occupying the premises before being excluded by the trespasser (s. 12(3)). A "protected intending occupier" of the premises is someone who requires the premises for use as a residence, either because she is the owner, or a tenant, or a person with a licence; and who has made a written statement to that effect witnessed by a Justice of the Peace or a commissioner for oaths (s. 12A).

See 1-15 for licences.

9-6 Armed with a statement, a displaced residential occupier and a protected intending occupier can use or threaten force—in other words, violence—in order to gain entry to premises. But this is subject to the general rule of law that the force used should be the minimum necessary. If excessive force is used, the person concerned may be guilty of a criminal offence or may commit a civil wrong for which he is liable to pay compensation.

9-7 On the other side of the coin, by s. 7 of the Criminal Law Act 1977, a person who has entered premises as a trespasser commits an offence if he does not leave when called on to do so by a displaced residential occupier or a protected intending occupier of the premises. This offence and the offence under s. 6 are each punishable by imprisonment for up to six months or a level 5 fine or both (ss. 6(5) and 7(5)).

See 1-48 for the standard levels of fines.

9-8 Under s. 8 of the Criminal Law Act 1977 it is also an offence for a person who is on any premises as a trespasser (and who entered the premises as a trespasser) to have with him a weapon of offence. The maximum punishment is imprisonment for 3 months or a level 5 fine or both (s. 8(3)).

Harassment

9-9 Under the Protection from Harassment Act 1997, it is an offence for a person to pursue a course of conduct which amounts to harassment of another, and which he knows or ought to know amounts to harassment. Isolated incidents cannot amount to harassment, because there must be a "course of conduct"; but "conduct" includes

Seen also 10-35 onwards for the civil effects of the Act.

speech, so the offence can be committed by a course of conduct which consists of saying things to a person (s. 7(4)). Harassment includes causing alarm or distress (s. 7(2)). The courts have considered the offence and have taken the view that the offence has a relatively narrow scope, and is designed to deal with stalking and similar behaviour, not such things as bullying by the police or oppressive litigation[1].

The offence of harassment has a maximum punishment of a level 5 fine or six months' imprisonment (s. 2). The 1997 Act also contains a more serious offence, known as putting people in fear of violence (s. 4). This consists of engaging in a course of conduct which puts someone in fear, on at least two occasions, that violence will be used against them. The maximum punishment is prison for up to five years or an unlimited fine, if the offence is dealt with in the Crown Court, or otherwise six months' imprisonment or a level 5 fine (s. 4(4)). 9-10

When a person is sentenced for the offence of harassment, the court has a special power to make a "restraining order", to prohibit them from carrying out further harassment (s. 5). 9-11

A separate offence, created by s. 40 of the Administration of Justice Act 1970, consists of harassing debtors. The offence consists of coercing another person to pay money claimed under a contract by: 9-12

- Harassing that person with demands for payment which are calculated to cause him or his family alarm, distress or humiliation.
- Falsely saying that it is a criminal offence not to pay.
- Falsely claiming that the person concerned is entitled to enforce payment in some official capacity.
- Using a document which falsely indicates that it is official.

Threats

A person who, without a lawful excuse, makes a threat to destroy or damage property belonging to someone else, is guilty of an offence. The offence can be dealt with in a magistrates' court, or in the Crown Court, where the maximum is ten years' imprisonment (Criminal Damage Act 1971, s. 2). Making a threat to damage or destroy a 9-13

1. *Tuppen v Microsoft Corp Ltd, The Times,* 15 November 2000

caravan, or other property, is thus a serious offence in the absence of some lawful excuse.

Disorderly behaviour

9-14 The Public Order Act 1986 contains a range of offences, of varying seriousness, designed to deal with disorderly behaviour. The following paragraphs explain three of the less serious offences.

9-15 By s. 4(1) of the Act:

> "A person is guilty of an offence if he—
>
> (a) uses towards another person threatening, abusive or insulting words or behaviour, or
>
> (b) distributes or displays to another person any writing, sign or other visible representation which is abusive, threatening of insulting,
>
> with intent to cause that person to believe that immediate unlawful violence will be used against him or another by any person, or to provoke the immediate use of unlawful violence by that person, or another, or whereby that person is likely to believe that such violence will be used or it is likely that such violence will be provoked."

9-16 In essence, then, an offence is committed when one person puts another in fear of violence, or tries to provoke violence, by means of threatening behaviour. Section 4 of the Act goes on to provide that the offence can be committed in public or in private, but that no offence is committed if the people involved are inside a dwelling. (They need not all be in the same dwelling.) The Act defines "dwelling" in such a way as to include a caravan used as living accommodation; and "violence" is widely defined, so as to include violence against property (s. 8). The maximum punishment is six months' imprisonment or a level 5 fine.

9-17 Under s. 4A of the 1986 Act, it is also an offence for a person to use threatening behaviour, or signs, with intent to cause harassment, alarm, or distress. The maximum punishment for the offence is a level 3 fine. It is a defence for the person concerned to show that he was inside a dwelling and had no reason to believe that his actions would be seen or heard by someone outside the dwelling.

9-18 Finally, under s. 5 of the 1986 Act:

> "(1) A person is guilty of an offence if he—
>
> (a) uses threatening, abusive or insulting words or behaviour, or disorderly behaviour, or

(b) displays any writing, sign or other visible representation which is threatening, abusive or insulting

within the hearing or sight of a person likely to be caused harassment, alarm or distress thereby."

For this offence the maximum sentence is a level 3 fine. There is a similar defence in relation to acts inside a dwelling: no offence is committed if the accused person proves that he was inside a dwelling and had no reason to believe that what he said or did would be heard or seen by people outside the dwelling. 9-19

All of the above offences can be committed in racially aggravated form, under the Crime and Disorder Act 1998, s. 31. An offence is racially aggravated if at the time of the offence the offender demonstrated hostility based on membership of the victim's racial group, or the offence is motivated by hostility towards members of a racial group. "Racial group" means a group of people "defined by reference to race, colour, nationality (including citizenship) or ethnic or national origins" (s. 28). Where an offence is racially aggravated, the maximum punishment is more severe. 9-20

Disorderly behaviour while drunk is the subject of a special offence, under s. 91(1) of the Criminal Law Act 1967: 9-21

"Any person who in any public place is guilty, while drunk, of disorderly behaviour may be arrested without warrant by any person and shall be liable....to a fine not exceeding level 3 on the standard scale."

A "public place" includes any "premises or place to which at the material time the public have or are permitted to have access..." (s. 91(4)). A caravan site may thus be a public place if the public have access to it. 9-22

See also 9-29 for public access.

Offences under the Theft Acts

The Theft Acts 1968 and 1978 define the offence of theft and some related offences, many involving dishonesty. 9-23

The offence of burglary, under s. 9 of the Theft Act 1968, consists of entering a building as a trespasser and stealing, or causing someone serious harm, or of entering a building as a trespasser with the intention of doing one of these things, or of raping a woman or causing damage to the building (s. 9(1) and (2)). For these purposes "building" includes "an inhabited vehicle or vessel"—whether or not the person living there is present when the offence is committed (s. 9(3)). The offence of burglary can thus be committed in relation to a caravan if it 9-24 is inhabited, even though the person living there is not present, though not if it is standing empty. The maximum sentence is 14 years' imprisonment (s. 9(4)).

9-25 It is, by s. 12 of the Theft Act 1968, an offence to take a "conveyance" without authority. The offence usually involves taking a car ("joy-riding") but it applies to other "conveyances" too[1]. Something is *not* a conveyance if it is "constructed or adapted for use only under the control of a person not carried in it" (s. 12(7)). A motor-home can thus be a conveyance, but a caravan or mobile home, in the ordinary sense, cannot be a conveyance. The result is that merely moving a caravan without authority is not an offence under s. 12—though stealing one (taking one dishonestly and with the intention of permanently depriving the owner of it) is an offence, because it is theft.

Criminal damage and arson

9-26 Under the Criminal Damage Act 1971 it is an offence to damage property, which includes both land and other property (s. 10). Damaging a caravan is thus an offence, whether or not the caravan is attached to the land.* The offence includes what would generally be referred to as vandalism, for example writing graffiti and breaking things (s. 1). The maximum sentence for criminal damage is 10 years' imprisonment. Where damage is caused by fire, the offence (which is otherwise the same) is known as arson.

* See 1-8 onwards on this question.

9-27 It is a defence for a person accused of criminal damage to show that:

- He honestly believed that the owner of the property had consented, or would have consented if he had known about the damage.
- He damaged the property in order to protect property of his own, or a right in property, and honestly believed that the property or right was in immediate need of protection and that the action he took was reasonable in the circumstances (s. 5(2)).

1. Including pedal cycles—though this is a less serious offence, the maximum punishment being a level 3 fine.

Motoring offences and caravan sites

Cars and other vehicles will almost inevitably be present on caravan sites. Motoring offences are intended to apply mainly on public roads, but some are framed so that they apply more widely. 9-28

Many motoring offences are created by the Road Traffic Act 1988, as amended by the Road Traffic Act 1991; for example dangerous driving (s. 2) and careless or inconsiderate driving (s. 3), and using a car without an MoT certificate (s. 47). These offences apply on a "road or other public place". "Road" is defined in s. 192(1) as "any highway and any other road to which the public have access". This raises a series of questions. First, is there a highway; that is, an established public right of way, for vehicles or pedestrians? If so, these offences will apply. If there is no highway, is there nonetheless a road to which the public have access? It is a question of fact whether a sufficient selection of the public have access which is tolerated by the owner of the road[1]. Finally, if the place in question is not a road, is it within the meaning of "other public place"? In one case[2] the court decided that a holiday and touring site was a "public place". The owners allowed in anyone prepared to abide by the site conditions. The site was open to the public and therefore a public place, so offences such as dangerous driving could be committed on the site. The position might have been different, however, if the owners of the site had put up a notice restricting access by the public at large. 9-29

See 8-34 for the meaning of "highway".

This definition of "road" is very similar to the one used in the Road Traffic Regulation Act 1984 (as amended by the New Roads and Streets Works Act 1991). This Act gives local authorities power to regulate traffic, for example by imposing speed limits. The power does not extend to other public places; but a road within a caravan site could be within the 1984 Act if it was used by the public and if public use was tolerated. If so, the local authority could, if they saw a need to do so, exercise their powers under the Act to regulate traffic. 9-30

In contrast, the offence of using or keeping a car on a public road (s. 1 of the Vehicles (Excise) Act 1971) is much narrower, since "public road" means a road which is repairable at public expense (s. 38). The offence can thus only be committed on highways which the local authority has a duty to maintain. 9-31

Within a caravan site, residents and their guests will be acting lawfully in driving and parking if they are acting in accordance with the permission given by the owner in pitch agreements and site rules, and express or implied permission to come on to the site for such 9-32

---

1. See *Kreft v Rawlinson, The Times,* 12 May 1984.
2. *DPP v Vivier* [1991] RTR 205; [1991] 4 All ER 18.

purposes as making deliveries. Drivers who are *not* covered by permission from the site owner may commit an offence under s. 34 of the Road Traffic Act 1988. This applies to land which is "common land, moorland or land of any other description not being land forming part of a road". As explained above, roads within a caravan sites may be outside this definition, either because they are highways or because the public has access—in which case there will be no offence under s. 34. But otherwise it will be an offence for motorists to park on the site without permission or other lawful authority, unless they go no more than 15 yards from a road where they may drive lawfully, and do so in order to park. The offence is not endorsable, and the maximum fine is level 3 on the standard scale.

Caravans on the road

9-33 Technical requirements for road vehicles of all kinds are laid down by delegated legislation[1]. Caravans are not the subject of special provisions, but are covered by the rules which apply to trailers and other vehicles generally. The law is detailed and complicated, but its main effect is explained below.

9-34 Trailers, including the trailers of articulated vehicles, may generally be up to 12 metres long (in some circumstances they may be longer) if they have four or more wheels, depending upon the weight of the towing vehicle, which must be a goods vehicle. Otherwise the maximum is 7 metres. The usual maximum widths for these classes of trailer are 2.55 and 2.3 metres. A caravan must be within these dimensions in order to be towed on a public road.

9-35 It must also comply with other requirements, for example those relating to ground clearance, braking and lighting. A larger caravan could be carried as a load on a trailer or lorry, but the amount of overhang would be limited since there is a general requirement that loads must not be dangerous[2]. If a trailer is wider than the vehicle towing it, and the sides project more than 400mm beyond the line of the front lights of the towing vehicle, the trailer must be fitted with lights[3].

9-36 For most vehicles towing trailers, the speed limits are 60 mph on motorways and dual carriageways and 50 mph on other roads (Schedule 6 to the Road Traffic Regulation Act 1984).

1. The Road Vehicles (Construction and Use) Regulations 1986, SI 1986/1078. These have since been amended on many occasions.
2. See regulations 7, 8 and 100 of the above Regulations.
3. Under the Road Vehicles Lighting Regulations 1989, SI 1989/1796.

Dogs

Two Acts are potentially of importance on caravan sites. These deal with guard dogs and dangerous dogs. 9-37

It is an offence under s. 1 of the Guard Dogs Act 1975 for a person to use or allow a guard dog at any premises unless the dog is under the control of a handler except when it is tied up. A warning notice must be on display at each entrance to the premises. A "guard dog" is any dog which is being used to protect premises, or property kept on the premises, or a person guarding the premises (s.7). 9-38

"Premises" has a special definition here. Agricultural land is excluded, and so is land within the curtilage of a dwelling house. It seems possible but not certain that a residential caravan would be regarded as a "dwelling-house" for these purposes, so that a dog could be used to protect a caravan without meeting the requirements of the Act on notices and handlers. But the Guard Dogs Act would apply if a dog were used to guard a caravan site as a whole. The maximum punishment for the offence is a level 5 fine. 9-39

See 2-31 on the meaning of "curtilage".

The Dangerous Dogs Act 1991 provides that if a dog is dangerously out of control in a public place the owner and (if different) the person in control of the dog is guilty of an offence (s. 3(1)). An offence is also committed if a dog is allowed to enter a place which is not a public place, and where it is not permitted to be, and there are grounds for reasonable apprehension that it will injure someone (s. 3(3)). In either case the offence is aggravated if the dog actually causes injury. A public place is "any street, road or other place....to which the public have access or are permitted to have access". The maximum punishment for the basic offence is six months' imprisonment or a fine of up to the statutory maximum; and for the aggravated offence the maximum is two years' imprisonment or an unlimited fine or both (s. 3(4)). 9-40

Assessment

On an organised site, residents will look first to site rules to regulate behaviour and prevent friction. But if it is needed the criminal law contains a wide range of offences, of varying seriousness, designed to prevent anti-social and harmful behaviour. The criminal law punishes not just damaging property and injuring people, but also the making of threats, and disorderly conduct. More subtle forms of misbehaviour are also within the scope of the criminal law; for example, harassment 9-41 which consists not of violence but of insults and other activities designed to make someone feel alarmed or distressed.

9-42 A particularly important safeguard is the Criminal Law Act 1977. This protects people living in caravans even when there is no other protection available, under the caravan sites legislation or landlord and tenant law.

See chapter 4 for the Caravan Sites Act 1968 and chapter 7 for landlord and tenant law.

Chapter 10—Civil law

Introduction

This chapter is concerned with the civil law—the law which determines when compensation and other remedies can be awarded by the civil courts. 10-0

Civil wrongs, or "torts", have names such as "trespass", "nuisance", and "negligence", and they define the circumstances in which one person can take legal action in the civil courts against another, to obtain compensation and other remedies such as an injunction. Torts sometimes overlap; but they do not cover every situation in which one person is responsible for injury or loss suffered by another. Each has its own rules, about such matters as: 10-1

See 1-45 for injunctions.

- Who can take legal action.
- What must be proved.
- What sorts of injury or loss are covered.

Much of the law is to be found not in legislation but in the common law.

See 1-0 for the meaning of "common law".

The following paragraphs describe some of the torts which may be relevant to site owners and residents on a caravan site. These ways of taking legal action are different from (though they may sometimes overlap with) the action which can be taken for breach of a contract such as a pitch agreement, or of a tenancy agreement. 10-2

See chapter 7 for contracts and leases.

Trespass

Trespass is a familiar term. Legally it consists of going on to land without any sort of permission or legal right. Who can complain of a trespass? The rule is that a person with the right to possession of the land can do so, even if they do not have an interest in it. An occupier of a caravan will usually be in a position to take action for trespass, because of the control she has over the pitch. Although her pitch agreement usually gives her no interest in the land, it does give her the right to possession, and this is sufficient. A site owner is similarly in a 10-3

See 1-43 for "possessing" land.

See 1-15 for interests in land.

position to take action for trespass against anyone who comes on to the site without the right to do so.

10-4 The amount of compensation which can be obtained for trespass will usually be very small if no actual damage has been caused. More important, perhaps, is the court's power to grant an injunction, when necessary, in order to stop persistent trespassing.

Liability to neighbours

10-5 The tort of "nuisance"—sometimes known as "private nuisance", to distinguish it from statutory nuisance—allows a person to take legal action against anyone interfering with the use or enjoyment of land. Such interferences may cause injury or damage, for example smoke which dirties washing or discolours paintwork, or they may merely cause annoyance, as noise or smells may do. A person who suffers injury or damage can take legal action to obtain compensation, or an injunction to stop the nuisance.

10-6 If a particular activity does not cause injury or damage, but merely annoyance, the question of whether it is legally a nuisance depends upon its reasonableness. The courts consider all the circumstances, particularly the character of the neighbourhood. Noise or smells which would be acceptable on an industrial estate might well be unacceptable in a quiet residential area.

10-7 A person affected by a nuisance has a right to "abate" it, that is, take action himself to stop it. The right to abate a nuisance is an alternative to legal proceedings and must be exercised with great care if it is attempted at all: usually this course is unwise. But, as an exception, it is well established that branches overhanging a person's land, or roots growing underneath it, can be trimmed at the boundary.

10-8 However, only a person with an interest in the land is entitled to complain about interference by others of his enjoyment of it. A site owner is in this position, as is a caravan resident who has a tenancy. But a resident who has only a pitch agreement, which is a contract with the site owner, does not have an interest in the land[1].

10-9 This is not the end of the matter, because the above rules, which come from the common law, have been added to by Acts dealing with "statutory nuisances". Such nuisances are generally for the local authority to deal with, by serving an "abatement notice"; but it is also open to a member of the public to take legal action by applying to a magistrates' court for an order to stop the nuisance, or prevent it from

---

1. See *Hunter v Canary Wharf Ltd* [1997] AC 655.

recurring. This procedure can be used to deal with many of the annoyances and interferences which could also be dealt with as private nuisances, such as noise, smells and smoke.

See 8-11 onwards, where the procedure is explained.

Liability to visitors

The Occupiers' Liability Act 1957 is concerned with injury or damage to people who are lawfully visiting land. The Act lays down that the occupier of land owes a duty of care to visitors. If she is in breach of the duty, by failing to take adequate care, and a visitor suffers injury or damage as a result, the occupier is liable to pay compensation. 10-10

By s. 1(3) of the Act the rules which apply to land apply in the same way to "any fixed or movable structure, including any vessel, vehicle or aircraft". This plainly includes caravans. A person is an occupier if he is in control of the land or structure in question. Normally, the residents on the site will be the occupiers of their own caravans (and the respective pitches) under the 1957 Act, while for the rest of the site the occupier will be the site owner. 10-11

Who is a "visitor", and so covered by the 1957 Act? On a caravan site, the word will include people who are expressly invited on to the site, for example residents' guests, and also people with implied permission, for example casual callers or people delivering newspapers[1]. The residents of caravans themselves are also "visitors" in relation to parts of the site under the control of the site owner, including roads, paths and communal parts of the site: their pitch agreements are their permission to come on to the site and to use the communal parts of it. The duty of care is thus owed to them. A person entering land in the exercise of a legal right is also a "visitor" (s. 1(6))[2]. 10-12

A visitor is entitled to compensation for injury or damage only if the occupier has failed to take adequate care. The duty to take care, which the Act calls the "common duty of care", is defined in s. 2(2) as: 10-13

> "...a duty to take such care as in all the circumstances of the case is reasonable to see that the visitor will be reasonably safe in using the premises for the purposes for which he is invited or permitted by the occupier to be there".

The Act goes on to provide for two particular situations: an occupier must be prepared for children to be less careful than adults, but may expect a person in the exercise of his calling (meaning his 10-14

---

1. See *Robson v Hallett* [1967] 2 QB 939.
2. For example, local authority staff exercising the power to enter a caravan site, under the Caravan Sites and Control of Development act 1960—see 2-77.

trade, profession or occupation) to appreciate and guard against any special risks (s. 2(3)).

10-15 Warnings by the occupier about dangers may enable him to say that he has taken enough care, but only if the warning is sufficient in all the circumstances to enable the visitor to be reasonably safe (s. 2(4)(a)). If an occupier has entrusted work to a contractor (not an employee) he may not be liable for any resulting injury to a visitor if he (the occupier) was acting reasonably in doing so, and if he has acted reasonably in selecting the contractor and checking that the work has been properly done (s. 2(4)(b)). A person injured may of course be able to take legal action against the contractor, even if she cannot do so against the occupier of the land.

See 10-21 on negligence.

10-16 The 1957 Act covers not just personal injuries but also damage. Thus a visitor to a caravan site whose car was damaged, as a result of an accident which occurred because of the site owner's lack of care, would be entitled to compensation.

Liability to people other than visitors

10-17 The Occupiers' Liability Act 1984 is concerned with people who are not "visitors", and so are not covered by the 1957 Act. In essence, the 1984 Act applies to trespassers and to people coming on to land in exercise of a private right of way.

10-18 A duty of care is also imposed under the 1984 Act, but it is lighter than the duty under the 1957 Act. The duty exists where the occupier knows about a source of danger, or has reasonable grounds to believe there is a danger, and knows or has reasonable grounds to know that someone might come near the danger; and in view of the risk of injury might reasonably be expected to offer some protection against the danger (s. 1(3)). The duty is "to take such care as is reasonable in all the circumstances" (s. 1(9)). The court can thus take into account the nature of the danger, and the characteristics of the persons affected.

10-19 Suppose for example that a deep trench is dug on a part of a caravan site where residents are not supposed to go but in fact, as the site owner knows, do go. The trench is not fenced off or lit; one dark night a trespassing resident falls in and is injured. The site owner may be liable to pay compensation under the 1984 Act.

10-20 The 1984 Act is unlike the 1957 Act in that it covers only injury, not damage to property; though the common law, which applied before the 1984 Act came into force, may allow compensation for damage to be obtained. The duty under the 1984 Act is not extended to cover the occupiers of "structures" such as caravans: it applies only to land.

Negligence

The tort of negligence lays down a broad duty of care, so that those who suffer as a result of a breach of the duty can obtain compensation. It has a wide application, and in one sense is the most important tort. It overlaps with nuisance and occupiers' liability. 10-21

Whether a duty of care exists in a given situation is a matter of law. The law generally recognises that a person is under a duty of care to those who are closely affected by his conduct. Whether the person concerned has broken the duty of care depends upon several factors, including the nature of the risks being run and whether it is reasonable for the person to run those risks. 10-22

The courts can award compensation for injury or damage to property caused by negligence. In limited circumstances, damages may be awarded for "economic loss", for example loss of profits to a business which may flow from an accident. 10-23

In practice, many cases involve road accidents, and these are a good illustration of how the law works. The courts recognise that a driver owes a duty of care to other road users; and a driver whose negligence causes an accident is liable to compensate those who suffer injury or damage as a result. A claim could arise in relation to a caravan site because someone was knocked over as a result of negligent driving. Equally, if the negligent repair of a caravan led to injury, there could be a claim for compensation. 10-24

It is a defence to a claim that no duty was owed to the person concerned, or that there was no breach of the duty of care; that the person making the claim consented to run the risk, or that the person making the claim was himself careless, and so partly to blame. In the latter situation, where the Law Reform (Contributory Negligence) Act 1945 applies, the court's decision is expressed as a percentage: the person injured might (for example) be held to be 50% to blame, and would therefore receive only 50% of the compensation which she would otherwise have received. 10-25

Animals Act 1971

The Animals Act 1971 imposes liability on the keeper of an animal for the damage it causes (including injury and damage to property) subject to certain conditions[1]. 10-26

1. The Act also imposes other sorts of liability, including liability for dogs which injure livestock.

10-27 Some animals are covered by the Act because they belong to a "dangerous species", by which the Act means a species not commonly domesticated in the British Isles. Others are covered when they cause damage if they meet all of the three conditions set out in s. 2(2):

- The damage is of a kind which the animals is likely to cause, or which, if caused by the animal, is likely to be severe.

- This was because of abnormal characteristics, not usually found in such animals, or found only at particular times or in particular circumstances. And—

- The abnormal circumstances were known to the keeper of the animal.

10-28 The "keeper" of an animal is the person who owns the animal, or has possession of it, or, if the person in possession of it is under 16, the head of the household (s. 6). It may difficult to show that all these conditions are satisfied: even if the animal is, say, a large and powerful dog, it is still necessary to show that the dog had abnormal characteristics of which the keeper was aware[1]. If the conditions are shown to be satisfied, the keeper is liable to pay compensation, even if he was not actually at fault. If the conditions are *not* satisfied, it may still be possible for a person who has suffered damage to obtain compensation by relying on the tort of negligence.

See 10-21.

Liability of a site owner for damage to caravans

10-29 Does a site owner have any liability towards the owner of a caravan which is stolen or damaged? The Court of Appeal considered this question in a case in 1986[2], in which a caravan was stolen from a site. The answer depended upon the legal nature of a pitch agreement. The court decided that there was no duty on the site owner to look after the caravan, and he was therefore not obliged to compensate the owner of the caravan for loss or damage caused by someone else.

1. See *Jaundrill v Gillett*, *The Times* 30 January 1996.
2. *Hinks v Fleet* [1986] 2 EGLR 243.

Defects in manufacture of caravans

The Consumer Protection Act 1987 allows a person who suffers injury, loss or damage as a result of a defective product to obtain compensation. A caravan is a product for these purposes, even if attached to the land (ss. 1 and 45(1)). According to the Act, there is a defect if: 10-30

See also 1-41 on British Standards

> "the safety of the product is not such as persons generally are entitled to expect" (s. 3)

A person claiming compensation must show that the product was dangerous and caused damage.

Compensation can be obtained for death or injury. If loss is caused because property is damaged, the manufacturer is not required to pay compensation for the loss of the product he manufactured; and compensation can only be obtained if the value of the damage exceeds £275 (s. 5). If, for example, a caravan caught fire due to faulty manufacture, and the occupant was injured, and clothes and other items of property damaged to a value of more than £275, compensation could be obtained. 10-31

Compensation can thus be claimed from the manufacturer of a defective product. The supplier of the product can also be liable under the Consumer Protection Act 1987 to pay compensation if he is asked to name the person from whom he obtained the goods but does not do so (s. 2(3)). This does not mean that a site owner or other person supplying a defective caravan is not liable to cause compensation; but where the Consumer Protection Act does not apply the basis for the liability is different. 10-32

See 10-21 for negligence, and chapter 7 for contracts.

Under s. 4 of the Act, a number of defences are available to a person from whom compensation is claimed, including that: 10-33

- The defect was attributable to some legal requirement.

- The defect was not in the product when it was put into circulation.

- The supply was not in a commercial context (for example, where a site owner lets someone use a caravan as a friendly act, not in the course of his business).

- Given the state of scientific knowledge at the time, the manufacturer could not be expected to have discovered the defect when the product was being made.

10-34 The point of the Act is to protect consumers; and it applies only where the product in question is ordinarily intended for private use and is intended to be used mainly for private purposes by the person claiming compensation (s. 5(4)). A site owner cannot generally claim under the Act for defective caravans bought from a manufacturer, since they will not be mainly for her private use. (She may, however, be able to take action for breach of contract.) A private person buying a caravan would normally be able to do so, if the caravan was his private use, even though he intended to let it out from time to time.

See chapter 7.

Protection from Harassment Act 1997

10-35 The Protection from Harassment Act 1997 makes harassment an offence. But, by s. 3(1), harassment is also a civil wrong, so that a person who has been subjected to (or threatened with) harassment can take action in the civil courts to obtain compensation or an injunctions or both.

See 9-9 for the offence, and what amounts to harassment

See 1-45 for injunctions.

10-36 The Act makes clear, in s. 3(2), that compensation can be awarded for:

> "...(among other things) any anxiety caused by the harassment and any financial loss resulting from the harassment."

10-37 If a person obtains an injunction, ordering someone not to harass him, a breach of the injunction can be punished by the court because it is a contempt of court. Since criminal courts are able to make "restraining orders", when sentencing a person for the offence of harassment, and to punish for breach of such orders, the Act enables both civil and criminal courts to act in much the same way in dealing with people who harass others.

10-38 The Protection from Harassment Act 1997 could be relevant on a caravan site where ill-feeling or other problems led one resident to engage in "stalking" or similar behaviour towards another. But it would not cover generally cover the sort of actions with which Part I of the Caravan Sites Act 1968 and the Protection from Eviction Act 1977 are designed to deal. However, it does allow a person affected to make a claim for compensation. Neither the 1968 nor the 1977 Acts do this; though under s. 27 of the Housing Act 1988 a tenant can obtain compensation for unlawful eviction.

See further 7-55.

Anti-social behaviour orders

For seriously anti-social behaviour, s. 1 of the Crime and Disorder Act 1998 introduced a new procedure. If it appears that a person, aged 10 or more: 10-39

> "(a)...has acted...in an anti-social manner, that is to say, in a manner that caused, or that was likely to cause, harassment, alarm or distress to one or more persons not of the same household as himself; and
>
> (b) that such an order is necessary to protect persons in the local government area in which the harassment, alarm or distress was caused or was likely to be caused from further anti-social acts by him"

—then the local authority or the police (but not ordinary members of the public) can apply to a magistrates' court for an anti-social behaviour order, or "ASBO".

Such proceedings are civil in nature[1]. They are intended to be used to deal with unruly, intimidating or bullying behaviour, perhaps marked by vandalism and drug- or alcohol-abuse. The Act is not designed to deal with one-off incidents: for an ASBO to be made, it must be clear that repetition of the behaviour is likely. Before an application can be made there must be consultations between the police and the local authority. The behaviour which the police or the local authority rely on in applying for an order may consist of criminal offences, but non-criminal behaviour may also be relied on. An ASBO must prohibit the person concerned from repeating his behaviour, and the order must last for at least two years. Breach of an order is an offence punishable by a maximum of five year's imprisonment. 10-40

An ASBO could be applied for in relation to a person living on a caravan site; but the procedure is intended for those who cause serious disruption, to the extent that intervention by the police and the local authority is called for. Action by the site owner for breach of site rules might lead to the removal of such a person, without the need for official action. 10-41

Contracts and notices excluding liability

The Unfair Contract Terms Act 1977 is relevant where a term in a contract sets out to exclude liability for breach of the contract.● The Act also deals with attempts to exclude liability for negligence in a 10-42

● See 7-30 onwards.

1. See *R v Manchester Crown Court, ex parte M, The Times* 9 March 2001.

contract—for example, a term in a pitch agreement saying that the site owner will not be liable if a resident suffers injury or damage due to her negligence. The Act contains two main rules:

- A person can never exclude liability for death or injury resulting from negligence (s. 2(1)).

"Negligence" includes liability under the Occupiers' Liability Acts: see 10-10 onwards.

- For other sorts of loss and damage, a person can exclude liability only in so far as it is reasonable to do so (s. 2(2)). (The Act lists some of the factors which are relevant to the question of reasonableness, including the strength of each party's bargaining position (s. 11, Schedule 2).)

10-43 Despite its name, the Act applies not just to contracts but also to notices designed to apply where there is no contract. Occupiers of land sometimes display notices which say that they will not be liable for injury or damage to visitors. The aim is to establish that people coming on to the land have been warned, and accept any risks that there may be, so that the occupier is not responsible. But, in relation to negligence, the Act makes these notices ineffective in the same circumstances as terms and conditions in contracts.

Assessment

10-44 The law treats site owners and residents rather differently, but both have the right to claim compensation in certain circumstances, and both are made responsible by the law for their behaviour and for what happens on the land which they control.

10-45 In practice, it may be persistent annoyances rather than major disasters which concern residents. Site rules will be the first recourse. Otherwise, residents who have pitch agreements are at a disadvantage in that they are not able to take action for private nuisance against neighbours and others who cause a disturbance. Statutory nuisance may assist, as explain in chapter 8, and the local authority may be prepared to take action. Full compensation may not be awarded; but this form of legal proceedings may succeed in putting an end to the nuisance, which may be first priority for the person affected.

10-46 For both site owners and residents, insurance against the risk of injury and loss—including the risk of being required to compensate someone else for their loss—will always be wise.

Appendix—materials

This Appendix contains the current text of the Caravan Sites and Control of Development Act 1960, the Caravan Sites Act 1968, and the Mobile Homes Act 1975 and 1983. Text has been omitted where provisions have been repealed, or apply only to Scotland, or deal with amendments to other legislation.

The Appendix also contains delegated legislation made under the Mobile Homes Act 1983, and Policy Planning Guidance Notes and Circulars by the DETR. In relation to the latter, some of the material reproduced consists of extracts relating to caravan sites and mobile home parks. In cases of doubt, reference should be made to the full text of the document. Square brackets identify up-dated references.

Caravan Sites and Control of Development Act 1960

PART I
CARAVAN SITES
Licensing of caravan sites

Prohibition of use of land as a caravan site without a licence

1.—(1) Subject to the provisions of this Part of this Act, no occupier of land shall after the commencement of this Act cause or permit any part of the land to be used as a caravan site unless he is the holder of a site licence (that is to say, a licence under this Part of this Act authorising the use of the land as a caravan site) for the time being in force as respects the land so used. A-0

(2) If the occupier of any land contravenes subsection (1) of this section he shall be guilty of an offence and liable on summary conviction to a fine not exceeding level 4 on the standard scale.

(3) In this part of this Act the expression "occupier" means, in relation to any land, the person who, by virtue of an estate or interest therein held by him, is entitled to possession thereof or would be so entitled but for the rights of any other person under a licence granted in respect of the land:

Provided that where land amounting to not more than four hundred square yards in area is let under a tenancy entered into with a view to the use of the land as a caravan site, the expression "occupier" means in relation to that land the person who would be entitled to possession of the land but for the rights of any person under that tenancy.

(4) In this Part of this Act the expression "caravan site" means land on which a caravan is stationed for the purposes of human habitation and land which is used in conjunction with land on which a caravan is so stationed.

Exemptions from licensing requirements

A-1 2. No site licence shall be required for the use of land as a caravan site in any of the circumstances specified in the First Schedule to this Act and that Schedule shall have effect accordingly.

Issue of site licences by local authorities

A-2 3.—(1) An application for the issue of a site licence in respect of any land may be made by the occupier thereof to the local authority in whose area the land is situated.

(2) An application under this section shall be made in writing and shall specify the land in respect of which the application is made; and the applicant shall, either at the time of making the application or subsequently, give to the local authority such other information as they may reasonably require.

(3) A local authority may on an application under this section issue a site licence in respect of the land if, but only if, the applicant is, at the time when the site licence is issued, entitled to the benefit of a permission for the use of the land as a caravan site granted under Part III of the Act of 1947 otherwise than by a development order.

(4) If at the date when the applicant duly gives the information required by virtue of subsection (2) of this section he is entitled to the benefit of such a permission as aforesaid, the local authority shall issue a site licence in respect of the land within two months of that date or, if the applicant and the local authority agree in writing that the local authority shall be afforded a longer period within which to grant a site licence, within the period so agreed.

(5) If the applicant becomes entitled to the benefit of such a permission as aforesaid at some time after duly giving the information required by virtue of subsection (2) of this section the local authority shall issue a site licence in respect of the land within six weeks of the date on which he becomes so entitled or, if the applicant and the local authority agree in writing that the local authority shall be afforded a longer period within which to grant a site licence, within the period so agreed.

(6) Notwithstanding anything in the foregoing provisions of this section, a local authority shall not at any time issue a site licence to a person who to their knowledge has held a site licence which has been revoked in pursuance of the provisions of this Part of this Act less than three years before that time.

Duration of site licences

A-3 4.—(1) Where permission for the use of any land as a caravan site has been granted under Part III of the Act of 1947 otherwise than by a development order, and has been so granted in terms such that it will expire at the end of a specified period, any site licence issued in respect of the land by virtue of the existence of that permission shall expire, and shall be stated to expire, at the end of that period; but, subject as aforesaid, a site licence shall not be issued for a limited period only.

(2) If after a site licence is issued the terms of the said permission are varied by the Minister on an appeal under section sixteen of the Act of 1947, the local authority who issued the licence shall make in the site licence any alteration required to secure that its terms comply with the provisions of the foregoing subsection.

Power of local authority to attach conditions to site licences

A-4 5.—(1) A site licence issued by a local authority in respect of any land may be so issued subject to such conditions as the authority may think it necessary or desirable to impose on the occupier of the land in the interests of persons dwelling thereon in caravans, or of any other class of persons, or of the public at large; and in particular, but without prejudice to the generality of the foregoing, a site licence may be issued subject to conditions—

(a) for restricting the occasions on which caravans are stationed on the land for the purposes of human habitation, or the total number of caravans which are so stationed at any one time;

(b) for controlling (whether by reference to their size, the state of their repair or, subject to the provisions of subsection (2) of this section, any other feature) the types of caravan which are stationed on the land;

(c) for regulating the positions in which caravans are stationed on the land for the purposes of human habitation and for prohibiting, restricting, or otherwise regulating, the placing or erection on the land, at any time when caravans are so stationed, of structures and vehicles of any description whatsoever and of tents;

(d) for securing the taking of any steps for preserving or enhancing the amenity of the land, including the planting and replanting thereof with trees and bushes;

(e) for securing that, at all times when caravans are stationed on the land, proper measures are taken for preventing and detecting the outbreak of fire and adequate means of fighting fire are provided and maintained;

(f) for securing that adequate sanitary facilities, and such other facilities, services or equipment as may be specified are provided for the use of persons dwelling on the land in caravans and that, at all times when caravans are stationed thereon for the purposes of human habitation, any facilities and equipment so provided are properly maintained.

(2) No condition shall be attached to a site licence controlling the types of caravans which are stationed on the land by reference to the materials used in their construction.

(3) A site licence issued in respect of any land shall, unless it is issued subject to a condition restricting to three or less the total number of caravans which may be stationed on the land at any one time, contain an express condition that, at all times when caravans are stationed on the land for the purposes of human habitation, a copy of the licence as for the time being in force shall be displayed on the land in some conspicuous place.

(3A) The local authority shall consult the fire authority as to the extent to which any model standards relating to fire precautions which have been specified under subsection (6) of this section are appropriate to the land.

(3B) If—

(a) no such standards have been specified; or

(b) any standard that has been specified appears to the fire authority to be inappropriate to the land,

the local authority shall consult the fire authority as to what conditions relating to fire precautions ought to be attached to the site licence instead.

(4) A condition attached to a site licence may, if it requires the carrying out of any works on the land in respect of which the licence is issued, prohibit or restrict the bringing of caravans on to the land for the purposes of human habitation until such time as the local authority have certified in writing that the works have been completed to their satisfaction; and where the land to which the site licence relates is at the time in use as a caravan site, the condition may, whether or not it contains any such prohibition or restriction as aforesaid, require the works to be completed to the satisfaction of the authority within a

stated period.

(5) For the avoidance of doubt, it is hereby declared that a condition attached to a site licence shall be valid notwithstanding that it can be complied with only by the carrying out of works which the holder of the site licence is not entitled to carry out as of right.

(6) The Minister may from time to time specify for the purposes of this section model standards with respect to the layout of, and the provision of facilities, services and equipment for, caravan sites or particular types of caravan site; and in deciding what (if any) conditions to attach to a site licence, a local authority shall have regard to any standards so specified.

(7) The duty imposed on a local authority by subsection (6) of this section to have regard to standards specified under that subsection is to be construed, as regarding standards relating to fire precautions which are so specified, as a duty to have regard to them subject to any advice given to the fire authority under subsection (3A) or (3B) of this section.

(8) In this section "fire precautions" means precautions to be taken for any of the purposes specified in paragraph (e) of subsection (1) of this section for which conditions may be imposed by virtue of that subsection.

Failure by local authority to issue site licence

A-5 6. Where a local authority, being required under section three of this Act to issue a site licence in respect of any land, fail to do so within the period within which they are required to issue a site licence by that section, no offence under section one of this Act shall be committed in respect of the land by the person by whom the application for the site licence was made at any time after the expiration of the said period and before a site licence is issued in pursuance of the said application.

Appeal to a magistrates' court against conditions attached to the licence

A-6 7.—(1) Any person aggrieved by any condition (other than the condition referred to in subsection (3) of section five of this Act) subject to which a site licence has been issued to him in respect of any land may, within twenty-eight days of the date on which the licence was so issued, appeal to a magistrates' court for the petty sessions area in which the land is situated; and the court, if satisfied (having regard amongst other things to any standards which may have been specified by the Minister under subsection (6) of the said section five) that the condition is unduly burdensome, may vary or cancel the condition.

(2) In so far as the effect of a condition (in whatever words expressed) subject to which a site licence is issued in respect of land is to require the carrying out on the land of any works, the condition shall not have effect during the period within which the person to whom the site licence is issued is entitled by virtue of the foregoing subsection to appeal against the condition nor, thereafter, whilst an appeal against the condition is pending.

Power of local authorities to alter conditions attached to site licences

A-7 8.—(1) The conditions attached to a site licence may be altered at any time (whether by the variation or cancellation of existing conditions, or by the addition of new conditions, or by a combination of any such methods) by the local authority, but before exercising their powers under this subsection the local authority shall afford to the holder of the licence an opportunity of making representations.

(2) Where the holder of a site licence is aggrieved by any alteration of the conditions attached thereto or by the refusal of the local authority of an application by him for the alteration of those conditions, he may, within twenty-eight days of the date on which written notification of the alteration or refusal is received by him, appeal to a magistrates' court

acting for the petty sessions area in which the land to which the site licence relates is situated; and the court may, if they allow the appeal, give to the local authority such directions as may be necessary to give effect to their decision.

(3) The alteration by a local authority of the conditions attached to any site licence shall not have effect until written notification thereof has been received by the holder of the licence, and in so far as such alteration imposes a requirement on the holder of the licence to carry out on the land to which the licence relates any works which he would not otherwise be required to carry out, the alteration shall not have effect during the period within which the said holder is entitled by virtue of the last foregoing subsection to appeal against the alteration nor, thereafter, whilst an appeal against the alteration is pending.

(4) In exercising the powers conferred upon them by subsection (1) and subsection (2) of this section respectively, a local authority and a magistrates' court shall have regard amongst other things to any standards which may have been specified by the Minister under subsection (6) of section five of this Act.

(5) The local authority shall consult the fire authority before exercising the powers conferred upon them by subsection (1) of this section in relation to a condition attached to a site licence for the purposes set out in section 5(1)(e) of this Act.

Provisions as to breach of condition

9.—(1) If an occupier of land fails to comply with any condition for the time being attached to a site licence held in respect of the land, he shall be guilty of an offence and liable on summary conviction to a fine not exceeding level 4 on the standard scale. A-8

(2) Where a person convicted under this section for failing to comply with a condition attached to a site licence has on two or more previous occasions been convicted thereunder for failing to comply with a condition attached to that licence, the court before whom he is convicted may, if an application in that behalf is made at the hearing by the local authority in whose area the land is situated, make an order for the revocation of the site licence to come into force on such date as the court may specify in the order, being a date not earlier than the expiration of any period within which notice of appeal (whether by case stated or otherwise) may be given against the conviction and if before the date so specified an appeal is so brought the order shall be of no effect pending the final determination or withdrawal of the appeal.

The person convicted or the local authority who issued the licence may apply to the magistrates' court which has made such an order revoking a site licence for an order extending the period at the end of which the revocation is to come into force, and the magistrates' court may, if satisfied that adequate notice of the application has been given to the local authority or, as the case may be, the person convicted, make an order extending that period.

(3) Where an occupier of land fails within the time specified in a condition attached to a site licence held by him to complete to the satisfaction of the local authority in whose area the site is situated any works required by the condition to be so completed, the local authority may carry out those works, and may recover as a simple contract debt in any court of competent jurisdiction from that person any expenses reasonably incurred by them in that behalf.

Transfer of site licences and transmission on death, etc

10.—(1) When the holder of a site licence in respect of any land ceases to be the occupier of the land, he may, with the consent of the local authority in whose area the land is situated, transfer the licence to the person who then becomes the occupier of the land. A-9

(2) Where a local authority give their consent to the transfer of a site licence they shall

endorse on the licence the name of the person to whom it is to be transferred and the date agreed between the parties to the transfer as the date on which that person is, for the purposes of this Part of this Act, to be treated as having become the holder of the licence.

(3) If an application is made under subsection (1) of this section for consent to the transfer of a site licence to a person who is to become the occupier of the land, that person may apply for a site licence under section three of this Act as if he were the occupier of the land, and if the local authority at any time before issuing a site licence in compliance with that application give their consent to the transfer they need not proceed with the application for the site licence.

(4) Where any person becomes, by operation of law, entitled to an estate or interest in land in respect of which a site licence is in force and is, by virtue of his holding that estate or interest, the occupier of the land within the meaning of this Part of this Act he shall, for the purposes of this Part of this Act be treated as having become the holder of the licence on the day on which he became the occupier of the land, and the local authority in whose area the land is situated shall, if an application in that behalf is made to them, endorse his name and the said date on the licence.

Duty of licence holder to surrender licence for alteration

A-10 11.—(1) A local authority who have issued a site licence may at any time require the holder to deliver it up so as to enable them to enter in it any alteration of conditions or other terms of the licence made in pursuance of the provisions of this Part of this Act.

(2) If the holder of a site licence fails without reasonable excuse to comply with a requirement duly made under this section he shall be liable on summary conviction to a fine not exceeding level 1 on the standard scale.

Responsibility of occupier of land subject to a licence or special tenancy

A-11 12.—(1) It sha11 be a condition of any licence or of any such tenancy as is mentioned in subsection (3) of section one of this Act that if any person in exercise of rights under the licence or tenancy does anything which would constitute an offence under that section if that person were the occupier of the land, the person who is the occupier of the land may take possession of the land and terminate the licence or tenancy and in determining whether the occupier of the land has permitted the land to be used as a caravan site account shall be taken of any powers exercisable by him under this subsection.

(2) The occupier of any land subject to a licence or subject to any such tenancy as is mentioned in subsection (3) of section one of this Act shall have the right, as against any person claiming under the licence or tenancy, to enter on the land and do anything on the land reasonably required for the purpose of complying with any conditions attached to a site licence issued with respect to the land.

...

Caravans on commons

Power of rural district councils to prohibit caravans on commons

A-12 23.—(1) This section applies to any land in the area of a district council which is or forms part of a common, not being land falling within any of the following descriptions, that is to say—

(a) land to which section one hundred and ninety-three of the Law of Property Act, 1925 (which relates to the rights of the public over certain commons and waste lands), for the time being applies;

(b) land which is subject to a scheme under Part I of the Commons Act, 1899 (under which schemes may be made for the regulation and management of certain commons);

(c) land as respects which a site licence is for the time being in force.

(2) The council of a district may make with respect to any land in their area to which this section applies an order prohibiting, either absolutely or except in such circumstances as may be specified in the order, the stationing of caravans on the land for the purposes of human habitation.

(3) Without prejudice to the provisions of section one of this Act, any person who stations a caravan on any land in contravention of an order under this section for the time being in force with respect to the land shall be guilty of an offence and liable on summary conviction to a fine not exceeding level 1 on the standard scale.

(4) It shall be the duty of a district council to take all reasonable steps to secure that copies of any order under this section which is for the time being in force with respect to any land in their area are so displayed on the land as to give to persons entering thereof adequate warning of the existence of the order, and the council shall have the right to place on the land such notices as they consider necessary for the performance of their duty under this subsection.

(5) An order under this section may be revoked at any time by a subsequent order made thereunder by the district council, or may be so varied either so as to exclude any land from the operation of the order or so as to introduce any exception, or further exception, from the prohibition imposed by the order.

(6) Where the whole or any part of any land with respect to which an order under this section is in force ceases to be land to which this section applies, the said order shall thereupon cease to have effect with respect to the said land or part; and where an order ceases under this subsection to have effect with respect to a part only of any land, the district council shall cause any copy of the order which is displayed on that part of the land with respect to which the order continues in force to be amended accordingly.

(7) The provisions of the Second Schedule to this Act shall, subject as therein provided, have effect with respect to orders under this section.

(8) In this section the word "common" includes any land subject to be enclosed under the Inclosure Acts, 1845 to 1882, and any town or village green.

(9) This section and the Second Schedule to this Act shall apply in relation to land in Wales as if for every reference to a district council or to the district council (however expressed), or which falls to be construed as such a reference, there were substituted a reference to Welsh county council or county borough council or (as the case may be) the Welsh county council or county borough council.

Provision of caravan sites by local authorities

Power of local authorities to provide sites for caravans

24.—(1) A local authority shall have power within their area to provide sites where caravans may be brought, whether for holidays or other temporary purposes or for use as permanent residences, and to manage the sites or lease them to some other person. A-13

(2) Subject to the provisions of this section, a local authority shall have power to do anything appearing to them desirable in connection with the provision such sites, and in particular—

(a) to acquire land which is in use as a caravan site, or has been laid out as a caravan site, or

(b) to provide for the use of those occupying caravan sites any services or facilities for their health or convenience, or

(c) to provide, in or in connection with sites for the accommodation of gipsies, working space and facilities for the carrying on of such activities as are normally carried on by them,

and in exercising their powers under this section the local authority shall have regard to any standards which may have been specified by the Minister under subsection (6) of section five of this Act.

(2A) Before exercising the power to provide a site conferred on them by subsection (1) of this section the local authority shall consult the fire authority, if they are not themselves the fire authority—

(a) as to measures to be taken for preventing and detecting the outbreak of fire on the site; and

(b) as to the provision and maintenance of means of fighting fire on it.

(3) The local authority shall make in respect of the use of sites managed by them, and of any services or facilities provided or made available under this section, such reasonable charges as they may determine.

(4) A local authority may make available the services and facilities provided under this section for those who do not normally reside in the area of the local authority as freely as for those who do.

(5) A local authority shall, in the performance of their functions under this section, have power, where it appears to them that a caravan site or an additional caravan site is needed in their area, or that land which is in use as a caravan site should in the interests of the users of caravans be taken over by the local authority, to acquire land, or any interest in land, compulsorily.

(6) The power of a local authority under the last foregoing subsection to acquire land, or any interest in land, compulsorily shall be exercisable in any particular case on their behalf authorised to do so by the Minister, and the Acquisition of Land Act 1981 shall have effect in relation to the acquisition of land, or any interest in land, under the said subsection.

(7) A local authority shall not have power under this section to provide caravans.

(8) In this section the expression "local authority" includes the council of a county in England and "gipsies" means persons of nomadic habit of life, whatever their race or origin, but does not include members of an organised group of showmen, or persons engaged in travelling circuses, travelling together as such.

...

Miscellaneous and supplemental

Registers of site licences

A-14 25.—(1) Every local authority shall keep a register of site licences issued in respect of land situated in their area, and every such register shall be open for inspection by the public at all reasonable times.

(2) Where under subsection (2) or subsection (4) of section ten of this Act a local author-

ity endorse on a site licence the name of any person in the circumstances described in those subsections, they shall record his name, and the date entered in the licence, in the register of site licences.

Power of entry of officers of local authorities

26.—(1) Subject to the provisions of this section, any authorised officer of a local authority shall, on producing, if so required, some duly authenticated document showing his authority, have a right at all reasonable hours to enter any land which is listed as a caravan site or in respect of which an application for a site licence has been made— A-15

(a) for the purpose of enabling the local authority to determine what conditions should be attached to a site licence or whether conditions attached to a site licence should be altered;

(b) for the purpose of ascertaining whether there is, or has been, on or in connection with the land any contravention of the provisions of this Part of this Act;

(c) for the purpose of ascertaining whether or not circumstances exist which would authorise the local authority to take any action, or execute any work, under this Part of this Act.

(d) for the purpose of taking any action, or executing any work, authorised by this part of this Act to be taken or executed by the local authority.

Provided that admission to any land shall not be demanded as of right unless twenty-four hours' notice of the intended entry has been given to the occupier.

(2) If it is shown to the satisfaction of a justice of the peace—

(a) that admission to any land has been refused, or that refusal is apprehended, or that the occupier of the land is temporarily absent and the case is one of urgency, or that an application for admission would defeat the object of the entry; and

(b) that there is reasonable ground for entering on the land for any such purpose as is mentioned in subsection (1) of this section,

the justice may by warrant under his hand authorise the local authority by any authorised officer to enter the land, if need be by force:

Provided that such a warrant shall not be issued unless the justice is satisfied either that notice of the intention to apply for the warrant has been given to the occupier, or that the occupier is temporarily absent and the case is one of urgency, or that the giving of such notice would defeat the object of the entry.

(3) An authorised officer entering any land by virtue of this section, or of a warrant issued thereunder, may take with him such other persons as may be necessary.

(4) Every warrant granted under this section shall continue in force until the purpose for which the entry is necessary has been satisfied.

(5) A person who wilfully obstructs any person acting in the execution of this section, or of a warrant under this section, shall be liable on summary conviction to a fine not exceeding level 1 on the standard scale.

...

Crown land

28. The provisions of this Part of this Act relating to site licences shall apply to land the occupier of which is not the Crown notwithstanding that an interest in the land belongs to A-16

Her Majesty in right of the Crown or of the Duchy of Lancaster, or to the Duchy of Cornwall, or belongs to a government department or is held in trust for Her Majesty for the purposes of a government department.

Interpretation

A-17 29.—(1) In this Part of this Act, unless the context otherwise requires—

"caravan" means any structure designed or adapted for human habitation which is capable of being moved from one place to another (whether by being towed, or by being transported on a motor vehicle or trailer) and any motor vehicle so designed or adapted, but does not include —

(a) any railway rolling stock which is for the time being on rails forming part of a railway system, or

(b) any tent;

"caravan site" has the meaning assigned to it by subsection (4) of section one of this Act;

"development order" means an order made under section thirteen of the Act of 1947 (under which orders may be made which, in some cases, themselves grant permission for development and, in other cases, provide that permission shall be granted on an application in that behalf);

"fire authority", in relation to any land, means the authority discharging in the area in which the land is situated the functions of fire authority under the Fire Services Act 1947;

...

"local authority" means a council of a London Borough or a district, the Common Council of the City of London and the Council of the Isles of Scilly but, in relation to Wales, means the council of a Welsh county or county borough;

"occupier" has the meaning assigned to it by subsection (3) of section one of this Act and "occupied" and "occupation" shall be construed accordingly;

"site licence" has the meaning assigned to it by subsection (1) of section one of this Act;

"the Minister" means the Minister of Housing and Local Government.

(2) Any reference in this Part of this Act to the carrying out of works shall include a reference to the planting of trees and shrubs and the carrying out of other operations for preserving or enhancing the amenity of land.

(3) For the purposes of any provision of this Part of this Act relating to the expiration of permission granted under Part III of the Act of 1947 for any use of land, permission granted for the use of land for intermittent periods shall not be regarded as expiring at any time so long as the permission authorises the use of the land for further intermittent periods.

(4) Any reference in this Part of this Act to permission granted under Part III of the Act of 1947 for the use of land as a caravan site shall be taken as a reference to such permission whether or not restricted in any way or subject to any condition or limitation, and any reference in this Part of this Act to such permission shall include a reference to permission deemed to be granted under the said Part III or granted on the designation of an enterprise

zone under Schedule 32 of the Local Government, Planning and Land Act 1980.

(5) In this Part of this Act references to the local planning authority shall, where appropriate, be taken as references to any local authority to whom any of the functions of the local planning authority under Part III of the Act of 1947 have been delegated.

Part repeal of s. 269, Public Health Act 1936

30.—(1) Section two hundred and sixty-nine of the Public Health Act, 1936 (which empowers local authorities in England and Wales, excluding London, to control by means of licences the use of movable dwellings within their areas) shall cease to have effect in relation to caravans; and in subsection (5) of that section, paragraph (ii) thereof (which exempts from the provisions of the said section a movable dwelling belonging to and regularly used by a travelling showman in the course of travelling for the purposes of his business) shall be omitted. A-18

...

PART III
GENERAL

...

Financial provisions

49. There shall be paid out of monies provided by Parliament— A-19

(a) any administrative expenses incurred by the Minister of Housing and Local Government or the Secretary of State in consequence of the passing of this Act, and

(b) any increase attributable to the provisions of this Act in the sums payable out of monies so provided under any other enactment.

Short title, interpretation, extent and commencement

50.—(1)This Act may be cited as the Caravan Sites and Control of Development Act, 1960. A-20

(2) In this Act "the Act of 1947" means the Town and Country Planning Act, 1947.

(3) This Act shall not extend to Northern Ireland.

(4) This Act shall come into force at the expiration of a period of one month beginning with the date on which it is passed.

SCHEDULES

FIRST SCHEDULE

CASES WHERE A CARAVAN SITE LICENCE IS NOT REQUIRED

(section 2)

Use within curtilage of a dwellinghouse

1. A site licence shall not be required for the use of land as a caravan site if the use is incidental to the enjoyment as such of a dwellinghouse within the curtilage of which the land is situated. A-21

Use by a person travelling with a caravan for one or two nights

A-22 2. Subject to the provisions of paragraph 13 of this Schedule, a site licence shall not be required for the use of land as a caravan site by a person travelling with a caravan who brings the caravan on to the land for a period which includes not more than two nights—

(a) if during that period no other caravan is stationed for the purposes of human habitation on that land or any adjoining land in the same occupation, and

(b) if, in the period of twelve months ending with the day on which the caravan is brought on to the land, the number of days on which a caravan was stationed anywhere on that land or the said adjoining land for the purposes of human habitation did not exceed twenty-eight.

Use of holdings of five acres or more in certain circumstances

A-23 3.—(1) Subject to the provisions of paragraph 13 of this Schedule, a site licence shall not be required for the use as a caravan site of land which comprises, together with any adjoining land which is in the same occupation and has not been built on, not less than five acres—

(a) if in the period of twelve months ending with the day on which the land is used as a caravan site the number of days on which a caravan was stationed anywhere on that land or on the said adjoining land for the purposes of human habitation did not exceed twenty-eight, and

(b) if in the said period of twelve months not more than three caravans were so stationed at any one time.

(2) The Minister may by order contained in a statutory instrument provide that in any such area as may be specified in the order this paragraph shall have effect subject to the modification—

(a) that for the reference in the foregoing sub-paragraph to five acres there shall be substituted a reference to such smaller acreage as may be specified in the order, or

(b) that for the condition specified in head (a) of that sub-paragraph there shall be substituted a condition that the use in question falls between such dates in any year as may be specified in the order, or subject to modification in both such respects.

(3) The Minister may make different orders under this paragraph as respects different areas, and an order under this paragraph may be varied by a subsequent order made thereunder.

(4) An order under this paragraph shall come into force on such date as may be specified in the order, being a date not less than three months after the order is made; and the Minister shall publish notice of the order in a local newspaper circulating in the locality affected by the order and in such other ways as appear to him to be expedient for the purpose of drawing the attention of the public to the order.

Sites occupied and supervised by exempted organisations

A-24 4. Subject to the provisions of paragraph 13 of this Schedule, a site licence shall not be required for the use as a caravan site of land which is occupied by an organisation which holds for the time being a certificate of exemption granted under paragraph 12 of this Schedule (hereinafter referred to as an exempted organisation) if the use is for purposes of recreation and is under the supervision of the organisation.

Sites approved by exempted organisations

5.—(1) Subject to the provisions of paragraph 13 of this Schedule, a site licence shall not be A-25
required for the use as a caravan site of land as respects which there is in force a certificate issued under this paragraph by an exempted organisation if not more than five caravans are at the time stationed for the purposes of human habitation on the land to which the certificate relates.

(2) For the purposes of this paragraph an exempted organisation may issue as respects any land a certificate stating that the land has been approved by the exempted organisation for use by its members for the purposes of recreation.

(3) The certificate shall be issued to the occupier of the land to which it relates, and the organisation shall send particulars to the Minister of all certificates issued by the organisation under this paragraph.

(4) A certificate issued by an exempted organisation under this paragraph shall specify the date on which it is to come into force and the period for which it is to continue in force, being a period not exceeding one year.

Meetings organised by exempted organisations

6. Subject to the provisions of paragraph 13 of this Schedule, a site licence shall not be A-26
required for the use of land as a caravan site if the use is under the supervision of an exempted organisation and is in pursuance of arrangements made by that organisation for a meeting for its members lasting not more than five days.

Agricultural and forestry workers

7. Subject to the provisions of paragraph 13 of this Schedule, a site licence shall not be A-27
required for the use as a caravan site of agricultural land for the accommodation during a particular season of a person or persons employed in farming operations on land in the same occupation.

8. Subject to the provision of paragraph 13 of this Schedule, a site licence shall not be A-28
required for the use of land as a caravan site for the accommodation during a particular season of a person or persons employed on land in the same occupation, being land used for the purposes of forestry (including afforestation).

Building and engineering sites

9. Subject to the provisions of paragraph 13 of this Schedule, a site licence shall not be A-29
required for the use as a caravan site of land which forms part of, or adjoins, land on which building or engineering operations are being carried out (being operations for the carrying out of which permission under Part III of the Act of 1947 has, if required, been granted) if that use is for the accommodation of a person or persons employed in connection with the said operations.

Travelling showmen

10.—(1) Subject to the provisions of paragraph 13 of this Schedule, a site licence shall not be A-30
required for the use of land as a caravan site by a travelling showman who is a member of an organisation of travelling showmen which holds for the time being a certificate granted under this paragraph and who is, at the time, travelling for the purposes of his business or who has taken up winter quarters on the land with his equipment for some period falling between the beginning of October in any year and the end of March in the following year.

(2) For the purposes of this paragraph the Minister may grant a certificate to any organisation recognised by him as confining its membership to bona fide travelling showmen; and a certificate so granted may be withdrawn by the Minister at any time.

Sites occupied by licensing authority

A-31 11. A site licence shall not be required for the use as a caravan site of land occupied by the local authority in whose area the land is situated.

Gypsy sites occupied by county councils or regional councils

A-32 11A. A site licence shall not be required for the use of land occupied by a county council, or in Scotland by a regional council, as a caravan site providing accommodation for gipsies.

Certification of exempted organisations

A-33 12.—(1) For the purposes of paragraphs 4, 5 and 6 of this Schedule the Minister may grant a certificate of exemption to any organisation as to which he is satisfied that its objects include the encouragement or promotion of recreational activities.

(2) A certificate granted under this paragraph may be withdrawn by the Minister at any time.

Power to withdraw certain exemptions

A-34 13.—(1) The Minister may on the application of a local authority by order provide that, in relation to such land situated in their area as may be specified in the order, this Schedule shall have effect as if paragraphs 2 to 10, or such one or more of those paragraphs as may be so specified, were omitted from this Schedule.

(2) An order under this paragraph—

(a) shall come into force on such date as may be specified therein, and

(b) may, on the application of the local authority on whose application it was made, be varied or revoked by a subsequent order made thereunder,

and, except in the case of an order the sole effect of which is to revoke in whole or part a previous order, the local authority shall, not less than three months before the order comes into force, cause a notice setting out the effect of the order and the date on which it comes into force to be published in the London Gazette … and in a local newspaper circulating in the locality in which the land to which the order relates is situated.

SECOND SCHEDULE

Further Provisions as to Orders Relating to Commons

(section 23)

Duty to consult conservators

A-35 1. Before making an order under section twenty-three of this Act with respect to land which is or forms part of a common of which conservators have been appointed under any local Act, or under any order made under an Act of Parliament, the district council shall consult with the conservators.

Procedure for making orders imposing prohibitions

A-36 2. Before making any order under the said section twenty-three, other than an order the sole effect of which is to revoke or vary a previous order under that section, the district council shall publish in one or more local newspapers circulating in the locality in which the land is situated a notice—

(a) stating the general effect of the order;

(b) specifying a place in the said locality where a copy of the draft order may be inspected by any person free of charge at all reasonable hours during a period of twenty-eight days from the date of the first publication of the notice; and

(c) stating that, within the said period, any person may by notice to the council object to the making of the order.

3.—(1) Not later than the date on which the said notice is first published the district council shall serve a copy thereof on every person entitled as lord of the manor or otherwise to the soil of the land unless the council are satisfied that the persons entitled to the soil of the land are numerous, or cannot after diligent inquiry be ascertained. A-37

(2) A notice under the foregoing sub-paragraph may be served on any person by sending it in a registered letter addressed to him at his usual or last known address.

4.—(1) If before the expiration of a period of twenty-eight days beginning with the date of the first publication of a notice under paragraph 2of this Schedule an objection to the making of the order to which the notice relates is duly made to the district council by any person entitled to the soil of the land, and the notice is not subsequently withdrawn, the district council shall not proceed with the making of the order. A-38

(2) Subject as aforesaid, the council may, at any time within one year after the expiration of the said period, make an order in the terms of the draft order; but if any objection to the making of the order was duly made within the said period by a person who was not entitled to the soil of the land, and the objection has not been withdrawn at the date on which the order is made, the order shall not take effect until it is confirmed by the Minister.

(3) Where the council submit an order to the Minister for his confirmation, they shall send to the Minister a copy of every such objection as is referred to in the last foregoing sub-paragraph; and the Minister, after considering every such objection and causing if he thinks fit a local inquiry to be held, may confirm or refuse to confirm the order and, if he confirms it, may do so subject to such modifications (if any) as he may think desirable.

Notice to lord of manor of other orders

5. Where the sole effect of an order under section twenty-three of this Act is to revoke or vary a previous order under that section (so that paragraphs 2 to 4 of this Schedule do not apply with respect to the making of the order) the district council shall serve such notices, and take such other steps, as appear to them to be appropriate for informing the persons entitled to the soil of the land of the effect of the order. A-39

Crown land

6.—(1) Where it is proposed to make an order of the kind described in paragraph 2 of this Schedule with respect to land in which there is a Crown or Duchy interest, and the nature of that interest is such that, but for this paragraph, the person to whom the interest belongs would be entitled under paragraph 3 of this Schedule to a copy of the notice referred to in that paragraph,— A-40

(a) the said paragraph 3 shall have effect as if it required the copy to be served instead on the appropriate authority; and

(b) sub-paragraph (1) of paragraph 4 of this Schedule shall not apply in relation to the order, but the council shall not make the order unless and until they have obtained the consent in writing thereto of the appropriate authority.

(2) In this paragraph "Crown or Duchy interest" means an interest belonging to Her Majesty in right of the Crown or of the Duchy of Lancaster, or belonging to the Duchy of Cornwall, or belonging to a government department, or held in trust for Her Majesty for

the purposes of a government department; and "the appropriate authority"—

(a) in relation to land belonging to Her Majesty in right of the Crown and forming part of the Crown Estate, means the Crown Estate of Commissioners, and, in relation to any other land belonging to Her Majesty in right of the Crown, means the government department having the management of that land;

(b)in relation to land belonging to Her Majesty in right of the Duchy of Lancaster, means the Chancellor of the Duchy;

(c) in relation to land belonging to the Duchy of Cornwall, means such person as the Duke of Cornwall, or the possessor for the time being of the Duchy of Cornwall, appoints; and

(d)in relation to land belonging to a government department or held in trust for Her Majesty for the purposes of a government department, means that department;

and if any question arises as to what authority is the appropriate authority in relation to any land, that question shall be referred to the Treasury, whose decision shall be final.

Caravan Sites Act 1968

PART I

PROVISIONS FOR PROTECTION OF RESIDENTIAL OCCUPIERS

Application of Part I

A-41 1.—(1) This Part of this Act applies in relation to any licence or contract (whether made before or after the passing of this Act) under which a person is entitled to station a caravan on a protected site (as defined by subsection (2) below) and occupy it as his residence, or to occupy as his residence a caravan stationed on any such site; and any such licence or contract is in this Part referred to as a residential contract, and the person so entitled as the occupier.

(2) For the purposes of this Part of this Act a protected site is any land in respect of which a site licence is required under Part I of the Caravan Sites and Control of Development Act 1960 or would be so required if paragraph 11 of Schedule 1 to that Act (exemption of land occupied by local authorities) were omitted, not being land in respect of which the relevant planning permission or site licence—

(*a*) is expressed to be granted for holiday use only; or

(*b*) is otherwise so expressed or subject to such conditions that there are times of the year when no caravan may be stationed on the land for human habitation.

(3) References in this Part of this Act to the owner of a protected site are references to the person who is or would apart from any residential contract be entitled to possession of the land.

Minimum length of notice

A-42 2. In any case where a residential contract is determinable by notice given by either party to the other, a notice so given shall be of no effect unless it is given not less than four weeks before the date on which it is to take effect.

Protection of occupiers against eviction and harassment

3.—(1) Subject to the provisions of this section, a person shall be guilty of an offence under this section— A-43

(*a*) if, during the subsistence of a residential contract, he unlawfully deprives the occupier of his occupation on the protected site of any caravan which the occupier is entitled by the contract to station and occupy, or to occupy, as his residence thereon;

(*b*) if, after the expiration or determination of a residential contract, he enforces, otherwise than by proceedings in the court, any right to exclude the occupier from the protected site or from any such caravan, or to remove or exclude any such caravan from the site;

(*c*) if, whether during the subsistence or after the expiration or determination of a residential contract, with intent to cause the occupier—

(i) to abandon the occupation of the caravan or remove it from the site, or

(ii) to refrain from exercising any right or pursuing any remedy in respect thereof,

he does acts calculated to interfere with the peace or comfort of the occupier or persons residing with him, or persistently withdraws or withholds services or facilities reasonably required for the occupation of the caravan as a residence on the site.

(2) References in this section to the occupier include references to the person who was the occupier under a residential contract which has expired or been determined and, in the case of the death of the occupier (whether during the subsistence or after the expiration or determination of the contract), to any person then residing with the occupier being—

(*a*) the widow or widower of the occupier; or

(*b*) in default of a widow or widower so residing, any member of the occupier's family.

(3) A person guilty of an offence under this section shall, without prejudice to any liability or remedy to which he may be subject in civil proceedings, be liable on summary conviction to a fine not exceeding level 5 on the standard scale or to imprisonment for a term not exceeding six months, or to both.

(4) In proceedings for an offence under paragraph (*a*) or (*b*) of subsection (1) of this section it shall be a defence to prove that the accused believed, and had reasonable cause to believe, that the occupier of the caravan had ceased to reside on the site.

(5) Nothing in this section applies to the exercise by any person of a right to take possession of a caravan of which he is the owner, other than a right conferred by or arising under the expiration or determination of a residential contract, or to anything done pursuant to an order of the court.

Provision for suspension of eviction orders

4.—(1) If in proceedings by the owner of a protected site the court makes an order for enforcing in relation thereto any such right as is mentioned in paragraph (*a*) of subsection (1) of section 3 of this Act, the court may (without prejudice to any power apart from this section to postpone the operation or suspend the execution of an order, and subject to the following provisions of this section) suspend the enforcement of the order for such period not exceeding twelve months from the date of the order as the court thinks reasonable. A-44

(2) Where the court by virtue of this section suspends the enforcement of an order, it may impose such terms and conditions, including conditions as to the payment or rent or other or other periodical payments or of arrears of such rent or payments, as the court thinks reasonable.

(4) In considering whether or how to exercise its powers under this section, the court shall have regard to all the circumstances, and in particular to the questions—

(a) whether the occupier of the caravan has failed, whether before or after the expiration or determination of the relevant residential contract, to observe any terms of conditions of that contract, any conditions of the site licence, or any reasonable rules made by the owner for the management and conduct of the site or the maintenance of caravans thereon;

(b) whether the occupier has unreasonably refused an offer by the owner to renew the residential contract or make another such contract for a reasonable period and on reasonable terms;

(c) whether the occupier has failed to make reasonable efforts to obtain elsewhere other suitable accommodation for his caravan (or, as the case may be, another suitable caravan and accommodation for it).

(5) Where the court makes such an order as is mentioned in subsection (1) of this section but suspends the enforcement of that order by virtue of this section, the court shall make no order for costs unless it appears to the court, having regard to the conduct of the owner or of the occupier, that there are special reasons for making such an order.

(6) The court shall not suspend the enforcement of an order by virtue of this section in the following cases, namely—

(a) where the proceedings are taken by a local authority within the meaning of section 24 of the Caravan Sites and Control of Development Act 1960;

(b) where no site licence under Part I of that Act is in force in respect of the site;

and where a site licence in respect of the site is expressed to expire at the end of a specified period, the period for which enforcement may be suspended by virtue of this section shall not extend beyond the expiration of the licence.

Supplementary

A-45 5.—(1) In this Part of this Act "the court" means the county court; and any powers of a county in such proceedings as are mentioned in section (1) of section 4 of this Act may be exercised with the leave of the judge by any registrar of the court, except in so far as rules of court provide otherwise.

(2) The power of the court under section 4 of this Act to suspend the enforcement of an order shall extend to any order made but not executed before the commencement of this Part of this Act.

(3) Nothing in this Part of this Act shall affect the operation of section 13 of the Compulsory Purchase Act 1965,

(4) Subsection (1) of section 12 of the Caravan Sites and Control of Development Act 1960 (power of site occupier to take possession and terminate a licence or tenancy in case of contravention of section 1 of that Act) shall have effect subject to the foregoing provisions of this Part of this Act.

(5) The Protection from Eviction Act 1977 (protection against eviction and harassment without due process of law) shall not apply to any premises being a caravan stationed on a protected site.

...

PART III
MISCELLANEOUS

Twin-unit caravans

13.—(1) A structure designed or adapted for human habitation which— A-46

(a) is composed of not more than two sections separately constructed and designed to be assembled on a site by means of bolts, clamps or other devices; and

(b) is, when assembled, physically capable of being moved by road from one place to another (whether by being towed, or by being transported on a motor vehicle or trailer),

shall not be treated as not being (or not having been) a caravan within the meaning of Part I of the Caravan Sites and Control of Development Act 1960 by reason only that it cannot lawfully be so moved on a highway when assembled.

(2) For the purposes of Part I of the Caravan Sites and Control of Development Act 1960, the expression "caravan" shall not include a structure designed or adapted for human habitation which falls within paragraphs *(a)* and *(b)* of the foregoing subsection if its dimensions when assembled exceed any of the following limits, namely—

(a) length (exclusive of any drawbar): 60 feet (18.288 metres);

(b) width: 20 feet (6.096 metres);

(c) overall height of living accommodation (measured internally from the floor at the lowest level to the ceiling at the highest level): 10 feet (3.048 metres).

(3) The Minister may my order by statutory instrument after consultation with such persons or bodies as appear to him to be concerned substitute for any figure mentioned in subsection (2) of this section such other figure as may be specified in the order.

(4) Any statutory instrument made by virtue of subsection (3) of this section shall be subject to annulment in pursuance of a resolution of either House of Parliament.

Offences

14.—(1) Where an offence under this Act committed by a body corporate is proved to have been committed with the consent or connivance of or to be attributable to any neglect on the part of, any director, manager, secretary or other similar officer of the body corporate or any person who is purporting to act in any such capacity, he as well as the body corporate shall be guilty of that offence and shall be liable to be proceeded against and punished accordingly. A-47

(2) Proceedings for an offence under this Act may be instituted by any local authority.

Financial provision

15. There shall be defrayed out of moneys provided by Parliament any increase which may arise in consequence of this Act in the sums payable out of moneys so provided in respect of rate support grant under the Local Government Act 1966. A-48

Interpretation

16. In this Act the following expressions have the following meanings that is to say— A-49

"caravan" has the same meaning as in Part I of the Caravan Sites and Control of Development Act 1960;

...

"local authority" has the same meaning as in section 24 of the Caravan Sites and Control of Development Act 1960;

"the Minister" means, in England other than Monmouthshire, the Minister of Housing and Local Government, and in Wales and Monmouthshire the Secretary of State'

"planning permission" means permission under Part III of the Town and Country Planning Act 1990.

Short title, commencement and extent

A-50 17.—(1) This Act may be cited as the Caravan Sites Act 1968.

(2) This Act, except Part II, shall come into force at the expiration of the period of one month beginning with the day on which it is passed, and Part II shall come into force on such date as the Minister may by order made by statutory instrument appoint.

(3) This Act does not extend to Scotland or Northern Ireland.

Mobile Homes Act 1975

...

Power to prescribe minimum standards

A-51 7.—(1) Without prejudice to his powers under section 5(6) of the Act of 1960, the Secretary of State may by order prescribe minimum standards with respect to the layout of, and the provision of facilities, services and equipment for protected sites within the meaning of Part I of the Act of 1968 on which there are mobile homes occupied as an only or main residence.

(2) An order made under subsection (1) above may apply generally or to a particular area or to protected sites in a particular category and may prescribe different minimum standard in relation to protected sites in different categories.

(3) The power of the Secretary of State to make orders under this section shall be exercisable by statutory instrument.

(4) An order under subsection (1) above shall be subject to annulment in pursuance of a resolution of either House of Parliament.

(5) Any power of the Secretary of State to make an order under any provision of this section shall include a power to make an order varying or revoking any order previously made under that provision.

...

Interpretation

A-52 9.—(1) In this Act the following expressions have the following meanings, that is to say—

"the Act of 1960" means the Caravan Sites and Control of Development Act 1960;

"the Act of 1968" means the Caravan Sites Act 1968;

...

"mobile home" has the same meaning as "caravan" in Part I of the Act of 1960 as amended by the Act of 1968.

...

Short title, commencement and extent

10.—(1) This Act may be cited as the Mobile Homes Act 1975. A-53

(2) This Act shall come into force at the expiration of the period of two months beginning with the day on which it is passed.

(3) This Act does not extend to Northern Ireland.

Mobile Homes Act 1983

Particulars of agreements

1.—(1) This Act applies to any agreement under which a person ("the occupier") is entitled— A-54

(a) to station a mobile home on land forming part of a protected site; and

(b) to occupy the mobile home as his only or main residence.

(2) Within three months of the making of an agreement to which this Act applies, the owner of the protected site ("the owner") shall give to the occupier a written statement which—

(a) specifies the names and addresses of the parties and the date of commencement of the agreement;

(b) includes particulars of the land on which the occupier is entitled to station the mobile home sufficient to identify it;

(c) sets out the express terms of the agreement;

(d) sets out the terms implied by section 2(1) below;

(e) complies with such other requirements as may be prescribed by regulations made by the Secretary of State.

(3) If the agreement was made before the day on which this Act comes into force, the written statement shall be given within six months of that date.

(4) Any reference in subsection (2) or (3) above to the making of an agreement to which this Act applies includes a reference to any variation of an agreement by virtue of which the agreement becomes one to which this Act applies.

(5) If the owner fails to comply with this section, the occupier may apply to the court for an order requiring the owner to comply.

(6) Regulations under this section—

(a) shall be made by statutory instrument; and

(b) may make different provisions which respect to different cases or descriptions of case, including different provisions for different areas.

Terms of agreements

A-55 2.—(1) In any agreement to which this Act applies there shall be implied the terms set out in Part I of Schedule 1 to this Act; and this subsection shall have effect notwithstanding any express term of the agreement.

(2) The court may, on the application of either party made within six months of the giving of the statement under subsection 1(2) above, order that there shall be implied in the agreement terms containing the matters mentioned in part II of Schedule 1 to this Act.

(3) The court may, on the application of either party made within the said period of six months, by order vary or delete any express term of the agreement.

(4) On an application under this section, the court shall make such provision as the court considers just and equitable in the circumstances.

Successors in title

A-56 3.—(1) An agreement to which this Act applies shall be binding on and endure for the benefit of any successor in title of the owner and any person claiming through or under the owner or any such successor.

(2) Where an agreement to which this Act applies is lawfully assigned to any person, the agreement shall enure for the benefit of and be binding on that person.

(3) Where a person entitled to the benefit of and bound by an agreement to which this Act applies dies at a time when he is occupying the mobile as his only or main residence, the agreement shall enure for the benefit of and be binding on—

(a) any person residing with that person ("the deceased") at that time being—

(i) the widow or widower of the deceased; or

(ii) in default of a widow or widower so residing, any member of the deceased's family; or

(b) in default of any such person so residing, the person entitled to the deceased's mobile home by virtue of the deceased's will or under the law relating to intestacy by subject to subsection (4) below.

(4) An agreement to which this Act applies shall not enure for the benefit of or be binding on a person by virtue of subsection (3)*(b)* above in so far as—

(a) it would, but for this subsection, enable or require that person to occupy the mobile home; or

(b) it includes terms implied by virtue of paragraph 5 or 9 of Part I of Schedule 1 to this Act.

Jurisdiction of the court

A-57 4. The court shall have jurisdiction to determine any question arising under this Act or any agreement to which it applies, and to entertain any proceedings brought under this Act or any such agreement.

Interpretation

A-58 5.—(1) In this Act, unless the context otherwise requires—

"the court" means—

(a) in relation to England and Wales, the county court for the district in which the protected site is situated or, where the parties have agreed in writing to

submit any question arising under this Act or, as the case may be, any agreement to which it applies to arbitration, the arbitrator; or

...

"local authority" has the same meaning as in part I of the Caravan Sites and Control of Development Act 1960;

"mobile home" has the same meaning as "caravan" has in that part in that Act;

"owner", in relation to a protected site, means the person who, by virtue of an estate or interest held by him, is entitled to possession of the site or would be so entitled but for the rights of any persons to station mobile homes on land forming part of the flight;

"planning permission" means permission under Part III of the Town and Country Planning Act 1990 or

...

"protected site" does not include any land occupied by a local authority as a caravan site providing accommodation for gipsies or, in Scotland, for persons to whom section 24(8A) of the Caravan Sites and Control of Development Act 1960 applies but, subject to that, has the same meaning as in Part I of the Caravan Sites Act 1960.

(2) In relation to an agreement to which this Act applies—

(*a*) any reference in this Act to the owner includes a reference to any person who is bound by and entitled to the benefit of the agreement by virtue of subsection (1) of section 3 above; and

(*b*) subject to subsection (4) of that section, any reference in this Act to the occupier includes a reference to any person who is entitled to the benefit of and bound by the agreement by virtue of subsection (2) or (3) of that section.

(3) A person is a member of another's family within the meaning of this Act if he is his spouse, parent, grandparent, child, grandchild, brother, sister, uncle, aunt, nephew or niece; treating—

(*a*) any relation ship by marriage as a relationship by blood, any relationship of the half blood as a relationship of the whole blood and the stepchild of any person as his child; and

(*b*) an illegitimate person as the legitimate child of his mother and reputed father;

or if they live together as husband and wife.

Short title, repeals, commencement and extent

6.—(1) This Act may be cited as the Mobile Homes Act 1983. A-59

(2) The enactments mentioned in Schedule 2 to this Act are hereby repealed to the extent specified in the third column of that Schedule.

(3) This Act shall come into force on the expiry of the period of one week beginning with the day on which it is passed.

(4) This Act does not extend to Northern Ireland.

...

SCHEDULE 1

AGREEMENTS UNDER THE ACT

(Section 2)

PART I

TERMS IMPLIED BY THE ACT

Duration of agreement

A-60 1. Subject to paragraph 2 below, the right to station the mobile home on land forming part of the protected site shall subsist until the agreement is determined under paragraph 3, 4, 5 or 6 below.

A-61 2.—(1) If the owner's estate or interest is insufficient to enable him to grant the right for an indefinite period, the period for which the right extends shall not extend beyond the date when the owner's estate or interest determines.

(2) If planning permission for the use of the protected site as a site for mobile homes has been granted in terms such that it will expire at the end of a specified period, the period for which the right subsist shall not extend beyond the date when the planning permission expires.

(3) If before the end of a period determined by this paragraph there is a change in circumstances which allows a longer period, account shall be taken of that change.

Termination by occupier

A-62 3. The occupier shall be entitled to terminate the agreement by notice in writing given to the owner not less than three weeks before the date on which it is to take effect.

A-63 4. The owner shall be entitled to terminate the agreement forthwith if, on the application of the owner, the court—

(*a*) is satisfied that the occupier has breached a term of the agreement and, after service of a notice to remedy the breach, has not complied with the notice within a reasonable time; and

(*b*) considers it reasonable for the agreement to be terminated.

A-64 5. The owner shall be entitled to terminate the agreement forthwith if, on the application of the owner, the court is satisfied that the occupier is not occupying the mobile home as his only or main residence.

A-65 6.—(1) The owner shall be entitled to terminate the agreement at the end of a relevant period if, on the application of the owner, the court is satisfied that, having regard to its age and condition, the mobile home—

(*a*) is having a detrimental effect on the amenity of the site; or

(*b*) is likely to have such an effect before the end of the next relevant period.

(2) In sub-paragraph (1) above) "relevant period" means the period of five years beginning with the commencement of the agreement and each succeeding period of five years.

Recovery of overpayments by occupier

A-66 7. Where the agreement is terminated as mentioned in paragraph 3, 4, 5 or 6 above, the occupier shall be entitled to recover from the owner so much of any payment made by him in pursuance of the agreement as is attributable to a period beginning after the termination.

Sale of mobile home

8.—(1) The occupier shall be entitled to sell the mobile home, and to assign the agreement, to a person approved by the owner, whose approval shall not be unreasonably withheld. A-67

(2) Where the occupier sells the mobile home, and assigns the agreement, as mentioned in sub-paragraph (7) above, the owner shall be entitled to receive a commission on the sale at a rate not exceeding such rate as may be specified in an order made by the Secretary of State.

(3) An order under this paragraph—

(*a*) shall be made by statutory instrument which shall be subject to annulment in pursuance of a resolution of either House of Parliament; and

(*b*) may make different provision for different areas nor for sales at different prices.

Gift of mobile home

9. The occupier shall be entitled to give the mobile home, and to assign the agreement, to a member of his family approved by the owner, whose approval shall not be unreasonably withheld. A-68

Re-siting of mobile home

10. If the owner is entitled to require that the occupier's right to station the mobile home shall be exercisable for any period in relation to other land forming part of the protected site— A-69

(*a*) that other land shall be broadly comparable to the land on which the occupier was originally entitled to station the mobile home; and

(*b*) all costs and expenses incurred in consequence of the requirement shall be paid by the owner.

PART II

MATTERS CONCERNING WHICH TERMS MAY BE IMPLIED BY COURT

1. The right of the occupier to quiet enjoyment or, in Scotland, undisturbed possession of the mobile home. A-70

2. The sums payable by the occupier in pursuance of the agreement and the times at which they are to be paid.

3. The review at yearly intervals of the sums so payable.

4. The provision or improvement of services available on the protected site, and the use by the occupier of such services.

5. The preservation of the amenity of the protected site.

6. The maintenance and repair of the protected site by the owner, and the maintenance and repair of the mobile home by the occupier.

7. Access by the owner to the land on which the occupier is entitled to station the mobile home.

...

Mobile Homes (Commissions) Order 1983, SI 1983/748

1. This order may be cited as the Mobile Homes (Commissions) Order 1983 and shall come into operation on 20th May 1983. A-71

A-72 2. The maximum rate of commission to which an owner shall be entitled, under the provisions of paragraph 8 of Part I of Schedule 1 to the Mobile Homes Act 1983, on the sale by an occupier of a mobile home shall be 10 per cent.

Mobile Homes (Written Statement) Regulations 1983, SI 1983/749

A-73 1. These regulations may be cited as the Mobile Homes (Written Statement) Regulations 1983 and shall come into operation on 20th May 1983.

A-74 2. The requirements with which a written statement has to comply for the purposes of section 1(2)(e) of the Mobile Homes Act 1983 are that it shall be in the form prescribed in the Schedule to these regulations or a form substantially to the like effect.

SCHEDULE

WRITTEN STATEMENT UNDER MOBILE HOMES ACT 1983

A-75 IMPORTANT—PLEASE READ THIS STATEMENT CAREFULLY AND KEEP IT IN A SAFE PLACE. IT SETS OUT THE TERMS ON WHICH YOU ARE ENTITLED TO KEEP YOUR MOBILE HOME ON SITE AND TELLS YOU ABOUT THE RIGHTS GIVEN YOU BY LAW. IF THERE IS ANYTHING YOU DO NOT UNDERSTAND YOU SHOULD GET ADVICE (FOR EXAMPLE FROM A SOLICITOR OR A CITIZENS ADVICE BUREAU).

PART I

A-76 1. You have an agreement to which the Mobile Homes Act 1983 applies.

2. The parties to the agreement are—
....(name and address of mobile home occupier)
....(name and address of site owner)

3. The agreement commenced on ....(fill in date).

4. The particulars of the land on which you are entitled to station your mobile home are
....
....

((5. The site owner's estate or interest in the land will end on.......................(fill in date); or
The site owner's planning permission for the site will end on......................(fill in date)
This means that your right to stay on the site will not continue after that date unless the site owner's interest or planning permission is extended.)) (Cross out words in double brackets if they do not apply).

PART II

INFORMATION

1. Because you have an agreement with a site owner which entitles you to keep your mobile home on his site and live in it as your home, the Mobile Homes Act 1983 gives you certain rights, affecting in particular your security of tenure and the sale of your mobile home. A-77

2. These rights, which are contained in the implied terms set out in Part III of this statement, apply automatically and cannot be overridden, so long as your agreement continues to be one to which this Act applies. A-78

3. A full explanation of your rights can be found in the booklet "Mobile Homes" produced jointly by the Department of the Environment, the Welsh Office and the Scottish Development Department. From 1st August 1983 the booklet is available free from Council offices and housing aid centres and you are advised to read it. A-79

4. If you are not sure what any of the terms of your agreement mean or how they will work in future, you should get advice at once from a solicitor or citizens advice bureau. A-80

5. If you are not happy with any of the express terms of your agreement (as set out in Part IV of this statement) you should discuss them with the site owner, who may agree to change them. But if you are still not satisfied you can challenge the agreement in two ways, as explained in paragraphs 6 to 9 below, provided you do so within 6 months of the time you are given this statement. A-81

6. A challenge can be made either in the county court (in Scotland, the sheriff court) or before an arbitrator (in Scotland, an arbiter). You can:— A-82

(a) ask for any of the express terms of the agreement (those set out in Part IV of this statement) to be changed or deleted;

(b) ask for further terms to be included in the agreement concerning the matters set out in Part II of Schedule 1 to the Act (see paragraph 9 below).

The site owner can also go to court or to an arbitrator to ask for the agreement to be changed in these two ways.

7. The appointment of an arbitrator may be provided for in one of the express terms of the agreement. If not, you and the site owner can still agree in writing to appoint an arbitrator to settle a dispute between you. A-83

8. The court or the arbitrator must make an order on terms they consider just and equitable in the circumstances. If you wish to challenge your agreement, you should get advice from a solicitor or citizens advice bureau. A-84

9. The matters set out in Part II of Schedule 1 to the Act are as follows:— A-85

(a) the right of the occupier to quiet enjoyment, or in Scotland, undisturbed possession of the mobile home;

(b) the sums payable by the occupier in pursuance of the agreement and the times at which they are to be paid;

(c) the review at yearly intervals of the sums so payable;

(d) the provision or improvement of services available on the protected site, and the use by the occupier of such services;

(e) the preservation of the amenity of the protected site;

(f) the maintenance and repair of the protected site by the owner, and the maintenance and repair of the mobile home by the occupier;

(g) access by the owner to the land on which the occupier is entitled to station the mobile home.

A-86 10. If no application to court or an arbitrator is made within the six months time limit, both you and the site owner will be bound by the terms of the agreement and will not be able to change them unless both parties agree.

PART III
IMPLIED TERMS

Under the Act, certain terms must be contained in your agreement. This part of the statement sets out those terms

Duration of agreement

A-87 1. Subject to paragraph 2 below, the right to station the mobile home on land forming part of the protected site shall subsist until the agreement is determined under paragraph 3, 4, 5 or 6 below.

A-88 2.—(1) If the owner's estate or interest is insufficient to enable him to grant the right for an indefinite period, the period for which the right subsists shall not extend beyond the date when the owner's estate or interest determines.

(2) If planning permission for the use of the protected site as a site for mobile homes has been granted in terms such that it will expire at the end of a specified period, the period for which the right subsists shall not extend beyond the date when planning permission expires.

(3) If before the end of a period determined by this paragraph there is a change in circumstances which allows a longer period, account shall be taken of that change.

Termination by occupier

A-89 3. The occupier shall be entitled to terminate the agreement by notice in writing given to the owner not less than four weeks before the date on which it is to take effect.

Termination by owner

A-90 4. The owner shall be entitled to terminate the agreement forthwith, if, on the application of the owner, the court—

(a) is satisfied that the occupier has breached a term of the agreement and, after service of a notice to remedy the breach, has not complied with the notice within a reasonable time; and

(b) considers it reasonable for the agreement to be terminated.

5. The owner shall be entitled to terminate the agreement forthwith if, on the application of the owner, the court is satisfied that the occupier is not occupying the mobile home as his only or main residence. A-91

6.—(1) The owner shall be entitled to terminate the agreement at the end of a relevant period if, on the application of the owner, the court is satisfied that, having regard to its age and condition, the mobile home— A-92

(a) is having a detrimental effect on the amenity of the site; or

(b) is likely to have such an effect before the end of the next relevant period.

(2) In sub-paragraph (1) above, the "relevant period" means the period of five years beginning with the commencement of the agreement and each succeeding period of five years.

Recovery of overpayments by occupier

7. Where the agreement is terminated as mentioned in paragraph 3, 4, 5 or 6 above, the occupier shall be entitled to recover from the owner so much of any payment made by him in pursuance of the agreement as is attributable to a period beginning after its termination. A-93

Sale of mobile home

8.—(1) The occupier shall be entitled to sell the mobile home and to assign the agreement to a person approved by the owner, whose approval shall not be unreasonably withheld. A-94

(2) Where the occupier sells the mobile home, and assigns the agreement, as mentioned in sub-paragraph (1) above, the owner shall be entitled to receive a commission on the sale at a rate not exceeding such rate as may be specified by an order made by the Secretary of State.

The maximum rate is presently fixed at 10% by the Mobile Homes (Commissions) Order 1983 (SI 1983/748).

Gift of mobile home

9. The occupier shall be entitled to give the mobile home, and to assign the agreement, to a member of his family approved by the owner, whose approval shall not be unreasonably withheld. A-95

Re-siting of mobile home

10. If the owner is entitled to require that the occupier's right to station the mobile home shall be exercisable for any period in relation to other land forming part of the protected site— A-96

(a) that other land shall be broadly comparable to the land on which the occupier was originally entitled to station the mobile home; and

(b) all costs and expenses incurred in consequence of the requirement shall be paid by the owner.

Part IV

Express Terms of the Agreement

A-97 *This part of the statement sets out the terms of the agreement settled between you and the site owner in addition to the implied terms.*

Terms to be filled in by site owner.

PPG3: Housing

[Extract]

Residential mobile homes

A-98 29. Residential mobile homes (park homes) may have a part to play in providing low cost accommodation for small households. Where there is a demand for such homes in an area, the local authority should take account of that in its forward planning for new housing.

A-99 30. Proposals for residential mobile homes will, like all planning applications, need to be considered on their own planning merits, taking into account their visual and other effects on the surrounding area. Where authorities consider that there is no fundamental planning objection to park homes, the use of planning conditions, together with the site licence system, backed up by the Department's model standards, can in appropriate cases provide an effective way of minimising the impact of a site on its surroundings and controlling conditions on the site itself.

A-100 31. Planning authorities should also bear in mind the special needs of houseboat dwellers.

PPG7: The Countryside: Environmental Quality and Economic and Social Development

[Extract]

ANNEX I

AGRICULTURAL AND FORESTRY DWELLING

. . .

Permanent agricultural dwellings

A-101 I5 New permanent dwellings should only be allowed to support existing agricultural activities on well-established agricultural units, providing:

(a) there is a clearly-established *existing* functional need (see paragraph I6);

(b) the need relates to a *full-time* worker, or one who is primarily employed in agriculture, and does not relate to a part-time requirement;

(c) the unit and the agricultural activity concerned have been established for at least three years, have been profitable for at least one of them, and are currently financially sound, and have a clear prospect of remaining so (see paragraph I10);

(d) the functional need could not be fulfilled by another dwelling on the unit, or any other existing accommodation in the area which is suitable and available for accommodation by the workers concerned; and

(e) other normal planning requirements, for example on siting and access, are satisfied.

I6. A *functional* test is necessary to establish whether it is essential for the proper func- A-102
tioning of the enterprise for one or more workers to be readily available at most times. Such a requirement might arise, for example, if workers are needed to be on hand day and night:

- in case animals or agricultural processes require essential care at short notice;
- to deal quickly with emergencies that could otherwise cause serious loss of crops or products, for example, by frost damage or the failure of automatic systems.

I7. In cases where the local planning authority is particularly concerned about possible A-103
abuse, it may be helpful to investigate the history of the holding, to establish the recent pattern of use of land and buildings and whether, for example, any dwellings or buildings suitable for conversion to dwellings have recently been sold separately from the farmland concerned. Such a sale could constitute evidence of lack of agricultural need.

I8. The protection of livestock from theft or injury by intruders may contribute on ani- A-104
mal welfare grounds to the need for an agricultural dwelling, although it will not by itself be sufficient to justify one. Requirements arising from food processing, as opposed to agriculture, cannot be used to justify an agricultural dwelling. Nor can agricultural needs justify the provision of new retirement homes for farmers.

I9. If a functional requirement is established, it will then be necessary to consider the A-105
number of workers needed to meet it, for which the scale and nature of the enterprise will be relevant.

I10. New permanent accommodation cannot be justified on agricultural grounds unless A-106
the farming enterprise is economically viable. A *financial* test is necessary for this purpose, and to provide evidence of the size of dwelling which the unit can sustain.

...

PPG12: Development Plans and Regional Planning Guidance

[Extract]

5.50 Local planning authorities should show in both structure and detailed development A-107
plans what regard they have had to their statutory duty under the Caravan Sites Act 1968

to provide adequate accommodation for gypsies residing in or resorting to their areas. Fuller advice is given in paragraph 7 of Annex D.

...

PPG21: Tourism

[Extract]

ANNEX B

HOLIDAY AND TOURING CARAVANS

A-108 1. This Annex is concerned only with the use of land for holiday and touring caravan sites; and not with residential or gypsy caravan sites, or with "new age travellers". However, similar considerations may also apply to holiday chalet developments.

A-109 2. Significant numbers of people spend their holidays touring with caravans or staying on "static" holiday caravan sites. Self-catering accommodation, 40% of which is accounted for by caravans, accounts for almost two-thirds of all commercial tourist bednights in England. In Britain as a whole, 13 million take holidays in caravans.

A-110 3. In drawing up development pans, local authorities should investigate whether there are adequate facilities for both the touring caravanner to have reasonable freedom to wander and explore and for the static holiday caravanner to have reasonable choice of sites. This objective needs to reconciled with the protection and preservation of those environments which attract holidaymakers in the first place; holiday caravan sites can be particular intrusive in the open landscape, in particular on the coast. Special consideration needs to be given to proposals for new sites, especially in designated areas (see paragraphs 5.12–5.16). But authorities should be in no doubt that holiday and touring caravan parks will remain an important part of the self-catering holiday sector, and can contribute as much to the local tourism economy as would conventional holiday accommodation, while using less land for the purpose.

A-111 4. *Caravan sites* require both a planning permission and a site licence, unless one of the small number of specific exemptions in Schedule 1 to the Caravan Sites and Control of Development Act 1960 applies. On the other hand, *tent camping* enjoys permitted development rights under the General Development Order for up to 28 days, and no site licence under the Public Health Act 1936 is needed for occupation for periods of less than 42 days, or for fewer than 60 in any year. The introduction of a small number of tents on an existing caravan site may not constitute a material change of use requiring planning permission. Whether the change of use is material is a matter of fact and degree. But the licensing requirement would apply after the 42-day period, or for more than 60 days in the year.

A-112 5. The traditional divisions between touring and motorised caravans and tents are becoming more blurred with the availability of more flexible accommodation, e.g. trailer tents. Local authorities may find themselves considering planning applications which combine the different types of touring accommodation in terms of "touring units". When submitting such applications, developers and site owners should be encouraged to be specific about the overall numbers. In considering applications in terms of "touring units", authorities should take into account the land-use implications of the different types of unit, in particular in relation to the use of local roads and to access. But it should often be possible to grant a permission which allows flexibility between the numbers of tents and touring units within an overall limit on the number of pitches. In such situations, two licences will continue to be required and will need to contain interdependent conditions to the same effect.

6. The General Development Order and the exemptions from licensing in the 1960 Act allow a measure of freedom for the touring caravanner. The facility for the larger caravanning organisations to certificate sites for use by up to 5 members' holiday caravans is a useful means of providing small sites in sensitive rural areas where larger sites would be unduly intrusive, and should help to contribute to the local economy in those areas. The use of these sites by other than the members of these organisations would be a breach of the terms of the general planning permission. In particularly sensitive areas, a local authority should bear in mind its power to make Article 4 directions to withdraw permitted development rights. In such cases a specific planning application will be required. A-113

7. The demand for sites has concentrated traditionally on the most popular holiday areas, particularly on the coast, although there is increasing demand inland. New sites should be sited so as to be effectively screened, and planned so as not to be visually intrusive. Sites should not as a rule be allowed immediately by the sea, but should be set back a short distance inland where they are not visible from or along the coast. Advice about developments in areas at risk of flooding is contained in DOE Circular 17/82 (WO 15/82)—shortly to be updated. Local planning authorities should take full account of the advice contained in PPG2 on Green Belts, PPG7 on the Countryside and the Rural Economy, PPG20 on Coastal Planning and the forthcoming PPG on Nature Conservation when considering planning applications for holiday caravan sites affecting designated areas such as National Parks, Areas of Outstanding Natural Beauty, the Heritage Coasts, Green Belts and Sites of Special Scientific Interest.

8. Through their local plans, planning authorities should examine the scope for encouraging holiday caravan site operators to improve the quality of their sites and to relocate sites away from particularly sensitive areas, such as the Heritage Coast (see paragraph 3.9). In some cases, to facilitate improvement or relocation, local planning authorities may need to consider whether some expansion of the area covered by a site should be allowed, so that improved layouts and better landscaping can be implemented. Local authorities may also need to consider the possibility of dividing large sites into smaller units to reduce the overall environmental impact. In these circumstances, to ensure the overall scale of the operation is not increased, local planning authorities should consider the use of planning conditions to limit the number of pitches on the site (see DOE Circular 1/8 (WO1/85)). A-114

9. Local planning authorities may attach conditions to planning permissions for holiday caravan sites. However with better caravan standards and the trend towards tourism as a year-round activity, authorities should give sympathetic consideration to applications to extend the opening period allowed under existing permissions. (See Annex C on Seasonal and Holiday Occupancy Conditions.) A-115

10. Guidance to local planning authorities about model standards which should be applied to the design and layout of sites and the facilities and amenities they should contain is given in DOE Circular 23/83 (WO 32/83) for touring caravans and in 14/89 (WO 23/89) for static holiday caravans. Access to sites should be carefully planned and should be designed to allow safe movement for cars and caravans to and from the site. Local planning authorities should consider planning applications against these standards for sites accessed from local roads, but where trunk roads are involved the Department of Transport or the Welsh Office should be advised of the proposals and will consider them against their Circular 4/88 (WO 42/88). A-116

...

Circular 23/83: Caravan Sites and Control of Development Act 1960[1]

A-117 1. We are directed by the Secretary of State for the Environment and the Secretary of State for Wales to refer to the Revised Model Standards for licensed caravan sites in England and Wales specified under the Caravan Sites and Control of Development Act 1960 which were brought to the attention of local authorities in DOE Circular 119/77 (Welsh Office Circular 42/77). We also refer to the use of site-licence control as an alternative to the procedures under the [Town and Country Planning Act 1990] when caravans are stationed on an unauthorised site; and to the provision of winter quarters for members of the Showmen's Guild of Great Britain who, although exempt from site licensing requirements, are still required to obtain planning permission for the sites they occupy.

Model standards

A-118 2. Although the current standards may have been taken to apply to sites used for touring caravans, that was not the intention, and the opportunity has now been taken to clarify the situation by the formulation of model standards for touring caravan sites. The 1977 Revised Model Standards will have effect hereafter as applying only to permanent residential sites, to static holiday caravan sites and to sites where there are both static and touring caravans but where the predominant use is for static holiday caravans.

A-119 3. In considering licences for sites which serve touring caravans, local authorities should have regard to the new Model Standards which have been published as an Annex to this Circular. These represent the standards normally to be expected, as a matter of good practice, on sites used wholly or predominantly by touring caravans which are not permanently placed on the site throughout the year or the holiday season.

A-120 4. Particular attention is drawn, however, to the possibility that lower standards in respect of communal toilet and washing facilities may be appropriate in some circumstances.

Effect on existing caravan sites

A-121 5. In the light of this Circular, local authorities should consider the alteration of conditions attached to site licences, after consultation with the holder of the licence, under the provisions of section 8(1) of the 1960 Act. The fire authority should also be consulted before any conditions appertaining to their interests are altered.

Emergency services

A-122 6. Local authorities are reminded that, when emergency services are called to a caravan site, valuable time can be saved if the site is readily identifiable. They may wish to ensure, by attaching a condition to that effect to the site licence, that a sign indicating the name of the site is displayed at the site entrance. Provided it comes within the specified size-limits, a sign of this type will usually benefit from the "deemed consent" provided by Class II in

---

1. Welsh Office Circular 32/83.

regulation 14 of the [Town and Country Planning (Control of Advertisements) Regulations 1992]

Site licence control as an alternative to enforcement procedures

7. Attention is drawn to the fact that the use of land as a caravan site (whether for residential or static holiday caravans, for touring caravans, or for gypsy caravans) is subject to a system of dual control. Consequently, a caravan site which is not authorised by a specific grant of planning permission for that use is likely to be in breach both of planning control, under the [Town and Country Planning Act 1990] and of site-licence control under the 1960 Act, so that the enforcement powers in both enactments would be available to the local authority in order to remedy the unlawful use of land. In such cases, local authorities should consider which method of enforcement is likely to be the more effective and appropriate, bearing in mind that enforcement of planning control under the [1990 Act] is likely to result in delay if the statutory right of appeal to the Secretary of State against an enforcement notice is exercised. A-123

...

ANNEX

CARAVAN SITES AND CONTROL OF DEVELOPMENT ACT 1960

SECTION 5—MODEL STANDARDS FOR TOURING CARAVAN SITES

I. Section 5(6) of the Act provides that the Secretary of State may from time to time specify Model Standards with respect to the lay-out of, and the provision of facilities, services and equipment for, caravan sites or particular types of caravan site; and that in deciding what (if any) conditions to attach to a site licence the local authority shall have regard to any standards so specified. Under section 5(1)(c) such conditions may regulate the positions in which caravans are stationed for the purposes of human habitation, and the placing or erection at any time when caravans are so stationed, of structures and vehicles of any description whatsoever and of tents. A-124

II. Section 7(1) of the Act provides that on an appeal against any condition of a site licence a magistrates' court, if satisfied (having regard amongst other things to any standards specified by the Secretary of State under section 5(6)) that a condition is unduly burdensome, may vary or cancel the condition. A-125

III. Section 24, which empowers local authorities to provide caravan sites, provides, in subsection (2), that in exercising their powers under the section the local authority shall have regard to any standards that may have been specified by the Secretary of State under section 5(6) of the Act. A-126

IV. Section 8(2) of the Local Government (Miscellaneous Provisions) Act, 1982 inserted provisions into sections 5, 8 and 24 of the Caravan Sites and Control of Development Act 1960 requiring local authorities to consult fire authorities when exercising their powers under that Act in relation to the issuing of site licences for caravan sites and the provision of local authority caravan sites. The local authority is now required to consult the fire authority as to the extent to which any model standards relating to fire precautions are appropriate in relation to the site. If the fire authority considers that the standards specified are inappropriate in relation to the site, the local authority is required to consult them as to what conditions relating to fire precautions ought to be attached to the site licence. The local authority is also required to consult the fire authority before altering any condition in a site licence that relates to fire precautions or before themselves providing a caravan site. A-127

A-128 V. In pursuance of his powers under section 5(6) of the Act, the Secretary of State now specifies Model Standards for sites for touring caravans. Although these represent the standards normally to be expected, as a matter of good practice, the Secretary of State does not wish them to be applied to all sites, regardless of the economic and other implications for the site operators, people using the site and public amenity. They should be applied with due regard to the particular circumstances of each case, including the physical character of the site, any services or facilities that may already be available within convenient reach, and other local conditions including the kind of holidays which the site is designed to offer. Where usage is restricted to caravans equipped with their own toilet and washing facilities, communal toilet and washing facilities may not be necessary and lower standards than specified may be desirable in some locations for the avoidance of visually intrusive structures or installations.

A-129 VI. These Model Standards are for sites used by touring caravans, by which is meant caravans which are not permanently placed on the site throughout the year or the holiday season. Where a site is used both for touring caravans and for static caravans, the local authority should judge whether to refer to the Revised 1977 Model Standards or to the following Standards according to the predominant use of the site. For example, where static caravans predominate, application of the Revised Model Standards of 1977 will be appropriate. Account should, however, be taken of the fact that significant changes in the nature of the use might warrant the alteration of site licence conditions.

CARAVAN SITES AND CONTROL OF DEVELOPMENT ACT 1960 SECTION 5
MODEL STANDARDS FOR TOURING CARAVAN SITES

Density

A-130 1. Site density should not exceed 75 units (caravans or motor caravans) per hectare (30 units per acre) calculated on the basis of the usable area rather than the total site area (i.e. excluding crags, lakes, roads, communal services etc.), provided that, where tent camping is also permitted, the maximum number of units stationed on the site at any one time should be reduced by the number of pitches occupied by main tents stationed for human habitation.

A-131 2. Where the number of units on the site is to be limited by condition, it may be appropriate to prescribe maxima by references to specified periods so as to permit up to 10 more units during such peak holiday periods as may be agreed between the site licensing authority and the licence holder without the provision of additional facilities, provided that:

(i) the provisions of paragraph 1 above are complied with; and

(ii) the standards relating to spacing, as set out in paragraphs 3–5 below, are complied with.

Spacing

A-132 3. Every unit should be not less than 6 metres from any other unit in separate family occupation and not less than 3 metres should be permitted between units in any circumstances.

A-133 4. Vehicles and other ancillary equipment should be permitted within the 6 metres space between units in separate family occupation but, in order to restrict the spread of fire, there should always be 3 metres clear space within the 6 metres separation.

5. Emergency vehicles should be able to secure access at all times to within 90 metres of any unit on the site.

Drinking water supply and waste water disposal

6. There should be an adequate supply of drinking water. Each pitch on a site should be no further than 90 metres from a water tap. At each tap there should be a soakaway or gulley. A-134

7. Waste water disposal points should be provided so that each pitch is no further than 90 metres from a waste water disposal point. The appropriate Water Authority should be consulted about the arrangements for disposal of water likely to be contaminated. A-135

Toilets: WCs and chemical closets

8. The scale of provision should be 1 WC and 1 urinal for men and 2 WCs for women per 30 pitches and their location should be to the satisfaction of the licensing authority. The pro rata scale can be reduced where sites have over 120 pitches (see also paragraph 9 below). Toilets may not be justified where sites have less than 10 pitches but on sites with between 10 and 30 pitches at least one WC and 1 urinal for men and 2 WCs for women should be provided. A-136

9. Where the provision of WCs is not feasible or justified entry should be confined to units with their own toilets or chemical closets should be provided. A-137

Disposal point for chemical closets

10. Whether or not WCs are provided, a properly designed disposal point for the contents of chemical closets should be provided together with an adjacent adequate supply of water for cleansing containers. The method of disposal will need to be considered in the light of the particular circumstances and should be to the satisfaction of the local authority and the appropriate Water Authority. Where appropriate, the water supply should be clearly labelled as non-potable. A-138

Washing points

11. There should be a minimum of 4 wash basins supplied with water per 30 units; 2 each for men and women. They should be adjacent to the toilets. A-139

Hot water: showers

12. Showers should not be obligatory on sites with less than 70 pitches. If showers are required, provision should be on the basis of 1 shower per 25 pitches and hot water should be available. A-140

Disabled persons

13. Particular consideration should be given to the needs of the disabled in the provision made for water points, toilets, washing points and showers. A-141

Electrical installations

14. Where there is an electrical installation other than Electricity Board works and circuits subject to Regulations under Section 60 of the Electricity Act 1947, it should be installed to the requirements of the Institution of Electrical Engineers' Regulations for Electrical Installations (the IEE Wiring Regulations) for the time being in force and, where appropriate, to the standard acceptable for the Electricity (Overhead Lines) Regulations A-142

1970, SI 1970 No. 1355. Any installation should be maintained in such a way as to prevent danger as far as reasonably practicable and should be periodically inspected and tested by a competent person in accordance with the IEE Wiring Regulations.

Refuse disposal

A-143 15. Adequate provision should be made for the storage, collection and disposal of refuse. (It is expected that site operators should normally be able to meet their responsibilities by making arrangements with the local authority.)

Fire precautions

A-144 16. No unit should be further than 90 metres from a fire point. At each point there should be two water (gas expelled) extinguishers each of 10 litres capacity and complying with British Standard 5423:1980, together with a means of raising the alarm in the event of fire (e.g. a manually operated sounder, gong or hand operated siren). All fire fighting equipment susceptible to damage by frost should be suitably protected.

A-145 17. Wherever there is a likelihood of fire spreading due to vegetation catching fire, suitable beaters, of the type used by the Forestry Commission, should also be provided at each fire point.

A-146 18. The fire points should be clearly marked and easily accessible. All firefighting equipment should be maintained in working order and kept available for use and for inspection by the licensing authority.

A-147 19. Each fire point should exhibit a conspicuous notice indicating the action to be taken in case of fire and the location of the nearest telephone. The notice should include the following:

On discovering fire

1. Raise the alarm
2. Ensure the affected unit is evacuated
3. Call the Fire Brigade (the nearest telephone is sited ... ...)
4. If practicable, attack the fire using the firefighting equipment provided.

Liquefied petroleum gas

A-148 20: Arrangements for the storage of Liquefied Petroleum Gas (LPG) on the site should be in accordance with the current national Code of Practice and regulations.

A-149 *Site notices*

21. A sign indicating the name of the site should be displayed at the site entrance.

A-150 22. Notices should be displayed prominently on the site indicating the action to be taken in the event of an emergency and show where the police, fire brigade, ambulance, and local doctors can be contacted, and the location of the nearest public telephone. Where practicable a telephone should be provided on the site and the full address of the site should be displayed near the telephone.

A-151 23. At sites subject to flood risk, warning notices should be displayed giving advice about the operation of the flood warning system.

A-152 24. At sites with overhead electric lines, warning notices should be displayed on the supports for the lines and at the site entrance. Where appropriate, these should warn against the danger of contact between the lines and the masts of yachts or dinghies.

A-153 25. A copy of the site licence with its conditions should be displayed prominently on the site.

Circular 14/89: Caravan Sites and Control of Development Act 1960—Model Standards[1] A-154

1. This Circular is being issued to draw your attention to the revised versions of the Model Standards for licensed caravan sites in England and Wales specified under the Caravan Sites and Control of Development Act 1960.

Amendment to the Model Standards

2. The Secretary of State for the Environment, in agreement with the Secretary of State for Wales, has now specified revised Model Standards. He has decided to make separate Model Standards for mobile homes on permanent residential sites, and for static holiday caravan sites. Copies of the two versions are attached. Where sites are mixed, the standards for residential sites apply. The other standards will need to be applied taking into account the features of individual sites. Local authorities should have regard to these amended Model Standards in deciding what, if any, conditions to attach to a caravan site licence. A-155

3. The most significant change in the Model Standards is the reduction of the spacing standard to prevent fire spread from 6m to 5m in the holiday caravan standard. The new standard applies only to caravans with aluminium exteriors. The Standards also cover permitted intrusions into the space between units. The revisions are based on research sponsored by the Department of the Environment, the Home Office and the National Caravan Council. The report of this research, entitled "Fire Spread Between Park Homes and Caravans" was published in 1989 by HMSO and a copy has already been sent to every local authority and fire authority. A-156

4. Other changes include more detailed specifications on electrical installations and fire safety measures, including the storage of Liquefied Petroleum Gas. There is no longer a requirement for central washing facilities on residential sites. Local authorities may also wish to be aware that the British Standards Institution is publishing a Guide on the Siting of Holiday Caravans and Park Homes (British Standard 6768) which should be available in the summer of 1990. A-157

Implementation of the amended Model Standards

5. Local authorities are reminded that the Model Standards represent the standards normally to be expected as a matter of good practice on sites for residential mobile homes or static caravan sites, or both. They are not intended to apply to other types of caravan site. They should be applied with due regard to the particular circumstances of each case including the physical character of the site, any services or facilities that may already be available within convenient reach, and any other local conditions. A-158

6. Local authorities should review the conditions attached to existing site licences to determine which, if any, of the amended Model Standards should apply. Consideration should be given to a carefully phased introduction of any new standards, after consultation with the site owners, the caravan occupiers and the fire authority as appropriate. A-159

---

1. Welsh Office Circular 23/89. The Model Standards have ISBN numbers: 011 7522171 for permanent residential sites and 011 752218X for holiday sites.

Consultation with fire authorities

A-160 7. Where the licensing authority is not also the fire authority, the latter should be consulted both on the site licence conditions and arrangements for inspection.

Site fragmentation

A-161 8. If a site owner sells the freehold of one or more plots on a site but retains the freehold of the others, this could lead to difficulties in ensuring adequate provision and maintenance of communal facilities such as fire fighting equipment. In such cases, the local authority may need to review the licence conditions.

CARAVAN SITES AND CONTROL OF DEVELOPMENT ACT 1960, SECTION 5
MODEL STANDARDS 1989: PERMANENT RESIDENTIAL MOBILE HOME SITES

A-162 I. Section 5(6) of the Act provides that the Secretary of State may from time to time specify Model Standards with respect to the lay-out and the provisions of facilities, services and equipment for caravan sites or particular types of caravan site; and that, in deciding what (if any) conditions to attach to a site licence, the local authority shall have regard to any standards so specified.

A-163 Section 7(1) provides that on appeal against any condition of a site licence a magistrates' court may, if satisfied, having regard amongst other things to any standards specified by the Secretary of State under section 5(6), that a condition is unduly burdensome, may vary or cancel the condition.

A-164 Section 24, which empowers local authorities to provide caravan sites, provides in subsection (2) that in exercising their powers under the section the local authority shall have regard to any standards that may have been specified by the Secretary of State under section 5(6) of the Act.

A-165 II. In pursuance of his powers under section 5(6) of the Act, the Secretary of State hereby specifies the following standards in relation to caravan sites on which some or all of the caravans are used as permanent residences by people other than gipsies or agricultural workers. They are Model Standards: they represent the standards normally to be expected as a matter of good practice on such sites. They are not intended to apply to any other type of caravan site—for example, sites which have only holiday caravans, or touring caravan sites. They should be applied with due regard to the particular circumstances of each case, including the physical character of the site, any services or facilities that may already be available within convenient reach, and other local conditions.

Site boundaries

A-166 1. The boundaries of the site should be clearly marked, for example by fences or hedges. In addition, the site owner should give the local authority a plan of its layout. It is recommended that a 3-metre wide area should be kept clear within the inside of all boundaries.

Density and space between caravans

A-167 2. Subject to the following variations, every caravan should be not less than 6 metres from any other caravan which is occupied separately and not less than 2 metres from a road. The point of measurement for porches, awnings etc. is the exterior cladding of the caravan.

- Porches may protrude 1m into the 6 metres and should be of the open type.

- Where awnings are used, the distance between any part of the awning and an adjacent caravan should not be less than 3 metres. They should not be of the type which incorporate sleeping accommodation and they should not face each other or touch.

- Eaves, drainpipes and bay windows may extend into the 6 metre space provided the total distance between the extremities of two adjacent units is not less than 5.25 metres.

- Where there are ramps for the disabled, verandahs and stairs extending from the unit, there should be 4.5m clear space between them and two such items should not face each other in any space. If they are enclosed, they may need to be considered as part of the unit and, as such, should not intrude into the 6m space.

- A garage, a shed or a covered storage space should be permitted between units only if it is of non-combustible construction (including non-combustible roof) and sufficient space is maintained around each unit so as not to prejudice means of escape in case of fire. Windows in such structures should not face towards the units on either side. Car ports and walkways should in no circumstances be allowed within the 6m space. For cars and boats between units, see standard (27).

3. The density should be consistent with safety standards and health and safety requirements. The gross density should not exceed 50 caravans to the hectare, calculated on the basis of the usable area (i.e. excluding lakes, roads, communal services and other areas unsuitable for the siting of caravans) rather than the total site area. A-168

Roads, gateways and footpaths

4. Roads and footpaths should be designed to provide adequate access for fire appliances. (Detailed guidance on turning circles etc is available from fire authorities.) Roads of suitable material should be provided so that no caravan is more than 50 metres from a road. Where the approach to the caravan is across ground that may become difficult or dangerous to negotiate in wet weather, each standing should be connected to a carriageway by a footpath with a hard surface. Roads should be not less than 3.7 metres wide, or, if they form part of a clearly-marked one-way traffic system, 3 metres wide. Gateways should be a minimum of 3.1 metres wide and have a minimum height clearance of 3.7 metres. Footpaths should not be less than 0.75 metres wide. Roads should have no overhead cable less than 4.5 metres above the ground. Roads and footpaths should be suitably lit. Emergency vehicle routes within the site should be kept clear of obstruction at all times. A-169

Hard standings

5. Every caravan should stand on a concrete hard-standing which should extend over the whole area of the caravan placed upon it, and should project a sufficient distance outwards from its entrance or entrances to enable occupants to enter and leave safely. A-170

Fire fighting appliances

Fire points

6. These should be established so that no caravan or site building is more than 30 metres from a fire point. They should be housed in a weather-proof structure, easily accessible and clearly and conspicuously marked "FIRE POINT". A-171

Fire fighting equipment

7. Where water standpipes are provided and there is a water supply of sufficient pressure and flow to project a jet a water approximately 5 metres from the nozzle, such water A-172

standpipes should be situated at each fire point. There should also be a reel which complies with British Standard 5306 part 1, with a hose not less than 30 metres long, having a means of connection to a water standpipe (preferably a screw thread connection) with a water supply of sufficient pressure and terminating in a small hand control nozzle. Hoses should be housed in a box painted red and marked "HOSE REEL".

A-173 8. Where standpipes are not provided but there is a water supply of sufficient pressure and flow, fire hydrants should be installed within 100 metres of every caravan standing. Hydrants should conform to British Standard 750. Access to hydrants and other water supplies should not be obstructed or obscured.

A-174 9. Where standpipes are not provided or the water pressure or flow is not sufficient, each fire point should be provided with either water extinguishers (2 x 9 litre) or a water tank of least 500 litres capacity fitted with a hinged cover, 2 buckets and 1 hand pump or bucket pump.

Fire warning

A-175 10. A means of raising the alarm in the event of a fire should be provided at each fire point. This could be by means of a manually operated sounder, e.g. metal triangle with striker, gong or hand operated siren. The advice of the fire authority should be sought on an appropriate system.

Maintenance

A-176 11. All alarm and fire fighting equipment should be installed, tested and maintained in working order by a competent person and be available for inspection by or on behalf of the licensing authority. A log book should be kept to record all tests and any remedial action.

A-177 12. All equipment susceptible to damage by frost should be suitably protected.

Fire notices

A-178 13. A clearly written and conspicuous notice should be provided and maintained at each fire point to indicate the action to be taken in the event of fire and the location of the nearest telephone. The notice should include the following:

"On discovering a fire

i. ensure the caravan or site building involved is evacuated

ii. raise the alarm

iii. call the fire brigade (the telephone is sited.....)

iv. attack the fire using the fire fighting equipment provided, if it is safe to do so.

It is in the interests of all the occupiers of this site to be familiar with the above routine and the method of operating the fire alarm and fire fighting equipment."

Fire hazards

A-179 14. Grass and vegetation should be cut at frequent and regular intervals where necessary to prevent it becoming a fire hazard to caravans, buildings or other installations on the site. Any such cuttings should be removed from the vicinity of caravans. The space beneath and between caravans should not be used for the storage of combustible materials.

Telephones
15. An immediately accessible telephone should be available on the site for calling the emergency services. A notice by the telephone should include the address of the site. A-180

Storage of liquefied petroleum gas (LPG)
16. LPG storage supplied from tanks should comply with Guidance Booklet HSG 34 "The Storage of LPG at Fixed Installations" or, where LPG is supplied from cylinders, with Guidance Note CS4 "The Keeping of LPG in Cylinders and Similar Containers" as appropriate. A-181

Where there are metered supplies from a common LPG storage tank, then Guidance Note CS11 "The Storage and use of LPG at Metered Estates" provides further guidance. In this case and where a British gas main supply is available, then the Gas Safety (Installation and use) Regulations 1984 and the Pipe-lines Act 1962 may also be applicable.

Exposed gas bottles or cylinders should not be within the separation boundary of an adjoining unit.

LPG installations should conform to British Standard 5482, "Code of Practice for domestic butane and propane gas burning installations, part 2: Installations in Caravans and non-permanent dwellings".

For mains gas supply, the 1984 Regulations will be relevant for installation downstream of any service pipe(s) supplying any primary meter(s) and such service pipes are subject to the Gas Safety Regulations 1972.

In cases where the site owner supplies gas to caravans on the site he may need an authorisation from OFGAS to do so under the Gas Act 1986.

Electrical installations
17. Sites should be provided with an electricity supply sufficient in all respects to meet all reasonable demands of the caravans situated on them. A-182

18. Any electrical installations, which are not Electricity Board works and circuits subject to regulations made by the Secretary of State under section 16 of the Energy Act 1983 and section 64 of the Electricity Act 1947, should be installed, tested and maintained in accordance with the provisions of the Institution of Electrical Engineers' (IEE) Regulations for Electrical Installations for the time being in force, and where appropriate, to the standard which would be acceptable for the purposes of the Electricity Supply Regulations 1988, Statutory Instrument No. 1057. A-183

19. Work on electrical installations and appliances should be carried out only by competent persons such as the manufacturer's appointed agent, the electricity supplier, a member of the Electrical Contractors' Association, a contractor approved by the National Inspection Council for Electrical Installation Contracting, or a qualified person acting on behalf of one of the above. The installations should be inspected periodically: under IEE Wiring Regulations, every year or such longer period (not exceeding 3 years) as is considered appropriate in each case. When an installation is inspected, it should be judged against the current regulations. A-184

The inspector should, within 1 month of such an inspection, issue an inspection certificate in the form prescribed in the IEE Wiring Regulations which should be retained by the site operator and displayed, supplemented or replaced by subsequent certificates, with the site licence. The cost of the inspection and report should be met by the site operator or licence holder.

20. If an inspection reveals that an installation no longer complies with the regulations extant at the time it was first installed, any deficiencies should be rectified. Any major alterations and extensions to an installation and all parts of the existing installation A-185

affected by them should comply with the latest version of the IEE Wiring Regulations.

A-186 21. If there are overhead electric lines on the site, suitable warning notices should be displayed at the entrance to the site and on supports for the line. Where appropriate, particular attention should be drawn to the danger of masts of yachts or dinghies contacting the line.

Water supply

A-187 22. All parks should be provided with a water supply in accordance with appropriate Water Byelaws and statutory quality standards.

Drainage, sanitation and washing facilities

A-188 23. Satisfactory provision should be made for foul drainage, either by connection to a public sewer or sewage treatment works or by discharge to a properly constructed septic tank or cesspool approved by the local authority.

A-189 24. Each caravan should have its own water supply and water closet. Each caravan standing should be provided with a connection to the foul drainage system; the connection should be capable of being made air-tight when not in use.

A-190 25. Every site and hard standing should be provided with an adequate drainage system for the complete and hygienic disposal of foul, rain and surface water from the site, buildings, caravans, roads and footpaths.

Refuse disposal

A-191 26. Every caravan standing should have an adequate number of suitable non-combustible refuse bins with close-fitting lids or plastic bags. Arrangements should be made for the bins to be emptied regularly. Where communal bins are also provided these should be of similar construction and housed within a communal bin store.

Parking

A-192 27. One car only may be parked between adjoining caravans provided that the door to the caravan is not obstructed. Suitably surfaced parking spaces should be provided where necessary to meet the additional requirements of occupants and their visitors. Plastic or wooden boats should not be parked between units.

Recreation space

A-193 28. Where children live on the site, space equivalent to about one-tenth of the total area should be allocated for children's games and/or other recreational purposes. This provision will normally be necessary because of the limited space available round the caravans, but may be omitted where there are suitable alternative publicly provided recreational facilities which are readily available.

Notices

A-194 29. A suitable sign should be prominently displayed at the site entrance indicating the name of the site.

A-195 30. A copy of the site licence with its conditions should be displayed prominently on the site.

A-196 31. Notices and a plan should be displayed on the site setting out the action to be taken in the event of an emergency. They should show where the police, fire brigade, ambulance and local doctors can be contacted, and the location of the nearest telephone. The notices should also give the name and location/telephone number of the site licence holder or his/her accredited representative. At sites subject to flood risk, warning notices should be displayed giving advice about the operation of the flood warning system.

32. All notices should be suitably protected from the weather and displayed where possible out of the direct rays of the sun, preferably in areas lit by artificial lighting. A-197

CARAVAN SITES AND CONTROL OF DEVELOPMENT ACT 1960, SECTION 5
MODEL STANDARDS 1989: HOLIDAY CARAVAN SITES

I. Section 5(6) of the Act provides that the Secretary of State may from time to time specify A-198
Model Standards with respect to the lay-out and the provisions of facilities, services and equipment for caravan sits or particular types of caravan site; and that, in deciding what (if any) conditions to attach to a site licence, the local authority shall have regard to any standards so specified.

Section 7(1) provides that on appeal against any condition of a site licence a magistrates' court, if satisfied, having regard amongst other things to any standards specified by the Secretary of State under section 5(6), that a condition is unduly burdensome, may vary or cancel the condition.

Section 24, which empowers local authorities to provide caravan sites, provides in subsection (2) that in exercising their powers under the section the local authority shall have regard to any standards that may have been specified by the Secretary of State under section 5(6) of the Act.

II. In pursuance of his powers under section 5(6) of the Act, the Secretary of State A-199
hereby specifies the following standards in relation to holiday caravan sites. They are Model Standards: they represent the standards normally to be expected as a matter of good practice on such sites. They are not intended to apply to any other type of caravan site—for example, sites which only have caravans for permanent residential use, touring caravan sites, gipsy sites or sites which are used by agricultural workers. They should be applied with due regard to the particular circumstances of each case, including the physical character of the site, any services or facilities that may already be available within convenient reach, and other local conditions.

Site boundaries

1. The boundaries of the site should be clearly marked, for example by fences or hedges. In A-200
addition, the site owner should give the local authority a plan of its layout. It is recommended that a 3-metre wide area should be kept clear within the inside of all boundaries.

Density and space between caravans

2. Subject to the following variations, the minimum spacing distance between caravans A-201
made of aluminium or other materials with similar fire performance properties should not be less than 5 metres between units, 3.5 metres at the corners. (See specimen layout at Appendix 1.) For those with a plywood or similar skin it should not be less than 6 metres. Where there is a mixture of holiday caravans of aluminium and plywood, the separation distance should be 6 metres; and where there is a mixture of permanent residential homes and holiday caravans, the separation distance should again be 6 metres. The point of measurement for porches, awnings etc. is the exterior cladding of the caravan.

- Porches may protrude 1m into the 5 metres and should be of the open type.

- Where awnings are used, the distance between any part of the awning and an adjacent caravan should not be less than 3 metres. They should not be of the type which incorporate sleeping accommodation and they should not face each other or touch.

- Eaves, drainpipes and bay windows may extend into the 5 metre space provided the total distance between the extremities of two adjacent units is not less than 4.5 metres.

- Where there are ramps for the disabled, verandahs and stairs extending from the unit, there should be 3.5m clear space between them and two such items should not face each other in any space. If they are enclosed, they may need to be considered as part of the unit and, as such, should not intrude into the 5 or 6 metre space.

- A garage, a shed or a covered storage space should be permitted between units only if it is of non-combustible construction (including non-combustible roof) and sufficient space is maintained around each unit so as not to prejudice means of escape in case of fire. Windows in such structures should not face towards the units on either side. Car ports and walkways should in no circumstances be allowed within the 5m or 6m space. For cars and boats between units, see standard (27).

A-202 3. The density should be consistent with safety standards and health and safety requirements. The gross density should not exceed 60 caravans to the hectare, calculated on the basis of the usable area (i.e. excluding lakes, roads, communal services and other areas unsuitable for the siting of caravans) rather than the total site area.

Roads, gateways and footpaths

A-203 4. Roads and footpaths should be designed to provide adequate access for fire appliances. (Detailed guidance on turning circles etc. is available from fire authorities.) Roads of suitable material should be provided so that no caravan is more than 50 metres from a road. Where the approach to the caravan is across ground that may become difficult or dangerous to negotiate in wet weather, each standing should be connected to a carriageway by a footpath with a hard surface. Roads should be not less than 3.7 metres wide, or, if they form part of a clearly-marked one-way traffic system, 3 metres wide. Gateways should be a minimum of 3.1 metres wide and have a minimum height clearance of 3.7 metres. Footpaths should not be less than 0.75 metres wide. Roads should have no overhead cable less than 4.5 metres above the ground. Roads and footpaths should be suitably lit. Emergency vehicle routes within the site should be kept clear of obstruction at all times.

Hard standings

A-204 5. Every caravan should stand on a concrete hard-standing which should extend over the whole area of the caravan placed upon it, and should project a sufficient distance outwards from its entrance or entrances to enable occupants to enter and leave safely.

Hard standing may be dispensed with if the caravans are removed during the winter, or if they are situated on ground which is firm and safe in poor weather conditions.

Fire fighting appliances

Fire points

A-205 6. These should be established so that no caravan or site building is more than 30 metres from a fire point. They should be housed in a weather-proof structure, easily accessible and clearly and conspicuously marked "FIRE POINT".

Fire fighting equipment

7. Where water standpipes are provided and there is a water supply of sufficient pressure and flow to project a jet a water approximately 5 metres from the nozzle, such water standpipes should be situated at each fire point. There should also be a reel which complies with British Standard 5306 Part 1, with a hose not less than 30 metres long, having a means of connection to a water standpipe (preferably a screw thread connection) with a water supply of sufficient pressure and terminating in a small hand control nozzle. Hoses should be housed in a box painted red and marked "HOSE REEL". A-206

8. Where standpipes are not provided but there is a water supply of sufficient pressure and flow, fire hydrants should be installed within 100 metres of every caravan standing. Hydrants should conform to British Standard 750. Access to hydrants and other water supplies should not be obstructed or obscured. A-207

9. Where standpipes are not provided or the water pressure or flow is not sufficient, each fire point should be provided with either water extinguishers (2 x 9 litre) or a water tank of least 500 litres capacity fitted with a hinged cover, 2 buckets and 1 hand pump or bucket pump. A-208

Fire warning

10. A means of raising the alarm in the event of a fire should be provided at each fire point. This could be by means of a manually operated sounder, e.g. metal triangle with striker, gong or hand operated siren. The advice of the fire authority should be sought on an appropriate system. A-209

Maintenance

11. All alarm and fire fighting equipment should be installed, tested and maintained in working order by a competent person and be available for inspection by or on behalf of the licensing authority. A log book should be kept to record all tests and any remedial action. A-210

12. All equipment susceptible to damage to frost should be suitably protected. A-211

Fire notices

13. A clearly written and conspicuous notice should be provided and maintained at each fire point to indicate the action to be taken in the event of fire and the location of the nearest telephone. The notice should include the following: A-212

"On discovering a fire

i. ensure the caravan or site building involved is evacuated

ii. raise the alarm

iii. call the fire brigade (the telephone is sited.......................)

iv. attack the fire using the fire fighting equipment provided, if it is safe to do so.

It is in the interests of all the occupiers of this site to be familiar with the above routine and the method of operating the fire alarm and fire fighting equipment."

Fire hazards

14. Grass and vegetation should be cut at frequent and regular intervals where necessary to prevent it becoming a fire hazard to caravans, buildings or other installations on the site. Any such cuttings should be removed from the vicinity of caravans. The space beneath and between caravans should not be used for the storage of combustible materials. A-213

Telephones

A-214 15. An immediately accessible telephone should be available on the site for calling the emergency services. A notice by the telephone should include the address of the site.

Storage of liquefied petroleum gas (LPG)

A-215 16. LPG storage supplied from tanks should comply with Guidance Booklet HSG 34 "The Storage of LPG at Fixed Installations" or, where LPG is supplied from cylinders, with Guidance Note CS4 "The Keeping of LPG in Cylinders and Similar Containers" as appropriate.

Where there are metered supplies from a common LPG storage tank, then Guidance Note CS11 "The Storage and use of LPG at Metered Estates" provides further guidance. In this case and where a British gas main supply is available, then the Gas Safety (Installation and Use) Regulations 1984 and the Pipe-lines Act 1962 may also be applicable.

Exposed gas bottles or cylinders should not be within the separation boundary of an adjoining unit.

LPG installations should conform to British Standard 5482, "Code of Practice for domestic butane and propane gas burning installations, part 2: Installations in Caravans and non-permanent dwellings".

For mains gas supply, the 1984 Regulations will be relevant for installation downstream of any service pipe(s) supplying any primary meter(s) and such service pipes are subject to the Gas Safety Regulations 1972.

In cases where the site owner supplies gas to caravans on the site he may need an authorisation from OFGAS to do so under the Gas Act 1986.

Electrical installations

A-216 17. Sites should be provided with an electricity supply sufficient in all respects to meet all reasonable demands of the caravans situated on them.

A-217 18. Any electrical installations, which are not Electricity Board works and circuits subject to regulations made by the Secretary of State under section 16 of the Energy Act 1983 and section 64 of the Electricity Act 1947, should be installed, tested and maintained in accordance with the provisions of the Institution of Electrical Engineers' (IEE) Regulations for Electrical Installations for the time being in force, and where appropriate, to the standard which would be acceptable for the purposes of the Electricity Supply Regulations 1988, Statutory Instrument No. 1057.

A-218 19. Work on electrical installations and appliances should be carried out only by competent persons such as the manufacturer's appointed agent, the electricity supplier, a member of the Electrical Contractors' Association, a contractor approved by the National Inspection Council for Electrical Installation Contracting, or a qualified person acting on behalf of one of the above. The installations should be inspected periodically: under IEE Wiring Regulations, every year or such longer period (not exceeding 3 years) as is considered appropriate in each case. When an installation is inspected, it should be judged against the current regulations.

The inspector should, within 1 month of such an inspection, issue an inspection certificate in the form prescribed in the IEE Wiring Regulations which should be retained by the site operator and displayed, supplemented or replaced by subsequent certificates, with the site licence. The cost of the inspection and report should be met by the site operator or licence holder.

A-219 20. If an inspection reveals that an installation no longer complies with the regulations extant at the time it was first installed, any deficiencies should be rectified. Any major alterations and extensions to an installation and all parts of the existing installation affected by them should comply with the latest version of the IEE Wiring Regulations.

21. If there are overhead electric lines on the site, suitable warning notices should be displayed at the entrance to the site and on supports for the line. Where appropriate, particular attention should be drawn to the danger of masts of yachts or dinghies contacting the line. A-220

Water supply

22. All parks should be provided with a water supply in accordance with appropriate Water Byelaws and statutory quality standards. A-221

Drainage, sanitation and washing facilities

23. Satisfactory provision should be made for foul drainage, either by connection to a public sewer or sewage treatment works or by discharge to a properly constructed septic tank or cesspool approved by the local authority. A-222

24. Properly designed disposal points for the contents of chemical closets should be provided with an adequate supply of water for cleaning the containers. A-223

25. For caravans without their own water supply and water closets, communal toilet blocks should be provided, with adequate supplies of water, on at least the following scales: A-224

Men: 1 WC and 1 urinal per 15 caravans

Women: 2 WCs per 15 caravans

1 wash basin for each WC or group of WCs

1 shower or bath (with hot and cold water) for each sex per 20 caravans

Toilet blocks should be sited conveniently so that all site occupants may have reasonable access to one by means of a road or footpath.

Refuse disposal

26. Every caravan standing should have an adequate number of suitable non-combustible refuse bins with close-fitting lids or plastic bags. Arrangements should be made for the bins to be emptied regularly. Where communal bins are also provided these should be of similar construction and housed within a communal bin store. A-225

Parking

27. One car only may be parked between adjoining caravans provided that the door to the caravan is not obstructed. Suitably surfaced parking spaces should be provided where necessary to meet the additional requirements of occupants and their visitors. Plastic or wooden boats should not be parked between units. A-226

Recreation space

28. Where children live on the site, space equivalent to about one-tenth of the total area should be allocated for children's games and/or other recreational purposes. This provision will normally be necessary because of the limited space available round the caravans, but may be omitted where there are suitable alternative publicly provided recreational facilities which are readily available. A-227

Notices

A-228 29. A suitable sign should be prominently displayed at the site entrance indicating the name of the site.

A-229 30. A copy of the site licence with its conditions should be displayed prominently on the site.

A-230 31. Notices and a plan should be displayed on the site setting out the action to be taken in the event of an emergency. They should show where the police, fire brigade, ambulance and local doctors can be contacted, and the location of the nearest telephone. The notices should also give the name and location/telephone number of the site licence holder or his/her accredited representative. At sites subject to flood risk, warning notices should be displayed giving advice about the operation of the flood warning system.

A-231 32. All notices should be suitably protected from the weather and displayed where possible out of the direct rays of the sun, preferably in areas lit by artificial lighting.

APPENDIX 1
HOLIDAY CARAVAN LAYOUTS

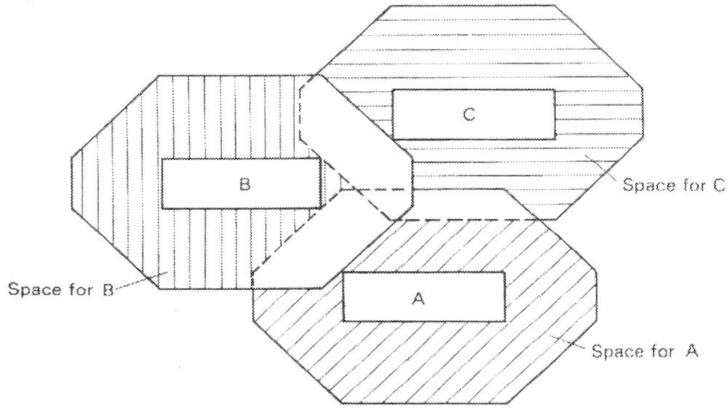

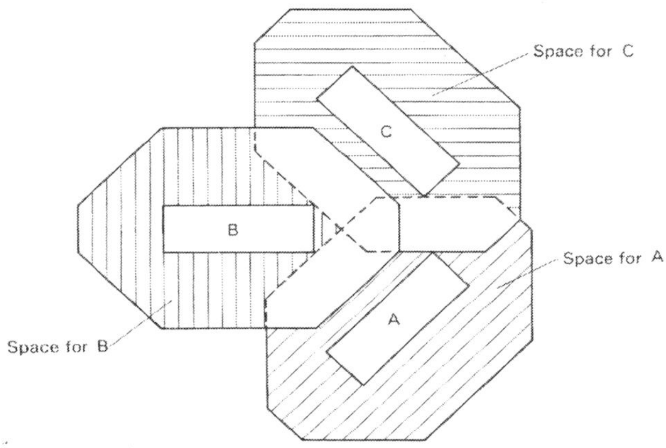

Circular No. 22/91: Travelling Showpeople[1]

1. This Circular gives advice to local authorities about planning considerations relating to travelling showpeople. A-232

Background
2. Showpeople are self-employed business people who travel the country holding fairs, chiefly during the summer months. Although their work is of a peripatetic nature, showpeople nevertheless require secure, permanent bases for the storage of their A-233

1. Welsh Office Circular 78/91.

equipment and more particularly for residential purposes. Such bases are most intensively occupied during the winter, when many showpeople will return there with their caravans, vehicles and showground equipment. For this reason, these sites have traditionally been referred to as "winter quarters". But increasingly showpeople's quarters need to be occupied by some members of the family permanently; older family members will stay on for most of the year and there are plainly advantages in children living there all year to benefit from uninterrupted education.

A-234 3. Most showpeople are members of the Showmen's Guild of Great Britain and are required by the Guild to follow a code of practice on the use of their sites. Membership of the Guild provides showpeople with exemption from the site licensing requirements of the Caravan Sites and Control of Development Act 1960 when they are travelling for the purpose of their business, or where they occupy quarters for some period between the beginning of October and the end of March in the following year. However they only enjoy permitted development rights under [Schedule 2 part 5 of the Town and Country Planning (General Permitted Development) Order 1995] when travelling for their business. They are therefore required to seek planning permission to establish all other sites. Furthermore, since showpeople are specifically excluded from the definition of gipsies under the Caravan Sites Act 1968, they do not benefit from the duty on local authorities under that legislation to provide gipsy accommodation.

A-235 4. The nature of showpeople's sites is unusual in planning terms. The sites illustrate the showpeople's characteristic self-sufficiency by combining residential, storage and maintenance uses. Typically a site comprises areas set aside for the showpeople's accommodation—usually caravans and mobile homes—and areas where vehicles and fairground equipment can be stored, repaired and tested. This means that the sites do not fit easily into existing land-use categories. Some of the difficulties showpeople have experienced with the planning system can be attributable to this.

A-236 5. In recent years many showpeople have had to leave traditional sites which have been displaced by other forms of development, sometimes following compulsory purchase. Some showpeople have had considerable difficulty in obtaining alternative sites with planning permission. This has caused overcrowding on some sites, and caused some showpeople to leave their home areas in attempts to find alternative sites—not always successfully. The problems showpeople have experienced in obtaining planning approval for their sites have led them sometimes to occupy land in breach of planning control, resulting in lengthy enforcement proceedings. This jeopardises the showpeople's livelihoods, and entails considerable cost to local authorities. The Government urges local planning authorities to pay close attention to this guidance with the aim of avoiding such conflict in the future.

Development plans

A-237 6. Local authorities should consider the needs of travelling showpeople when preparing their local plans and unitary development plans. They should identify existing sites which have planning permission, whether occupied or not, and should make a realistic assessment of the amount of accommodation required, including that made necessary by displacement, to provide the basis for relevant and appropriate plan policies. Where there has been a tradition of sites occupied by showpeople, and/or a local need for sites has been demonstrated, plans may make specific proposals for sites which would be suitable locations for showpeople's quarters.

A-238 7. Sites should be reasonably flat, have good vehicular access, and be reasonably convenient for schools and other community facilities. They should be identified having regard to environmental considerations, including the potential nuisance to neighbours from vehicular movement and the maintenance and testing of equipment. Wherever possible sites should be identified in locations with convenient and safe access to the road network; discussion with the local highway authority may prove helpful. Sites on the outskirts of built-up areas may satisfy these criteria but, where such locations are proposed, care should be taken to avoid visual encroachment into the open countryside. Sites with substantial natural screening may be particularly appropriate.

Handling of applications

8. Where the development plan is relevant to the development proposal, local planning authorities should determine planning applications in accordance with the plan unless material considerations indicate otherwise. In those cases where the development plan is not relevant, for example because the plan does not contain a policy relating to the provision of showpeople's quarters, or any other policy material to the application, the application should be determined on its merits. The relevant material considerations in these circumstances include the particular characteristics of showpeople's quarters and the circumstances that prompted the application. Nothing in this advice contradicts that contained in other circulars and Planning Policy Guidance Notes restricting development in specially protected areas. For example, very special circumstances have to be demonstrated to justify allowing development not normally appropriate in the Green Belt. (Full guidance about Green Belts is in PPG2.) A-239

9. Local authorities should ensure adequate publicity for planning applications for sites for travelling showpeople. (The Government's commitment that every planning application in England and Wales should receive some publicity will be given effect early in 1992.) As an alternative to refusal, local planning authorities should consider whether granting planning permission subject to conditions would provide sufficient control over particular details of a showpeople's site to overcome difficulties which have been identified. Conditions should always be necessary, relevant to planning and to the development permitted, enforceable, precise and reasonable in all other respects. Conditions can be particularly useful in ensuring adequate landscaping and screening of sites. A-240

10. In appropriate circumstances local planning authorities may also wish to consider imposing conditions to limit the proportion of a site which may be covered by fairground equipment, and the hours during which such equipment may be tested, in order to minimise the visual impact of the site and to safeguard local amenity from the effects of noise. However, local planning authorities should avoid imposing conditions prohibiting either residential use or the maintenance of equipment (or unduly restricting the hours during which this can be carried out): clearly, such conditions would effectively nullify the benefit of any permission for a permanent base. A-241

11. When local planning authorities are minded to grant planning permission for the use of land as a site for travelling showpeople, but consider that conditions might not be appropriate to ensure that the land continues to be available for use for that purpose, it is open to authorities, applicants and owners of the land to enter into an agreement under section 106 of the Town and Country Planning Act 1990 (as substituted by section 12 of the Planning and Compensation Act 1991) to limit the future occupation and use of the site. Where sites have been provided, and a continuing need for them can be demonstrated, local planning authorities should take full account of this factor in considering planning applications for alternative forms of development which would showpeople of such accommodation. A-242

12. Local planning authorities should bear in mind that the security of planning permission for the permanent use of a site for occupation by travelling showpeople is important to make worthwhile the investment required to provide sewerage and other services A-243

and to encourage the showpeople to undertake tasks such as screening and landscaping. Accordingly, conditions should be used to limit permissions to a temporary period only where the applicants themselves propose temporary development, or in exceptional cases where a "trial run" is warranted, or where the alternative would clearly be an outright refusal of planning permission.

Breaches of planning control

A-244 13. If there is a breach of planning control, local authorities are encouraged to regard showpeople in the same manner as other small businesses and self-employed people when they consider possible enforcement action. The guidance in paragraphs 13 to 16 of PPG 18 ("Enforcing Planning Control") applies equally to showpeople's sites. The same considerations apply to discontinuance action under sections 102 and 103 of the Town and Country Planning Act 1990.

General

A-245 14. In all cases the essential point is for local planning authorities to be ready to discuss the showpeople's needs with the showpeople themselves at an early stage, both while local plans and unitary development plans are being prepared, as well as in the development control context. Pre-application discussions can be particularly useful and may help to avoid misunderstandings or even confrontation at a later stage. The aim should be to help the showpeople to help themselves; this should allow the showpeople to secure the kind of sites they require and help to avoid the use of sites in breach of planning control.

A-246 15. When local planning authorities own a site where showpeople are based, and a need arises for it to be used for other purposes, they can assist showpeople by giving early notice and wherever possible not requiring the site to be vacated until alternative land has been secured. Where showpeople are in need of sites, local authorities are urged to give every assistance in finding permanent sites for purchase or rental whether publicly or privately owned. Local authorities should make full use of the registers of unused and under-used land owned by public bodies. Sometimes it may be possible for local authorities to acquire land for showpeople's sites under section 24 of the Caravan Sites and Control of Development Act 1960 (or to appropriate for this purpose land which they already hold) and lease it to the Showmen's Guild for the use of their members.

A-247 16. On all matters likely to affect travelling showpeople, including the preparation of local plans and unitary development plans as well as development control, local authorities are advised at an early stage to contact the General Secretary, the Showmen's Guild of Great Britain, Guild House, 41 Clarence Street, Staines TW18 4SY. The Guild will be able to provide advice about where the need for sites is most acute and to advise on the particular on-site requirements of travelling showpeople. The Guild can also make available site layout, model standards and other information to assist local authorities in assessing detailed aspects of site provision.

...

Circular No. 1/94: Gypsy Sites and Planning[1]

Introduction

1. This Circular revises guidance on the planning aspects of sites for caravans which provide accommodation for gypsies. It applies equally to local authorities' own sites and to applications for planning permission from gypsies themselves or from others wishing to develop land as a gypsy caravan site. Its main intentions are— A-248

—to provide that the planning system recognises the need for accommodation consistent with gypsies' nomadic lifestyle;

— to reflect the importance of the plan-led nature of the planning system in relation to gypsy site provision in the light of the Planning and Compensation Act 1991 ("the 1991 Act"); and

— to withdraw the previous guidance indicating that it may be necessary to accept the establishment of gypsy sites in protected areas, including Green Belts.

2. This Circular does not affect the advice given generally in other Departmental Circulars and Planning Policy Guidance Notes (PPGs). Those which may be of particular relevance are— A-249

—PPG1 ("General Policy and Principles")

—PPG2 ("Green Belts")

—PPG7 [("The Countryside: Environmental Quality and Economic and Social Development")]

—PPG12 [("Development Plans")]

—PPG12 (Wales) ("Development Plans and Strategic Planning Guidance in Wales")

—Draft PPG13 ("Transport")

—PPG16 and PPG16 (Wales ("Archaeology and planning")

—PPG18 ("Enforcing Planning Control")

—PPG (forthcoming) ("Nature Conservation")

—DOE Circular 1/92 (WO 1/92) ("Planning Controls over Sites of Special Scientific Interest")

—DOE Circular 28/77 (WO 51/77), subject to the cancellations made by this Circular (see paragraph 34).

3. The Government announced on March 31, 1993 its intention to introduce legislation to reform the Caravan Sites Act 1968 ("the 1968 Act") when Parliamentary time is available. In particular, the Government proposes to repeal the statutory duty of local authorities to provide accommodation on caravan sites for gypsies residing in or resorting to their areas. Local authorities would continue to have discretionary powers to provide such sites under the Caravan Sites and Control of Development Act 1960 ("the 1960 Act"). The Government also proposes to repeal the Secretary of State's powers to "designate" an area of a A-250

1. Welsh Office Circular 2/94.

local authority (for example, on the grounds that provision for gypsies in its area was adequate); to repeal his powers to direct an authority to provide more local authority sites; and to repeal his powers to pay grant to authorities for the provision of sites. Provisions implementing these proposals were included in the [Criminal Justice and Public Order Act 1994].

A-251 4. The proposed repeal of local authorities' duty to provide gypsy sites is expected to lead to more applications for private gypsy sites. The Government recognises that many gypsies would prefer to find and buy their own sites to develop and manage. More private sites should release pitches on local authority sites for gypsies most in need of public provision.

A-252 5. "Gypsies" are defined in section 16 of the 1968 Act as "persons of nomadic habit of life, whatever their race or origin". References to gypsies in this Circular are references to gypsies in that sense. The term does not include members of an organised group of travelling showpeople or circus people, travelling together as such. Planning advice relating to travelling showpeople is given in DoE Circular 22191 (WO 7819 1).

A-253 6. Gypsies make up a tiny proportion of the population of England and Wales, but their land-use requirements need to be met. Many gypsies are self-employed people, sometimes occupied in scrap and scrap-metal dealing, laying tarmacadam, seasonal agricultural work, casual labouring, and other employment associated with their itinerant lifestyle. The gypsy community also includes groups of long-distance travellers who nowadays earn their living mainly from trades such as furniture dealing, carpet selling and other related occupations. Local planning authorities need to be aware of the accommodation and occupational needs of gypsies, having regard to their statutory duties, including those in respect of homelessness under Part III of the Housing Act 1985.

Development Plans

A-254 7. At an early stage in the preparation of structure plans, local plans, and unitary development plans ("development plans"), it will be important for local planning authorities to be ready to discuss gypsies' accommodation needs with the gypsies themselves, their representative bodies and local support groups. A list of some relevant addresses is given in Annex A. Other important sources of advice are County Council Gypsy Liaison Officers. Planning departments may need to consult other departments and agencies with an interest, particularly highways authorities.

A-255 8. In preparing or amending their development plans, local planning authorities should indicate how they have taken account of their duty under the 1968 Act to make adequate provision for gypsies residing in or resorting to their areas. They should set out their land-use policies and proposals for fulfilling that statutory duty, for as long as it remains.

A-256 9. After the proposed repeal of this duty, local planning authorities should continue to indicate the regard they have had to meeting gypsies' accommodation needs. Repeal of the statutory duty will make it all the more important that local planning authorities make adequate gypsy site provision in their development plans through appropriate use of national and/or criteria-based policies. Structure plans and Part I of unitary development plans should continue to set out broad strategic policies, and provide a general framework for site provision. Local plans and Part II of unitary development plans should continue to provide detailed policies.

A-257 10. It is important that policies for gypsy site provision are set out clearly in development plans to avoid any potential for disagreements with the settled population which might otherwise arise because of inappropriate location or inadequate explanation of proposed development. With such policies in place in plans, there will be more certainty for all concerned when planning applications are determined by local planning authorities or appeals are considered by the Secretary of State.

Provision and location of sites

11. In deciding what level of provision is necessary, it is essential for authorities to have up- A-258
to-date information and to maintain records of trends through regular counts, particularly where the gypsy population varies appreciably. When preparing their development plans, authorities should take into consideration the number of gypsy caravans in their areas, particularly the six-monthly counts by local authorities, which are collected and published by the Department of the Environment and the Welsh Office. This information will also help determine the geographical distribution of caravans, and different needs between summer and winter months. Authorities should also consider making full use of the registers of unused and under-used land owned by public bodies as an aid to identifying suitable locations. Vacant land or surplus local authority land may be appropriate. Locations awaiting development in the future may also be suitable for a limited period.

12. Local plans and Part II of unitary development plans should wherever possible A-259
identify locations suitable for gypsy sites, whether local authority or private sites. Where this is not possible, they should set out clear, realistic criteria for suitable locations, as a basis for site provision policies. They should also identify existing sites which have planning permission, whether occupied or not, and should make a quantitative assessment of the amount of accommodation required. A tradition of sites occupied by gypsies and the demonstration of a local need will help authorities to make proposals for sites in suitable locations.

13. As a rule it will not be appropriate to make provision for gypsy sites in areas of A-260
open land where development is severely restricted, for example, Areas of Outstanding Natural Beauty, Sites of Special Scientific Interest, and other protected areas. Gypsy sites are not regarded as being among those uses of land which are normally appropriate in Green Belts. Green Belt land should therefore not be allocated for gypsy sites in development plans. PPG2 gives guidance on Green Belt policy.

14. In deciding where to provide for gypsy sites, local planning authorities might, for A-261
example, consider locations outside existing settlements, but within a reasonable distance of local services and facilities, e.g. shops, hospitals and schools. Sites on the outskirts of built-up areas may be appropriate, provided that care is taken to avoid encroachment on the open countryside. Many sites may be found in rural or semi-rural settings, but care needs to be taken to ensure consistency with agricultural and countryside policies, including those set out in PPG 7 on the protection of the best and most versatile agricultural land.

15. Sites, whether public or private, should be identified having regard to highways A-262
considerations, this may be achieved through early contact with Regional Operating Units of the Department of Transport, or, in Wales, the Welsh Office Highways Directorate. Guidance on access is given in draft PPG13 ("Transport"). In setting their policies, local planning authorities should have regard to the potential for noise and other disturbance from the movement of vehicles to and from the site, the stationing of vehicles on the site, and on-site business activities.

16. Many gypsies prefer to run their businesses from the site on which their caravans A-263
are stationed. Local planning authorities should, wherever possible, identify in their development plans gypsy sites suitable for mixed residential and business uses, having regard to the safety of the occupants and their children. If mixed sites are not practicable, authorities should consider the scope for identifying separate sites for residential and for business purposes in close proximity to one another. Some sites or parts of sites unsuitable for residence might be suitable for parking vehicles or storing materials.

Site characteristics and services

A-264 17. Given the variety of occupations in which gypsies are engaged, there is no simple profile of an ideal gypsy site, but there are a number of characteristics which may help local planning authorities to identify appropriate sites, whether publicly or privately owned. Three main types of site are referred to here for guidance: (1) sites for settled occupation; (2) temporary stopping places; and (3) transit sites. Even families who settle on sites may travel periodically, especially during the summer months, so there is often a need for transit sites for gypsies who are passing through a particular area.

A-265 18. Descriptions of various kinds of site are given for illustrative purposes in Annex B. For all kinds of site, consideration must be given to vehicular access from the public highway, as well as provision for parking, turning and servicing on site, and road safety for occupants and visitors. Landscaping and planting with trees and shrubs will help sites blend into their surroundings, give structure and privacy, and maintain visual amenity.

A-266 19. Private sites for settled occupation are generally small, accommodating pitches for individual or extended families without on-site business activities. Small sites can often be less obtrusive. Temporary stopping places and transit sites might also be small, except on routes frequented by those gypsy groups which travel in large numbers.

Applications

A-267 20. In order to encourage private site provision, local planning authorities should offer advice and practical help with planning procedures to gypsies who wish to acquire their own land for development. Wherever possible, gypsies should be encouraged to consult authorities on planning matters before buying land on which they intend to camp and for which planning permission would be required. Pre-application discussions are particularly important to avoid misunderstanding. The aim should be as far as possible to help gypsies to help themselves, to allow them to secure the kind of sites they need, and thus help avoid breaches of planning control. In particular, questions of road access, the availability of services, potential conflict with statutory undertakers or agricultural interests, and any significant environmental impacts should be resolved at the earliest opportunity.

A-268 21. Where a development plan contains policies relevant to a proposal for a gypsy site, authorities must determine the planning application in accordance with the plan unless material considerations indicate otherwise. If the plan is not relevant, applications should be determined in the light of all material considerations. Authorities should recognise that they may receive applications from gypsies without local connections which could not reasonably have been foreseen in their development plan policies. Authorities should not refuse private applications on the grounds that they consider public provision in the area to be adequate, or because alternative accommodation is available elsewhere on the authorities' own sites.

A-269 22. As with any other planning applications, proposals for gypsy sites should continue to be determined solely in relation to land-use factors. Whilst gypsy sites might be acceptable in some rural locations, the granting of permission must be consistent with agricultural, archaeological, countryside, environmental, and Green Belt policies (see paragraphs 2, 13 and 14, above). The aim should always be to secure provision appropriate to gypsies' accommodation needs while protecting amenity.

A-270 23. The appropriate use of planning conditions can enable some development proposals to proceed where it might otherwise be necessary to refuse permission. Conditions should be imposed only where they are necessary, relevant to planning and to the development to be permitted, enforceable, precise and reasonable in all other respects. General advice on the use of conditions is given in DOE Circular 1/85 (WO 1/85). A number of measures may be introduced to overcome planning objections to particular proposals. They might include ensuring adequate landscaping, and limiting which parts of a site may be used for business operations, in order to minimise the visual impact and limit the effect of noise. In certain circumstances, conditions might also be appropriate to specify the maximum number of days for which gypsy caravans might be permitted to stay on a transit site.

24. In some cases, for example where the applicants themselves propose to use a site for A-271
only a limited time, or where land is to be redeveloped on some occasion in the future, it may be appropriate to impose a condition allowing use for only a specified period. But unless such circumstances prevail, permission should generally be given for an indefinite period.

25. Where an authority's planning objectives cannot be achieved by imposing a plan- A-272
ning condition (because, for example, they relate to development, roads or buildings other than those covered by the planning application), it may be appropriate to enter into a planning obligation under section 106 of the Town and Country Planning Act 1990 ("the 1990 Act") (as substituted by section 12 of the 1991 Act). Advice on the use of such obligations is given in DOE Circular 16/91 (WO 53191) ("Planning Obligations").

Enforcement

26. If planning permission is required but not obtained for a gypsy site and the local A-273
planning authority are considering possible enforcement action, they should be guided by the policy advice in PPG 18 ("Enforcing Planning Control"). Local planning authorities should regard gypsies in the same manner as small businesses when considering possible enforcement action. The existence or absence of policies for gypsy sites in development plans could constitute a material consideration in matters of enforcement.

27. Local planning authorities have a range of enforcement power's available to them A-274
where the breach of planning control is sufficiently serious to justify taking action. Two powers may be particularly appropriate. *First*, the amended "stop notice" provisions, in section 183 of the 1990 Act, now enable the authority to serve a stop notice at the same time as the related enforcement notice; and, where circumstances justify it, to bring a stop notice into immediate effect, and to prohibit the use of any of the land specified in the enforcement notice for a residential caravan site. *Second*, the authority may apply for an injunction, in the High Court or County Court, to restrain an actual or apprehended breach of planning control, under section 187B of the 1990 Act. An injunction can be sought irrespective of whether the identity of the person is known. Detailed guidance about these two powers is given in Annexes 3 and 4, respectively, to DOE Circular 21/91 (WO 76/91).

28. Once an enforcement notice has taken effect in relation to land specified in it, the A-275
local planning authority now have improved powers (in the amended section 178 of the 1990 Act) to enter the land and carry out the requirements of the notice themselves, in default of the owner or occupier. The authority may also recover from the person who is then the owner of the land any expenses they reasonably incur in taking remedial action themselves. Guidance about these powers is given in paragraphs 49 to 51 of Annex 2 to DOE Circular 21/91 (WO 76/91).

Caravan use not requiring a planning application

29. Some kinds of activity will not fall within the definition of "development" in section 55 A-276
of the 1990 Act and will not therefore require planning permission. Any gypsy living in a dwellinghouse will not require planning permission to use a caravan within the curtilage of the dwellinghouse, provided that the purpose is incidental to the enjoyment of the dwellinghouse as such. A caravan within the curtilage of a dwellinghouse may have a

number of ancillary uses for which planning permission would not be required. For example, it could be used for additional living accommodation, provided that it remained part of the same planning unit as the dwellinghouse and the unit remained in single family occupation.

Permitted development

A-277 30. There are a number of circumstances in which gypsies, like any other users of the planning system, may carry out development for which a general permission is granted by the [General Permitted Development Order 1995, "the GPDO"]. Such development does not require a planning application. Types of permitted development are specified in Schedule 2 to the GPDO. Some types which may benefit gypsies are described below.

A-278 31. The provision on land of caravans required temporarily in connection with and for the duration of permitted operations (other than mining) being carried out on, in, under or over that land, or on adjoining land—which might include, for example, agricultural or building work—is permitted development (Class A of Part 4 of Schedule 2 to the [GPDO]).

A-279 32. The use of land for caravans may be permitted development in some of the cases, specified in Schedule 1 to the 1960 Act, where a site licence is not required (Class A of Part 5 of Schedule 2 to the [GPDO]). Such cases include—

—the use of land as a caravan site for up to 28 days a year for (a) a single caravan staying no more than two nights at any time on sites of less than five acres; and (b) for up to three caravans on larger sites;

—the use of agricultural or forestry land as a temporary caravan site for accommodation used in connection with seasonal working on that land; and

—the use of a caravan site on land forming part of, or adjoining, land where permitted building or engineering operations are being carried out, where accommodation is for people employed in connection with the operations.

Licensing

A-280 33. Under the 1960 Act, a caravan site, whether or not it is for gypsies, is likely to need a site licence. The district or borough council is responsible for issuing the site licence and must do so once planning permission is granted. The licence will contain conditions which specify how a particular site should be regulated and equipped, in the interests of health, safety and amenity. Details of the licensing conditions may be discussed while the application for planning permission is being considered, so that the licence can be issued as soon as permission is granted.

...

Financial and manpower implications

A-281 35. This Circular repeats and revises existing guidance. Its contents are not expected to have significant manpower or resource implications for local planning authorities in advance of proposed legislative changes repealing the authorities' duty to provide gypsy sites. Planning applications will continue to attract planning application fees.

...

ANNEX B

CHARACTERISTICS OF SITES

(for illustrative purposes only)

1. The ideal sites for long-term use will have access from properly surfaced roads. Individual pitches might have hardstandings for existing caravans, and additional parking space for extra caravans, cars and lorries, where necessary. There may need to be working spaces, and areas for clothes-drying and other domestic purposes, and a safe playing area for children. A reasonable level of services would be expected, including electricity and drinking water supplies, washing facilities, sewage disposal, and regular refuse collections. Each pitch would have access to its own drinking water supply and sanitation. Suitable means of marking site boundaries would include fencing or natural vegetation such as hedges or trees. Spare capacity would enable the accommodation of visiting families passing through an area or attending family events. A-282

2. The better temporary stopping places will have a hard-surfaced entrance or access road, hardstanding for caravans and vehicles, a convenient drinking water supply, a means of sewage disposal. and a refuse collection point. A typical site might have an impassable barrier such as hedging or an embankment to delineate its boundaries. A-283

3. For transit sites, some provision to minimise impact and avoid health hazards should include a refuse collection point, access to a drinking water supply, and sewage disposal. A drained and stable surface, particularly at entrances and where vehicles and caravans are likely to be parked, might also be desirable. A-284

Circular No. 18/94: Gypsy Sites and Unauthorised Camping

Introduction

1. This Circular offers guidance on the provisions in sections 77 to 80 of the Criminal Justice and Public Order Act 1994 ("the 1994 Act") which affect gypsies and unauthorised campers. The Act received Royal Assent on November 3, 1994, and sections 77 to 80 came into force on the same day. A-285

Definition of "gipsies"

2. Section 24 of the Caravan Sites and Control of Development Act 1960 ("the 1960 Act") as amended by section 80 of the 1994 Act, provides that "gipsies": A-286

> means persons of nomadic habit of life, whatever their race or origin, but does not include members of an organised group of travelling showmen, or of persons engaged in travelling circuses, travelling together as such".

3. The courts have recently clarified the definition of the word "gipsies" in s. 16 of the Caravan Sites Act 1968 ("the 1968 Act"), which was repealed by section 30 of the 1994 Act. In *R v South Hams District Council, ex parte Gibb* and two other applications—*The Times*, 8 June 1994; *The Independent*, 15 June 1994—the Court of Appeal held that "gipsies" meant persons who wandered or travelled for the purpose of making or seeking their livelihood, and did not include persons who moved from place to place without any connection between their movement and their means of livelihood. All references to "gypsies" in this Circular are references to "gypsies" this sense. A-287

Powers to control unauthorised camping

A-288 4. Section 77 of the 1994 Act empowers a local authority[1] to direct persons residing unlawfully in vehicles within the area of that local authority on highway land, other unoccupied land or occupied land without the consent of the occupier to leave the land and remove their vehicles and any other property they have with them on the land. It is an offence for a person, knowing that such a direction has been given to him, to fail to comply with it as soon as practicable. It is also an offence for a person so directed to re-enter the land concerned with a vehicle within three months of the date of the direction. In any proceedings brought for an offence, it is a defence for an accused person to show that his failure to comply with a direction or his re-entry of land was due to mechanical breakdown, illness or other immediate emergency. If a person who has been directed to leave does so as soon as practicable, and does not re-enter the land within three months of the date of the direction, no offence is committed.

A-289 5. Section 78 of the 1994 Act provides that a magistrates' court may, on a complaint by a local authority, make an order requiring the removal from land of any vehicle and property and any person residing in it, and authorising an authority to enter the land and remove the vehicle and property. It is an offence for a person wilfully to obstruct any person authorised to carry out the order. This power is modelled closely on the power that was available to authorities for areas designated under the 1968 Act, although it should be noted that sections 77 and 78 apply to any unauthorised camper, not just to gypsies.

Policy of toleration towards unauthorised gypsy encampments

A-290 6. The Secretaries of State recognise that in some circumstances it may be in the public interest to evict an unauthorised gypsy encampment and, they accept that this must remain a matter for local discretion. The Secretaries of State consider that it would usually be legitimate for a local authority to exercise the new eviction powers when gypsies camped unlawfully in their area refuse to move onto an authorised local authority site. Where gypsies are camped unlawfully on council land and are not causing a level of nuisance which cannot be effectively controlled, an immediate forced eviction might result in unauthorised camping on a site elsewhere in the area which could give rise to greater nuisance. Accordingly, authorities should consider tolerating gypsies' presence on the land for short periods and could examine ways of minimising the level of nuisance on such tolerated sites, for example, by providing basic services for gypsies, e.g. toilets, a refuse skip and a supply of drinking water.

A-291 7. Local authorities should also try to identify possible emergency stopping places, as close as possible to the transit routes used by gypsies, where gypsy families would be allowed to camp for short periods. Authorities should consider providing basic services on these temporary sites.

A-292 8. Where gypsies are unlawfully camped on Government-owned land, it is for the local authority, with the agreement of the land owning Department, to take any necessary steps to ensure that the encampment does not constitute a hazard to public health. It will continue to be the policy of the Secretaries of State that Government Departments should act in conformity with the advice that gypsies should not be moved unnecessarily from unauthorised encampments when they are causing no nuisance.

A-293 9. The Secretaries of State continue to consider that local authorities should not use their powers to evict gypsies needlessly. They should use the powers in a humane and

1. In England, a county council, a district council, a London borough council, the Common Council of the City of London and the Council of the Isles of Scilly; and in Wales, a county council or district council until 1 April 1996 (and a county council or county borough council thereafter).

compassionate fashion and primarily to reduce nuisance and to afford a higher level of protection to private owners of land.

Local authorities' obligations under other legislation

10. Social services departments and local housing authorities are reminded of their A-294
obligations under Part III of the Children Act 1989 (Local Authority Support for Children and Families); and Part Ill of the Housing Act 1985 (Housing the Homeless). The Secretaries of State expect authorities to take careful account of these obligations when taking decisions about the future maintenance of authorised gypsy caravan sites and the eviction of persons from unauthorised sites.

11. Local education authorities should bear in mind their statutory duty to make appro- A-295
priate educational provision available for all school-age children in their area, whether resident temporarily or permanently. As noted in paragraph 33 of Circular 11/88 and paragraph 9 of Circular 11,19-1 from the Department for Education (formerly the Department of Education and Science) and paragraph 6 of the annex (revised annually) to Welsh Office Circular 52/90, this duty embraces traveller children. Local education authorities should take careful account of the effects of an eviction on the education of children already enrolled, or in the process of being enrolled, at a school. Where an authority decides to proceed with an eviction, and any families concerned move elsewhere in the same area, alternative educational arrangements must be made in accordance with the requirements of the law appropriate to the children's ages, abilities and aptitudes.

12. The Secretaries of State also expect local authorities who decide to proceed with A-296
evictions to liaise with other local authorities who may have statutory responsibilities to discharge in respect of those persons who are being evicted.

13. Local authorities should also bear in mind that families camped unlawfully on land A-297
may need or may be receiving assistance from local health or welfare services. When they have decided to proceed with an eviction they should liaise with the relevant statutory agencies, particularly where pregnant women or newly-born children are involved, to ensure that those agencies are not prevented from fulfilling their obligations towards these persons.

Repeal of Part II of the Caravan Sites Act 1968

14. Section 80(1) of the 1994 Act, repeals: A-298

(a) the duty of local authorities to provide and manage sites (sections 6 and 7 of the 1968 Act);

(b) the requirement for a county council to consult the relevant district council before adopting a proposal to acquire or appropriate land for such a site (section 8);

(c) the Secretary of State's powers to direct a local authority to provide a site (section 9) and to designate the area of a local authority (section 12); and

(d) the powers for a designated authority to deal with unauthorised camping (sections 10 and 11).

15. Section 80(2) of the 1994 Act amends section 24 of the 1960 Act so as to allow a local A-299
authority to provide working space on gypsy caravan sites. Section 80(4) of the 1994 Act ensures that the repeal of the definition of the word "gipsies" in section 16 of the 1968 Act does not affect the interpretation of that word in the definition of a "protected site" in section 5(1) of the Mobile Homes Act 1983, or in any document embodying planning permission granted under the Town and Country Planning Act 1990 before 3 November 1994.

16. Section 80(3) of the 1994 Act makes transitional arrangements for those cases where A-300

the Secretary of State has issued a direction under section 8(3)(a) of the 1968 Act to a local authority to abandon a proposal for a gypsy caravan site, or under section 8(3)(c) of the 1968 Act to make an application to him for planning permission.

A-301 17. Directions under section 8(3)(a) of the 1968 Act will remain valid; directions under section 8(3)(b) and (c) of the 1968 Act will cease to have effect. However, where a local authority has made an application for planning permission to the Secretary of State before 3 November 1994, they may elect either to withdraw that application or to request the Secretary of State to determine it. In the latter case, the application would be treated as having been referred to the Secretary of State under section 77 of the Town and Country Planning Act 1990. Local authorities with outstanding directions under section 8(3)(c) of the 1968 Act, may, therefore, wish to notify their decision to the relevant Government Office for their region, or to the Welsh Office.

A-302 18. Section 80(5) of the 1994 Act repeals the power of the Secretaries of State for the Environment and for Wales to pay grant to local authorities in respect of capital expenditure for gypsy caravan sites under section 70 of the Local Government, Planning and Land Act 1980, except for the purposes of applications for grant received by the Secretaries of State before 3 November 1994. The repeal of section 70 does not apply to Scotland.

Future management of local authority gypsy caravan sites

A-303 19. Section 7 of the 1968 Act made provision for a sharing of functions between county councils and non-metropolitan district councils: county councils were required to acquire or appropriate land, set charges for the use of sites and contribute towards the costs incurred by district councils in managing the sites. District councils were required to provide and manage the site. The majority of public sites in non-metropolitan districts are owned by county councils and managed by district councils.

A-304 20. The Secretaries of State consider that the repeal of section 7 of the 1968 Act removes from district councils the delegation to manage sites on land owned by county councils. County councils become responsible for managing these sites by virtue of section 24 of the 1960 Act. Nonetheless, the Secretaries of State consider that authorities have adequate powers to make suitable arrangements for the maintenance and management of sites depending on local circumstances. In particular, section 101 of the Local Government Act 1972 empowers a local authority to arrange for the discharge of its functions by another local authority. Such an arrangement would enable a district council to continue to manage a site and the county council to contribute towards their expenses.

A-305 21. The Secretaries of State consider it important that authorities should maintain their existing gypsy caravan sites, or should make suitable arrangements for their maintenance by leasing them to other persons who are willing and able to maintain them.

A-306 21. The Secretaries of State also expect authorities to continue to consider whether it is appropriate to provide further permanent caravan sites for gypsies in their areas. Section 24 of the 1960 Act enables county councils, district councils and London borough councils to establish and manage sites or to lease them to another person and, as amended by section 80(2) of the 1994 Act, to provide working space on gypsy caravan sites.

"Gypsy Sites and Planning"

A-307 23. Local authorities are reminded of the advice in Department of the Environment (DOE) Circular 1/94 (Welsh Office (WO) Circular 2/94), "Gypsy Sites and Planning", dealing with the planning aspects of sites for gypsy caravans.

Bi-annual counts of gypsy caravans

24. The Department of the Environment and the Welsh Office intend to continue to ask local authorities to provide data for the compilation of the bi-annual counts of gypsy caravans in England and Wales on the same basis as at present. A-308

...

Financial and manpower implications

26. This Circular advises local authorities of the repeal of their duty to provide gypsy caravan sites and of the introduction of new discretionary powers to control unauthorised camping. Its contents are considered unlikely to have any net manpower or resource implications for local authorities. A-309

...

Circular 11/95: The Use of Conditions in Planning Permissions

[Extract]

Seasonal occupancy conditions

115. Occasionally it may be acceptable to limit the use of land for a particular purpose to certain seasons of the year. For example, where planning permission is being granted for a caravan site, the local planning authority may think it necessary to impose a condition to ensure that during the winter months the caravans are not occupied and are removed for storage to a particular part of the site or away from the site altogether; a suitable form of condition to secure seasonal use is given in model condition 43. Where such a condition is imposed, particular care should be taken to see that the condition allows a reasonable period of use of the caravans in each year. A similar approach may be taken where it is necessary to prevent the permanent residential use of holiday chalets which by the character of their construction or design are unsuitable for continuous occupation. Seasonal occupancy conditions may also be appropriate to protect the local environment, for example, where the site is near a fragile habitat which requires peace and quiet to allow seasonal breeding or winter feeding to take place. A-310

...

APPENDIX A

SUGGESTED MODELS OF ACCEPTABLE CONDITIONS FOR USE IN APPROPRIATE CIRCUMSTANCES

Caravans: Seasonal Sites

43. [No caravan on the site shall be occupied][No caravan shall remain on the site] between [date] in any one year and [date] in the succeeding year. A-311

Table of Authorities

1. Acts of Parliament

2. Delegated legislation

3. Cases

4. Other materials

Index

See also the *Glossary*, at the end of chapter 1, for words and phrases which are particularly relevant to the legislation on caravan sites.